Praise for *Miles to Go*

"*Miles to Go* awakens fond memories of my many road trips by car and Greyhound bus along the 'Mother Road,' Route 66!"—MARTIN SHEEN

"*Miles to Go* fills my heart with the freedom of being back on the road. Reading Brennen Matthews's story has time traveled my mind to when I drove Route 66 as a teenager and transported me back to all the unique places, the rich characters, and the smell of freedom that only America has to offer. What a joy to feel that once more. Route 66 is the artery of Americana and is now calling my name again. Here I go . . ."—JIM BELUSHI

"If there is a route to take to get to know America it's Route 66. If there is a book to read before you take it, it's *Miles to Go*."—ANDY GARCIA

"Brennen Matthews and his family's journey on America's Route 66 is viewed and filtered through their unique cultural and personal lens. *Miles to Go* lets you ride along with them as they experience the landscape, characters, and quirky stops along the way across one of the most famous and evocative roads in the world."—JOHN OATES

"*Miles to Go* picks up the spirit of the original pioneers and leads a family across the 'Mother Road' to find America!"—ROBERT PATRICK

"A spectacular book and a must-have for all fans of the Mother Road!"—DANNY BOY O'CONNOR

"Hop in and buckle up. Brennen Matthews's *Miles to Go* is a ride you won't soon forget."—RICHARD RATAY, author of *Don't Make Me Pull Over! An Informal History of the Family Road Trip*

"In *Miles to Go*, we don't just drive the highway looking out the window. We stop, interact with people, and learn things we were not expecting. . . . This Route 66 journey doesn't just immerse us in the sights, sounds, and experiences of the road. As guests on the journey, we're encouraged to think about what it means to live in America and be an American."—BILL THOMAS, chairman of the Route 66 Road Ahead Partnership

"*Miles to Go* is a compelling portrayal that draws the reader along the 2,448 miles of historic Route 66 from town to town and personality to personality. . . . The stories are honest, and the colorful characters encountered are exactly, and yet sometimes surprisingly, as you might expect"—KEN BUSBY, director of the Route 66 Alliance

"With the turning of each page, I rediscover Route 66 and the people that make it special. As *Miles to Go* presents a view of America through the filter of Route 66, as viewed by travelers from Africa, I found it a most intriguing read."—JIM HINCKLEY, author of *Travel Route 66: A Guide to the History, Sights, and Destinations Along the Main Street of America*

"Brennen Matthews has written a lively, delightful story that is told through the eyes of one who comes from abroad and is new to the Route. Surprisingly fresh and insightful, *Miles to Go* serves up a new and tasty slice of Route 66 pie. Get it. Read it. Share it."—JIM ROSS, author of *Route 66 Crossings: Historic Bridges of the Mother Road*, *Route 66 Sightings*, and *Roadside USA: Route 66 and Beyond*

"The story is told through the eyes of a family from Africa, a modern day de Tocqueville rambling through America's heartland. I hope that folks will not only read this book but be inspired to act and heed the call of the road, to explore America's highways and backroads, from Route 66 to the Lincoln Highway and more."—STEPHANIE STUCKEY, CEO of Stuckey's Corporation

"A must read for seasoned roadies and those going for their first time."—JIM CONKLE, publisher of *Route 66 Pulse*

"Everyone who's even considering traveling the Route should read this book. . . . Brennen Matthews takes you and his family on his first trip down the Mother Road. You feel as though you're seeing every site for the first time as he does and riding every mile with him, wondering what's around the next curve. It's the first time in twenty years I was actually in awe of the Route."—DAVID KNUDSON, executive director of the National Historic Route 66 Federation

Miles to Go

Miles *to* Go

AN AFRICAN FAMILY IN SEARCH
OF AMERICA ALONG ROUTE 66

Brennen Matthews

Foreword by **Michael Wallis**

University of New Mexico Press | Albuquerque

ISBN 978-0-8263-6401-2 (paper)
ISBN 978-0-8263-6402-9 (electronic)

Library of Congress Control Number: 2022933140

Founded in 1889, the University of New Mexico sits on the traditional homelands
of the Pueblo of Sandia. The original peoples of New Mexico—Pueblo, Navajo, and
Apache—since time immemorial have deep connections to the land and have made
significant contributions to the broader community statewide. We honor the land
itself and those who remain stewards of this land throughout the generations and
also acknowledge our committed relationship to Indigenous peoples. We gratefully
recognize our history.

Cover photograph courtesy of Jennifer Mallon
Designed by Felicia Cedillos
Composed in ScalaOT
All maps courtesy of the author.

CONTENTS

FOREWORD

Michael Wallis

The book you are about to read has been needed for a long time. Author Brennen Matthews tells "a tale of living life and taking chances" on US Route 66, the legendary highway that has been celebrated by multitudes of travelers from around the world. Much has been written about Route 66, but this book offers a fresh look from Brennen; his wife, Kate; and their young son, Thembi—together, a mixed-race family—as they examine America from their eyes, from their African perspective.

To take the pulse of the nation, the family chose America's most enduring artery and headed straight for Route 66. They wanted to taste, feel, hear, and experience genuine America—raw and uncensored. And that is precisely what they found on the Mother Road, as John Steinbeck dubbed the highway in his haunting novel *The Grapes of Wrath*. They shunned the turnpikes and freeways and cruised America's Main Street.

What they found is that the historic highway winding from Chicago to Santa Monica, through three time zones and eight states—Illinois, Missouri, Kansas, Oklahoma, Texas, New Mexico, Arizona, and California—has new life and meaning. More than 85 percent of Route 66 can still be traveled and enjoyed, and its necklace of towns, cities, and enticements are as alluring as ever. Arguably the most famous highway in the world, Route 66 is forever reinventing itself. Never static but fluid and elastic, it remains a road of movement and change.

Travelers may still view distinct layers of history along the various alignments of Route 66 in all eight states. They discover palpable examples of the Roaring Twenties, the bittersweet 1930s, the World War II years, and the postwar heyday of the highway. They also encounter the scars and desolation from the limbo years, when the interstate highways threatened the old road with extinction. Finally, they experience firsthand the highway of today's popular revival period—an episode of Route 66 history that appears to have no end in sight.

That is because Route 66 is America's most beloved road. It remains a road for everyone—the filthy rich and dirt poor, blue bloods, rednecks, foreign and domestic tourists, bona fide open-road travelers, poets, priests, fugitives, and dreamers. Politically, it is mostly red states book-ended by blue states, so the color should run purple—and purple can be such a lovely color. To many travelers, a journey along this historic path of concrete and asphalt, which stretches across two-thirds of the continent, is as comforting and familiar as a visit to Grandma's house. Some have sweet memories of the road, while others harbor lingering images of overheated radiators, ice storms, bloody wrecks, and speed traps. Yet no one can say that this highway is in any way ordinary.

Route 66 is forever reinventing itself. Businesses open and close. Highway landmarks appear and then vanish. Heroes and heroines of the road come and go. Retirement, death, and bad times take their toll. Change is both inevitable and necessary. Change offers challenges. Change keeps the road alive and well.

The highway has yielded plenty of saints and also a good many sinners. A microcosm of the nation, the old road has plenty of scar tissue, much to brag about, and a bright future. It is an unfinished story—a work in progress. Route 66 will always be incomplete.

And as a son of 66, I believe in the value of understanding the entire history of the highway. We simply must know and understand our past before we can manage the present and aspire to a future. The old road is a mirror of the nation reflecting our society and culture. That includes the good, the bad, the ugly, the holy, the shades of gray, and the cold hard truth of life. That has always been the case. That will never change.

It was certainly true when the highway was born back in 1926—when all roads of the time were less than hospitable, particularly if the traveler happened to be black or red or brown or anything other than lily white.

From the birth of Route 66 through its golden years, a mixed-race family, such as Brennen's, would not have been welcomed at most eateries, gas stations, rest stops, or motels along the route.

In the difficult 1930s, Dust Bowl pilgrims, tenant-farm refugees, and disenfranchised and broken souls poured onto the road. All of them headed west, following the scent of oranges and lemons, answering the siren call of the ocean surf, escaping from the harsh reality of economic depression and drought and foreclosure. All of them going to the San Joaquin Valley, Bakersfield, Fresno, San Bernardino, or Los Angeles. All of them moving toward the growing fields, the ripe orchards and groves, the lush vineyards, the factories and airplane plants, and the sunny beaches of a new promised land.

For a large number of people, traversing Route 66 was never an idyllic journey. Our highway may have earned the title Mother Road, but sometimes—and too often—she could be an abusive mother and a delinquent and uncaring parent. Ask the hordes of Okies and Arkies, the dirt-poor farmers and tenants, the unemployed city workers who were billy-clubbed, spat upon, shunned, cursed, abused, cheated, and lied to by others blinded by fear and ignorance and hatred.

Today, as in the past, nothing is predictable on Route 66. There is plenty of adventure—indeed, the potential for an escapade lurks around every curve and bend in the road. That accounts for much of the old road's attraction. For travelers from across the nation, as well as a growing number of visitors from throughout the Americas, Europe, and the Pacific Rim, this is an American highway that will never die.

Just keep in mind that it is a path for travelers who hanker for the hidden places off the well-beaten tourist path. Such a journey is much more personal than what the slabs of monotony called superhighways offer. On Route 66, travelers are not as distant from the ecology of the land and from the people who live there as they are when driving an interstate highway. On the old roads, travelers are physically closer and more connected to the land and the people.

Route 66 has evolved into a revered icon. It is a destination in itself. A trek down the highway is in order for all those who find time sacred and want to experience the America that used to be—America before the nation became generic. A tremendous revival has made Route 66 a symbol for all endangered two-lane roads. Although we cannot get along without our superhighways, it is good to know that Route 66 is still there as an alternative for those who value time and want to slow down and take the pulse of the land.

I am so pleased by the resurgence of interest in Route 66, a movement that started in 1990 when my book *Route 66: The Mother Road* first appeared. The success of this book later led me to join the great creative teams at Pixar Animation Studios to help create the first *Cars* film. When the film was in theaters, business increased by as much as 30 percent on long stretches of Route 66. I also acted as the consultant working with the Disney Imagineers to create Cars Land, the twelve-acre version of the fictional village of Radiator Springs come to life next to Disneyland in California. And, of course, I was delighted to provide the voice of Sheriff in all the *Cars* films and at Cars Land.

And now I am so proud and pleased to help unveil this new and exceptional Route 66 book—*Miles to Go: An African Family in Search of America along Route 66.*

I recognize an abundance of books have been published about Route 66 since my book first appeared in 1990, but I also know that there is always a demand and a need for more. Each book is different from the rest and contributes to the greater Route 66 story. The combination of all the books fuels the unprecedented renewal of interest in the Mother Road.

This book is truly an invaluable addition to the body of work about the historic path of well-worn concrete and asphalt. In telling the story of his African family's journey on Route 66, Brennen Matthews has made an important contribution to the legacy of the highway. He offers both a new voice and a new look at the Mother Road. Like the highway itself, the story Brennen so skillfully weaves is not in any way predictable. Nothing about this work is contrived. It is tailor made for open-road travelers and dreamers on a quest.

PROLOGUE

We discovered Route 66 by accident. It had been exactly eight months since our move to Toronto, where we had hibernated through the long Canadian winter, and the thaw of spring had triggered a restlessness. Sitting in front of my computer one day, looking for the best route to drive to sunny California, Route 66 jumped out at me. I mean, it literally exploded from the screen with its over-the-top, bizarre roadside attractions, fascinating history, and beautiful, quiet scenic roads and landscapes. I had heard of the fabled highway, but like most people, knew nothing about it. And other than a visit to New York, my wife, Kate, had not spent any time in America and was keen to explore. I schooled in Michigan for a few years when I was twenty, and had lived in California for a stint in my late teens, so Kate viewed me as a veteran expert. Never mind that it had been almost fifteen years since I last set foot in the States. But I had a growing hunger to get out on the open road, the wind in my hair, the vehicle pointed west, and the days unplanned. It felt good when we finally committed ourselves to the trip.

But before I share our journey into America, with all of its memorable moments, unexpected stumbles, and revelations, I must tell you a little of our story—Brennen, Kate, and Thembi's story—of becoming a family, of our unique life voyage, and of the shared desire to traverse our planet and explore. It's the story of our hopes and dreams and fears and uncertainties, and how they all coalesced at a moment in time when we made the decision that would take us west across America on that old road.

———

THE FIRST TIME that I remember meeting Kate was in the library during December exams week. It was 1997 and everyone at Daystar University was hunkered down, cramming for end-of-term tests. Outside, the hot wind blew wildly across the African plains in Athi River, Kenya; I was done for the night, and out of boredom wandered over to the bookshelves to search for something to read. I must have been pacing back and forth too much, as a soft but irritated voice said, "Can I help you find something?" That is the first time that I recall setting eyes on her. In front of me, books were sprawled across a small desk where the most beautiful girl sat, staring at me. She had big brown eyes, full lips, high cheekbones, and long, neat braids—and she had my attention. Unfortunately, she was not quite as impressed with me, and basically asked me to stop distracting her from her studying with my "annoying" movements. I asked her if I could walk her down to her dorm when the library closed. She said no.

Kate, however, remembers our first meeting somewhat differently. She remembers striking up a conversation with me on the university bus one day while on the forty-five-mile drive from Nairobi to the campus on the dry, windswept Athi Plains. Our school bordered Nairobi National Park. As the only full-time Caucasian student in a sea of African pupils, I obviously stood out. I have no memory of this meeting. Regardless, during the five days of exam week, every date that I made with Kate got canceled. I decided that it was perhaps not meant to be.

Ready for a much-needed break after exams, I headed home for the holidays. But our stars must have been aligned, because our paths intersected unexpectedly several days later, three hundred miles away, at a local hangout in our hometown of Mombasa. Mombasa is the country's second-largest city and located on the scenic shores of the Indian Ocean. This time, however, there was an immediate connection, and our relationship grew quickly. We were engaged seven months later and married in July 1999, right after graduation. We were young, attractive, carefree, and ready to take on the world.

Over the next decade, our lives took on the exciting new responsibilities of adulthood. I had completed my master's degree and entered a high-profile career in the global charity sector. My work took us to many countries, working with international nonprofit organizations and local communities on improving health care, food security, economic growth, and education. The work was intense but enjoyable, and I felt like I was making the world a better place. Kate, who had graduated with a bachelor of commerce, also worked with various charities and companies in whichever country we happened to find ourselves. These were fun and insouciant years as a young married couple, and our energy and zest for life was boundless. But after nine years of marriage, something even more exciting was afoot. Kate was pregnant and our lives were about to change forever.

Thembi—meaning "trusted one" in Xhosa—was born one early sticky Nairobi morning in February 2008. After several hours of difficult and strenuous labor, our doctor announced that both Kate and the baby were in serious distress and an emergency C-section was inevitable. Kate was whisked off in a flurry of urgency to the operating room while I was left to wait and worry.

After what felt like an eternity, the operating room door finally swung open and the doctor announced, "Brennen, I would like to introduce you to your son, Thembi." At that moment, the reality of being a parent rushed over me with immediate clarity. I was a father. Inside of a large spaceship-like glass box was the most amazing thing I had ever seen. Sleeping softly, eyes closed, wrapped up tightly in a swaddle, was my son. He had fought hard to be here, having to be resuscitated three times. He was beautiful. He was perfect. He was mine.

Being a new father came with many new lessons, life changes, and a realization that things I felt were so important before Thembi's birth, like my career, were no longer as significant. I was tired of the politics and uncertainties in the nonprofit world and wanted a change. I also wanted to travel less for work and be home more with my fledgling family. So, taking a leap of faith, I switched careers and became a full-time writer—a terribly frightening decision. I had indulged in freelance work for magazines and newspapers for years; I always loved seeing my stories in print and cherished opportunities as they arose, but I had never entertained the idea of making writing my career.

In late 2009, an opportunity arose to launch a new regional travel and lifestyle magazine out of Nairobi, *Destination Magazine*, and we jumped at it. We packed up our oceanside house in Mombasa and made the long drive north to Kenya's chaotic capital city and set to work establishing our new life. Kate joined the magazine's team as the digital editor, while I helmed it as the editor in chief. The publication opened up fresh and exciting opportunities. We featured fantastic travel and tourism destinations, shared candid celebrity interviews, and brought important investigative stories to readers that impacted lives. I never knew who, what, or where was next, and the adventure of it all was intoxicating.

However, after half a decade of this bliss, another new chapter was about to start. I turned forty and began a season that has brought more challenges and changes than I could have ever expected. The first half of my adult life had been incredibly busy, pushing and proving myself daily in all of my different roles—husband, director, father, writer, editor, friend. Our family of three had lived beautiful, easeful moments, and painful, difficult ones. I was happy and grateful. But still, turning forty brought with it an introspection—I was halfway to eighty. Was I half-done? This new phase ushered in sobering reflections of lost youth and innocence, as well as melancholy moments for all things never to be experienced again. And so, in the summer of 2015, we decided that we needed a fresh scene, away from Africa, and a chance to recharge our batteries. In another leap of faith, we made the decision to move to North America, where we hoped to find a fresh calling in which to invest two years of our lives before returning to Kenya. So the saying goes: Life is what happens when we are making our plans.

Leaving home is never easy, and while we were eager for change, the move was wrought with emotion. Adjusting to North American life in Toronto came with its trials and errors, challenges and adjustments, but we had some small wins. Thembi joined a great private school in our neighborhood, and our early days were spent exploring our quaint new community, characterized by its many leafy forests and endless hiking and biking trails. But something still plagued us: What did we really want to do with our lives? Kate and I were about to celebrate seventeen years of marriage, and we were both struggling to get a footing in our new reality.

After a great deal of soul-searching and discussion, Kate had an idea— we'd go on a road trip and clear our minds and hearts. Initially, I was resistant. We were not working, so our finances were guarded; we had no clear direction, so our carefreeness was muted; and I was fearful for my family and our future. I did not want to make such a trip without knowing what my actual *next* move was. But the more I deliberated, the more that getting out on the road made sense. We had already invested countless hours on highways exploring the little towns within driving distance, but we hungered for a longer time away from our new home to seek inspiration. We knew where we would go—across the United States to California—and *now* we knew how we would get there: Route 66.

America is a land of opportunity, a place of endless diversity and constant self-reinvention. Before Route 66, there was the opening of the West by the railroad and the redefining of tourism via the ingenuity of people like Fred Harvey and Mary Colter. There was the Oklahoma land runs of 1889 and a myriad of fascinating and iconic characters who forever live in legend and lore. America holds a billion stories. Kate and I have always been tremendously intrigued by what lies around every corner, and the more we delved into our route plan and discovered what magical things waited for us, the more excited we became. Little did we know that this odyssey across America, from the prairies of Illinois to the sunny coast of California, would change our lives forever.

This is the story of how the most famous road in America has influenced so many lives and futures. It is a tale of living life and taking chances, of being given the gift of a quest and of taking on America full tilt. But more than anything else, *Miles to Go* is our story, the tale of a family from Africa taking to Middle America and consuming it completely.

INTRODUCTION

The tale of Route 66, also known as the Will Rogers Highway, America's Main Street, and the Mother Road, has a definite beginning and an equally well-defined ending—the enactment of the federal highway system in 1926 and Route 66's completed decommissioning in 1985. However, its story is not necessarily a simple one to tell. In fact, this story is not merely about a basic road that was built to ferry people from one location to another at all, but about a way of seeing and living life that has stubbornly refused to die. And so, with time and the changes that it brings, Route 66 has also morphed and adapted, offering salvation to some, ease of travel to others, and a romantic road for the multitudes to get out and see the "real" America in all its forms and fashions.

In the early part of the twentieth century, the use of automobiles became increasingly widespread, and the resulting need for better roads in America became quickly apparent. The poorly marked routes of dirt and gravel roads that had served as "highways" had ultimately outrun their life span, and something needed to be done. In response, Congress passed the Federal Aid Road Act of 1916, a measure that provided $75 million in matching funds to states to aid in the creation of a national network of roads. The program was then extended in 1921. During this time, Cyrus Stevens Avery, a real estate investor and insurance man from Tulsa, Oklahoma, who also served as a Tulsa County commissioner, had himself been lobbying for new and improved roads. By 1921, Avery was selected to become president of the Associated Highways Association of America, and two years later, in 1923, he was appointed as the Oklahoma state highway commissioner. Avery was a rising statesman.

With 1924 drawing to a close, the American Association of State Highway Officials (renamed American Association of State Highway and Transportation Officials in 1973) proposed a new method of identifying routes that crisscrossed America, using a numbering system. Those heading east to west were ascribed even numbers, and those heading north to south were assigned odd numbers. Important highways were assigned numbers ending in 0. A twenty-one-member Joint Board on Interstate Highways was formed to oversee the creation of this whole network that connected existing local roads into highways, giving small farming towns access to their urban neighbors (and related markets). Avery, a member of the board, was tasked with identifying the most important routes of this new interstate highway system. This responsibility gave him considerable influence over what eventually fell under the United States highway system, including a major roadway that linked Chicago and Los Angeles and passed through his hometown of Tulsa. As a matter of fact, Oklahoma ended up with more Route 66 than any other state except New Mexico.

After months of deliberation, the new federal highway system was in place, and what remained to do was number the new route. Initially, Missouri and Illinois state officials wanted the highway going from Chicago to Los Angeles to be assigned the number 60. However, Kentucky also wanted the highway that passed through their state to be given number 60, due to the importance of numbers ending in 0. After a great deal of debate and controversy over the number, Avery and his team relinquished the designation and settled on 66, which was unassigned at the time. Why 66? Avery liked the sound of the number and thought that it would be easy to remember. Avery is now lovingly referred to as the Father of Route 66.

Today, we ponder the "good ole days" and romanticize a history that was not always fair or easy on those who lived it. Route 66, first commissioned on November 11, 1926, was largely used in the 1930s by those fleeing the Dust Bowl in the southern Plains states (Oklahoma, Arkansas, Kansas, Missouri, and Texas) that resulted in starvation and ruined lives for an incredible number of families. Route 66 represented their best (and often only) chance for survival. It is estimated that during the 1930s, some 2.5 million people migrated west in the hope of finding agricultural employment, leaving the Plains states behind. This was even more significant to the development of 66, as proactive residents in the towns and cities that the migrants passed through recognized that they needed somewhere to sleep, eat, get their overladen vehicles repaired, and to simply take a break from the difficult travel. As such, the Route 66 economy was truly born, and towns along the highway blossomed and grew with the influx of travelers.

By the 1940s, the military was investing enormously in the development of training bases, with the majority of the construction and troop training designated to take place in California. As a consequence, the War Department (as it was called before merging with other military departments to become part of the Department of Defense) needed to improve the available highways in order to allow for rapid mobilization in the event of a war. This, once again, resulted in a dramatically increased economy for many of the towns along Route 66, as well as some major upgrades to the road. In places like Hooker Cut in Missouri, whole sections of mountain were removed to create space for a divided-lane highway, a significant improvement from the original two-lane route. In 1946, the song "(Get Your Kicks on) Route 66," written by Bobby Troup and sung by Nat King Cole, was released and became a huge hit. The success of the song poignantly reflected the spirit of this postwar generation and their captivation with going west and "following their dreams," so much so that "Get your kicks on Route 66" became a popular catchphrase, and the most enduring travel story of Route 66, set to music.

As the 1950s rolled in and America began to stabilize with the end of World War II, there were tremendous strides in transportation and roadway development. Now more and more Americans owned a car, and with these newer, sleeker, faster automobiles came the need for more smooth-paved roads and places to go. Tracing its way from Chicago to California, Route 66 represented freedom and a chance to break from the norm and get out and meet life head-on. There was always a new adventure to be had and new places to see, and Route 66 was there to make it possible. After the economic devastation of the Dust Bowl era and two world wars, Route 66 represented, to the people of this period, a renewed spirit of optimism and a restored sense of the possible. The 1960s television series *Route 66* further propelled the popularity of the route by bringing it up close and personal, into American living rooms and lives each week.

Of course, by now, towns along the route were seasoned in rising up to meet every new opportunity, and with the extra spending power of the times, flashier diners, coffee shops, new motels, and novel attractions were born. Business owners used a wide array of ideas to attract customers and get them off the road. Nothing was too outlandish or insane—actually, the crazier, the better—and sky-high giant Muffler Men, impossibly vibrant neon signage, campaigns of endless billboards along the highway, and much more were unleashed on the traveling public.

As the road passed through natural wonders like Arizona's meteor crater, and across the bone dry but fiercely beautiful Mojave Desert of California, other tourist beacons arose to meet it. It was during this period, Route 66's heyday, that McDonald's opened its first restaurant in San Bernardino (1940) and its second in Des Plaines, Illinois (1955). For the towns and businesses along Route 66, things looked good. But it was not to last.

Today, the actual highway technically no longer exists. America's Main Street began its decline in 1956 with the signing of the Federal-Aid Highway Act by President Dwight D. Eisenhower, who envisioned a highway system that would rival Germany's grand autobahn. With the advent of the more straightforward, much faster highway system, many towns on Route 66 simply died, cut off from the busy traffic of the new shiny tarmac. And so, when following the road now, motorists must carefully trace their way through the winding, twisting, turning direction that 66 once took. But that is where the fun is!

For many travelers, motoring down 66 creates an overwhelming sense of following in the important and ever-changing footsteps of history. Every inch of roadway has been traversed by an innumerable number of hopefuls and dreamers, each with their own stories and aspirations, each expectant that their brighter future is just over the ridge, a characteristic that is most certainly unique to America. That is not to say that other nations do not offer their citizens, and immigrants alike, a multitude of life-changing opportunities. They do, of course, but there has always been something magnetic about America that draws dreamers seeking a better life. It is a land that romantically represents all that is possible in life, as its roads have inspired risk takers to follow the next bend to adventure.

But this is not a story just about Route 66—not entirely, anyhow. It is the story of our family's search for, and discovery of, quintessential America, while journeying down the most famous highway in the world. Route 66. With each mile that we traveled through diverse landscapes, the countless people that we encountered from all walks of life, and the unexpected circumstances that we constantly found ourselves in, we discovered the unquenchable, full-hearted spirit of America, and our own inspiration to keep moving forward. A life that has been lived is a life with some miles under its hood. We hope our story will inspire you to venture into the unknown too.

Part 1

In Search of Americana

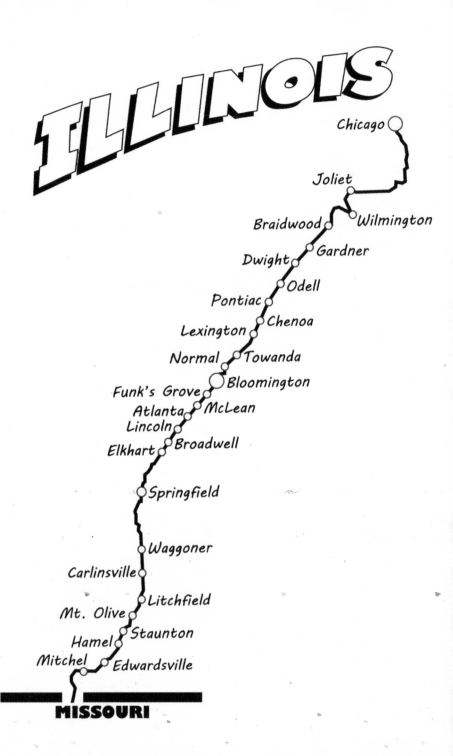

1

IT WAS AN early August morning when Kate, Thembi, and I first set foot in the small town of Wilmington, Illinois. Dark, menacing clouds threatened to rain down on what had started out as an idyllic day. The town's quaint streets seemed strangely quiet, only disturbed by the odd passing vehicle slowing down to shoot a welcoming wave from an open window. There was a dreamlike stillness that intensified a song from a family of birds in a nearby treetop. Loud pops of thunder in the distance further intensified the emotive atmosphere.

We had driven our Volkswagen SUV into Illinois with hungry anticipation. Iconic USA, with its quirky and colorful diners, museums, restored petrol stations, and roadside attractions all glimmering in the sunshine and bustling with warm and welcoming people, would await us. Glowing travelogues had promised us that the "real" America still existed, and we only need show up to get a taste. And now there we were, standing alone on a cracked, deserted parking lot next to a timeworn, closed-up diner—the once-popular Launching Pad Drive-In—without another soul in sight, nor any brilliant sunshine to illuminate our first Route 66 stop.

Nevertheless, our Great American Road Trip on Route 66 had properly commenced, and the fabled Gemini Giant, an enormous Muffler Man statue named after NASA's second human spaceflight program (begun in 1961), towered before us. His green and gray paint chipped and slightly faded, he still stood, having endured the years and all the good and bad that time had brought to tiny Wilmington. There was a lifelike quality about this giant. At twenty-one feet tall and weighing 438 pounds, he could be imposing, but at that moment, he just seemed sad. The gloom of the day was reflected in the stoic expression on his fiberglass face, as if he held on tightly to a million stories. Someone had managed to wedge an American football into the bottom of his space helmet. It must have taken some real effort, but this didn't seem to bother him. He came from a time when spacemen had broad shoulders.

I cannot count how many times that, while preparing for this road trip, we stared at his picture in books and magazines, and on more websites than I can recall, but we were still totally unprepared to come face-to-face with Gemini. There was something distinctive, human even, about this enormous relic from a bygone era that moved us.

In the same manner, the beginning of a road trip—especially on a legendary route like 66, which has been touted for decades as the most famous road in America—held something tantalizing and magical for me and for my family. Now a footnote from a simpler time, similar to the route itself, Gemini seemed somehow reflective beside the then-defunct Launching Pad (originally the Dari Delite), a diner that had once attracted hungry patrons from as far away as Chicago, fifty-nine miles to the north. The words "Route 66" were artfully splashed on a nearby wall, their big, bold letters filled with images of a red sports car, a humble town clock, an American flag, and Gemini himself—a picture of Route 66's story in Illinois. The air was crackling with history.

A half dozen blocks on down the route, near the center of town, another fiberglass creature, much smaller in size, awaited our admiration. A bright-green eighty-pound Sinclair DINO, a remnant of the long-successful marketing run of the Sinclair Oil Corporation, stood atop the front corner of a classic porcelain enamel, streamlined box-style building that was once a Sinclair station. First opened in the 1960s, the building was now being used as an unremarkable-looking tire store.

Around the corner from the jolly brontosaurus's watchful gaze, we stumbled upon the Mar Theatre, a quaint cinema dating back to the 1930s, with its simple but distinctive art deco style mostly intact. They were showing one of the *Toy Story* films.

Thembi, who was eight at this time, said, "We need to come back here at night," his eyes fixed on the beautiful marquee and its many light bulbs.

A couple of blocks away, near the bridge that carries the route across the Kankakee River, stood a plain two-story building that, like many other structures in town, is easy to miss. Only a large plaque beside the door of the historic Eagle Hotel identified it, and its simple, dated appearance belied the fact that it's one of the oldest commercial buildings on all of Route 66.

While the route officially begins on East Adams Street in bustling downtown Chicago, it seemed fitting that we began our journey in Wilmington, under the shadow of the world's most famous Muffler Man. We were standing where so many had stood before us, and yet, it had felt as though we were discovering a history, a piece of America that was rare and especially our own.

With 2,389 miles left to go, we had a deep sense of anticipation of what lay ahead.

2

"THERE ARE MORE on the other side." A smiling woman motioned with her hand as she noticed me taking photographs of the life-size statues of 1950s icons James Dean, Marilyn Monroe, and Betty Boop, which welcomed diners to Braidwood's Polk-a-Dot Drive-In.

With the Launching Pad long since closed and the early hour of the day, we found ourselves in Braidwood, down the road from Gemini and Wilmington, looking for some breakfast. At first, I was a bit embarrassed to be playing tourist, but the woman was so casual, almost dismissive, that I quickly realized that she must encounter camera-happy visitors like us all the time.

The Polk-a-Dot Drive-In was opened in 1956 by Chester "Chet" Fife. In its first incarnation, the drive-in was actually a bus that Fife purchased and painted in rainbow-colored polka dots, hence the name. But as business picked up, the Polk-a-Dot finally moved to its current location in 1962, where it continues to serve up classic American food like milkshakes, french fries, hamburgers—everything greasy right off the grill. With its signature white and light-blue theme colors and undeniable '50s vibe, the diner represents, for many, a picture of Americana that continues to define the nation globally. It's not difficult to visualize a busy Saturday evening there, with laughing teenagers, decked out in their coolest attire, driving up to the Polk-a-Dot in freshly waxed heavy-bodied cars, probably borrowed from their fathers, keen to show off their wheels and share in the local gossip. The diner's signature neon sign spinning slowly around, calling to the youth in the small Illinois town. Chuck Berry or Elvis blaring from the sound system.

Lost in my thoughts, I turned to walk around the restaurant but quickly jumped aside as a bright-red Toyota sedan crashed up over the curb and into the parking area, nearly making me a part of its front bumper. Three heavyset travelers emerged, almost frantically, from the traumatized little car, yelled at each other for a moment or two in rapid French, and then jumped back in. A torrent of choice words flooded my head, but before they could leave my mouth, the impudent motorists disappeared like a bad dream, back down the unassuming road from which they had come. I looked to the waitress in expectation of shared shock, but she simply continued to wipe the diner's glass door, unfazed, focused on getting the restaurant ready for its first customers of the day.

It finally started to drizzle as thunder rumbled above. The air was humid, and the sky held the promise of heavier precipitation. Rain can have a way of altering the mood of a place and creating a depressing scene. Still, that morning, at the start of Route 66, in the solitude of small-town America, the gray and melancholy somehow enhanced the romance of the experience and made us feel more alive, more a part of something bigger than ourselves. There is something to be said about being lost in reverie. Not then, though. We needed sunshine. We were on the road and it was summertime. Hurrying back to the vehicle, I spotted Kate cozying up next to Elvis, taking a selfie. Raindrops covered her smiling face and dripped down her cheeks.

"What are you doing?" I hollered over. "It's raining, get in the car."

"I want to take pictures with the people I meet on the trip."

"People? It's a statue!" Maybe there was something in the air.

Undaunted, she rushed over to the Blues Brothers and struck a pose, joining in with their wacky dancing stance, one leg in the air. Looking at the photograph later in the car, it actually looked like the trio was dancing together, as though she were the third sibling. It made me laugh.

Across the road lay a peculiar scene. An assortment of misfit characters—a pink elephant, a giraffe, a polar bear, and a red bull with white horns and golf balls for eyes—smiled goofily in our direction from their chest-level, fenced-in enclosure. This was the Braidwood Zoo, a quirky folk-art installation established in 2012—although the term "zoo" may have been a generous term when the local creators were dreaming of this attraction.

"Dad, is that a giant white rat?" Thembi asked, pointing to one of the large creatures covered in what looked like shreds of white nylon. In fact, I wasn't quite sure what we were looking at.

I paused longer than he was comfortable with. "That one, next to the really skinny . . . I think that's an emaciated cow."

It took some asking around before we discovered the identity of all of the inhabitants of this urban zoo. But that morning on North Front Street, Braidwood's portion of the Mother Road, the spectacle was right at home.

———

AFTER OUR ENCHANTING entry into northern Illinois, we drove south, through Gardner, with its two-man jail, and stopped to check out the beautifully restored Ambler's Texaco Gas Station at the intersection of old US Route 66 and Illinois Route 17 in the village of Dwight. Once known as Vernon's Texaco Station, as well as Becker's Marathon Gas Station, the spot got its current and most famous name from Basil "Tubby" Ambler, who had operated it from 1938 to 1966. The historic filling station, which was originally built in 1933, is now a very popular photo op and the quintessential Route 66 Illinois stop.

An older gentleman was seated idly next to the bay doors, seemingly waiting to welcome guests. The village was quiet—the rain had dissipated as quickly as it had started—and it looked like we were his first visitors of the soggy morning. He appeared happy to see us. He introduced himself as Carl and told us that he was a volunteer. He worked at the station once a week and loved meeting travelers from around the world.

"So are you going all the way to California?" he asked.

"Yes, we are," we answered proudly. "So far, we've really enjoyed what we've seen in Illinois."

He looked pleased. "And you say you are all from Africa? Even you?" He gazed at my blond hair and blue eyes with suspicion. It was not the first time in my life I had been asked this.

"Yep, even me," I said.

"And what brought you over here from Africa?"

"We wanted a change."

"And you decided that Route 66 was that change?" he asked slowly. He sounded baffled.

I smiled. It was a fair question.

It was our first time engaging with the unofficial American tradition of retirees spending a portion of their free time volunteering at historic landmarks. It was a little uncomfortable; we felt a bit like we were intruding on his peaceful day and being a nuisance. But Carl couldn't have been friendlier.

"You know, I've never done the whole trip myself," he said. "I would like to, but it's just never worked out. I have done most of Illinois, though. My son lives in Springfield and I have a daughter who does real estate down in Edwardsville. I try to take Route 66 when we go down to visit with them."

As the minutes wound by, we chatted about Dwight and the town gossip. Carl was a fount of knowledge about local happenings. Kate and I listened and laughed, soon drawn into local politics and family dramas. Thembi busied himself looking around the two-bay garage. He was impressed by all of the aged tools and equipment amassed to remind visitors of the station's historic past.

"Dad, look at this!" Thembi called. He was seated up high in a bright-red 1914 Ford Model T fire truck, pleased with himself and the experience. Kate strolled over and joined him, climbing into the passenger seat.

Carl smiled and was about to regale us with some information about the vehicle when a carload of new visitors with a Michigan license plate arrived. They looked delighted with their Route 66 find as they rushed past us, toward a plywood hole-in-the-face cutout of a welcoming service attendant, and began to take pictures.

Carl's attention shifted and it was clear that he was eager to speak with them. We thanked him for his time and decided to move on.

The heavy skies were slowly lifting, and the initial excitement of being on the highway was giving way to hunger, so we bought some pie and coffee from the Old Route 66 Family Restaurant across the road and stopped at a small park to enjoy our breakfast. There were a number of picnic tables that faced Route 66, offering a great view of the road. We sat underneath a large wooden canopy and listened to the insects come alive as the day began to slowly dry out. We were all alone, save for a few vintage vehicles that drove slowly past the park entrance. It had been a morning of chitchat and we were a bit talked out, so we sat and enjoyed being outdoors in Illinois, together in comfortable silence.

After an hour, we were done with breakfast and back on the two-lane highway, continuing south toward Odell. It was a journey of only twenty minutes from Dwight, but the deeper we ventured into Illinois, the more aware we became of the state's classic history, and the inherent need to slow down and embrace it. In today's crazy, manic world of always being on the go, it was rejuvenating to cast back sixty-five years and imagine how people once lived their lives.

We entered the town unexpectedly. That is one of the unique aspects of Illinois's section of the Mother Road; there are dozens of small towns that appear one after the other, the perfect introduction to the many Main Streets of America. We took left and right turns through the small community until we came upon one of the most photographed restored fueling stations in the state, the classic Standard Oil Gas Station.

Constructed in 1932 by local contractor Patrick O'Donnell—and modeled after 1916 Standard Oil stations in Ohio—the station originally sold Standard oil and gas for a mere twenty cents per gallon. In 1940, it switched to Phillips 66 fuel and, in order to compete with the other nine stations that fought for business along Odell's busy stretch of 66, O'Donnell added a two-bay garage for storage and service. Four years later, a bypass was constructed around the portion of Odell that housed the gas stations, and business began to dry up. By 1952, the station was in trouble and was leased by Robert Close, who owned a neighboring café. Close would go on to purchase the station two years later when O'Donnell died. In 1997, the station, through support from the Route 66 Association of Illinois Preservation Committee, was listed on the National Register of Historic Places. Then finally, in 1999, the association purchased the station from the Close family and donated it to the Village of Odell for the purpose of historic restoration. Now the tiny glimpse into seven decades ago is open as the town's welcome center and offers information and a myriad of memories.

Inside, we were taken aback by old black-and-white photographs and surprisingly simple vintage advertising that decorated the walls. Both Kate and I love period advertising. There is something so innocent, so unassuming about it, especially in our world of immediate information and knowledge at the click of a button. Consumers are jaded now and spoiled for choice, but back in the 1940s and '50s, things were different. It was the time when 20,679 physicians supposedly claimed that Lucky Strike cigarettes were good for you, and Cocaine Toothache Drops were only fifteen cents a pop.

An elderly, white-haired lady stood behind the counter, patiently waiting for us to make our way over. When we did, she was excited to tell us about her town and life on the Mother Road.

"I remember my father first took me on Route 66 back in 1944. He took me out of school, and we traveled for two weeks," said Mary, the volunteer at the tiny, picture-perfect refurbished fueling station. "Nowadays you wouldn't get away with doing that. But when I was a kid, things were much more relaxed and nobody really cared."

"That must have been really exciting! How far did you make it?" Kate asked.

"All the way to the ocean!" She beamed. "The road was much quieter back then and there were a lot more mountains." She paused and seemed lost in her thoughts.

"It's amazing how much things have changed," Mary continued. "But even back when I drove 66 with my dad, it was something memorable. Now we have people coming in here from all over the world. It has always been a very special road."

Thembi, who was listening quietly to Mary's stories about travels with her own father, was soon distracted by a frosted cooler behind us. It was packed with ice-cold beverages.

"Dad, can we get a Route 66 soda?" Thembi asked.

"A what?" I had never heard of the brand, but we were quickly discovering that Route 66 was a lucrative brand gimmick for many businesses.

"We've just had breakfast," I responded. "It's a bit too early for soda, Thembi."

"They are very tasty," Mary chimed in. "I really like the root beer."

"Why don't we all get one?" Kate suggested. "That way we can taste three of the flavors."

Route 66 Sodas is a Chicago-based brand of pop that uses sugarcane to sweeten their tasty drinks. They obviously know their market, as their products are found up and down the historic highway at strategic locations, tempting Route 66 enthusiasts like us—who don't generally drink a lot of pop—to try out their well-placed goods.

"I'll try the lime flavor," said Kate, while Thembi decided on the root beer and I landed on the grape.

Outside the Odell Standard Oil Gas Station, Kate, Thembi, and I stopped to enjoy our drinks and take in our serene surroundings. There was not a car or person in sight. A calm stillness characterized the town; not even the leaves on the trees shifted. It was hard to imagine that at a point in history not impossibly long ago, during Route 66's prime, the road in front of us was so busy with traffic that it was dangerous to cross. In 1934, the town had to build a pedestrian tunnel under Route 66, just so that people could get to the other side of America's Main Street safely. The tunnel, which is blocked now and no longer in use, is a reminder of how essential the old highway was at one time for those on the move. But it is also an indication of how quickly small-town America can be—and was—left behind.

To one side of the old station was a sign noting distances to various destinations: Chicago—87 miles; LA—2,361 miles. While it felt as though we had already been embraced by the road, we had, for all intents and purposes, gone nowhere. It was, for a moment, both exhilarating and overwhelming. Away from the crowds and the maddening realities of life back in Toronto, or Nairobi for that matter, time and monotony had forgotten us.

3

PONTIAC IS A warm and friendly town, designed to allow visitors to experience as much nostalgia, in easy walking distance, as possible. We liked the feel of the place right away and decided to stick around for a bit. For a small place, Pontiac has a lot to see: four well-designed and well-planned museums, twenty murals, several memorials, and lots of outdoor attractions, all within a manageable stroll. The town is only an hour and fifty minutes southwest of Chicago, but there in the heartland, big-city life seemed a world away.

"So where are you from?" asked Elizabeth, a retiree and volunteer at the Route 66 Association of Illinois Hall of Fame & Museum.

"We're from Africa. Do you know Kenya?"

"Well, I've heard of it, but I am not sure if we've ever had anyone visit from there. Please sign our guest book. We have signatures from all around the world. Maybe even someone in there from Africa," she noted with a smile.

The museum, located in the city's historic firehouse (built in 1900), was very well organized, and we had been advised by all of the guidebooks that it was one of the best on the route. The exhibits, as well as the actual layout of the venue, represented all eight Route 66 states in beautifully penned history and photography. The museum also housed famed Route 66 artist and cartographer Bob Waldmire's 1972 Volkswagen Microbus, which was the inspiration for the character Fillmore in the animated film *Cars*. Waldmire, who lived a somewhat unconventional life and traveled up and down the route in his VW van, came to prominence with his Route 66–focused art and his continual support for the preservation of the Mother Road. His efforts eventually won him the National Historic Route 66 Federation's John Steinbeck Award in 2004. The vehicle is roped off with a Do Not Touch sign on the side, but you can get a good glimpse of its inside, which is cluttered with Waldmire's artwork, books, Route 66 memorabilia, and other knickknacks that only very lightly reveal a snapshot of his life and character.

Michael Wallis once shared a story with me about Bob Waldmire that reveals a bit more about the artist's animated personality. Wallis recalled a day in the early 1990s when he pulled into Glenrio, Texas, to pay his respects to the ghost town. "As I walked around the derelict buildings, I picked up a bit of faint conversation riding the wind. I dipped in and around a few of the old buildings, sort of absorbing the town as I always did, when I began to pick up a little bit of conversation. I wasn't quite sure what the talk was, but it was punctuated by bursts of laughter. I was curious, because where I was coming from is where the paved road ends. So I walked down the road a little ways, and through the grass growing up all over the path, I could see somebody on the ground right in the middle of the road, and it was Bob. He was wearing his ubiquitous shorts and sandals and no shirt. Just a smiling Bob, lying on his back, and he was holding up, with his two hands above him, this great tortoise, this desert tortoise. It was a big thing, big as a football. He was holding it up, and they were having a conversation. More one sided of course, because Bob was doing all the verbalizing, but apparently, they were communicating quite well, because every once in a while, Bob would just let out a great holler and laugh. They were just having a great time, he loved nature so much, he really became part of nature. He was just wonderful that way, and so, although I hadn't seen him in a while, I decided right there at that moment, not to go down and talk to Bob. It looked like he was having such a good time with that tortoise, so I simply backed up and walked away."

As we wove our way around the exhibits, more and more wide-eyed visitors sauntered through the museum doors, creating a bit of a crowd. Up until then, we had been lucky to soak in the displays largely on our own. Not really ones for the masses, we headed outside to look around the rest of Pontiac. The gray clouds were completely gone now, and a pure blue sky welcomed us, as did a blistering heat and scorching sun. With the early-morning gloom burned off, the day had really begun.

In the parking lot at the rear of the museum, we found a big yellow school bus that had been converted into living quarters—Bob Waldmire's famous school bus home. It sat silent, permanently displayed, paying homage to its hippie owner. A mural of a large Route 66 shield adorned the redbrick wall next to a vintage sign for the Wishing Well Motel, a long-gone property built in 1941 that once stood proud in Countryside, Illinois. This mural is the oldest in Pontiac, and its popularity was evident from the number of people we saw going out of their way to pose in front of it for a selfie or group photo. We wandered across to the other side of the lot and checked out some of the other amazing lifelike murals that ornament this pretty town, each depicting a piece of the past.

We followed the colored footprints painted on the sidewalk that promised to lead us to various lures, trying to stay within the shape of the feet as we walked. Thembi was committed to spotting as many as he could of the fifteen colorful miniature art cars that are scattered around downtown, all uniquely decorated by various local artists. And just in case, also strategically placed around town were benches where visitors could sit and ponder this wonderful little city. Thembi was having a hard time keeping pace with his little legs but was making a grand time of the stroll. His laughter and joy were infectious. He was in his element, exploring, collecting memories as he went.

Down the road a short walk from the museum, past the town's elaborate, historic Livingston County Courthouse, Humiston-Riverside Park drew our attention, with its gorgeous swinging bridge—a suspended pedestrian crossway—spanning the Vermilion River. The bridge, built in 1978, is the newest of the three swinging bridges to call the city home. The oldest was constructed in 1898 by the Joliet Bridge Company. It was a serene setting, with an expansive grassy lawn, fat buzzing bumblebees, brightly colored singing birds, and a group of young people whiling away their summer day. The park appeared to jump right out of a storybook, but then again, so did much of Pontiac.

Thembi inspected the base of some nearby trees, on the lookout for insect life, one of life's enduring interests, while Kate gazed at the brown, slow-flowing river from the center of the bridge. I was busy taking pictures, increasingly frustrated with my inability to capture beauty on film in the way that my eyes were seeing it. I was suddenly aware that I had company.

"Hey, mister, whatcha doin'?"

A dozen young girls had found a distraction from their lazy day. Me.

Before I could answer, I was surrounded. "I'm ready, you can take my picture now," the bravest girl insisted, posing as though for the cover of Vogue.

Amused, I smiled at them but said nothing. I continued to explore and photograph. They stayed on my trail.

"No, pick me! I'm prettier and, besides, I can dance," exclaimed another, breaking out her best moves. The rest giggled and then started an elaborate, albeit poorly choreographed, performance.

Kate called from the bridge, drawing my attention.

"Where's he going?" the smallest asked, concerned.

"I don't know," said the cover model.

I felt like the pied piper as they followed me to the water. "Mister, do you live in Pontiac? Are you from here?"

"No," I answered slowly, "we're visiting from far away." I kept moving. They followed.

"It looks like you have a fan club," Kate joked. "Those little girls really want your attention." She laughed.

While they were a bit brash, I was impressed with their confidence to interact so freely with a stranger. I reflected back on my own youth—I'm not sure that I would have ever had the mettle to intercept an unfamiliar adult and petition to have my photo taken. The self-assuredness, or audacity, of this young generation well surpasses my own, certainly at their tender age. Or perhaps it was just an American thing.

I gathered my troops together. It was time to go. The kids were disappointed, as their diversion from the day's tedium was about to disappear.

"Hey, mister, is that your family? Do you have to go? Okay, but next time you're back in Pontiac, will you take our picture?"

4

LATER THAT DAY, as we passed through sleepy Lexington and its picturesque Memory Lane attraction—a one-mile stretch of original 1926 pavement, built almost a hundred years ago but still drivable today—my stomach began to lurch. I had been battling a flu for several days and was thankful that I had 66 to distract me. There are few things worse than being sick when traveling. I needed a break from the car and wanted to stretch my legs and get some fresh air. Just ahead of us was Towanda, home of the infamous Dead Man's Curve, a sharp bend in the road that from the 1920s to the 1950s was infamously treacherous for speeding motorists, catching many by surprise and leading them to an untimely end. This section was so dangerous that, along with several other accident-prone areas along the old highway, it gave Route 66 the unfortunate moniker of Bloody 66.

We stopped at a greasy roadside restaurant—the only eatery on this town's little stretch of the road—and ordered a bit of lunch. I watched as Thembi and Kate took down a hamburger and some potato chips with ease, but I found the smell of grease and grilled food extremely nauseating. I ducked outside into the sunshine and waited for them to finish. A line of antique vehicles motored past toward the city of Bloomington, slowly taking their time, enjoying the attention that they received from pedestrians and fellow motorists. At the rear of the convoy, an older couple in a red convertible smiled and waved, obviously delighted with the shared love of nostalgic automobiles. We were not long behind them.

Bloomington, which early settlers called Bloom Grove, traces its history to 1830, when the county seat was established, and is today a midsize city with a population of about seventy-seven thousand. But even that modest size was a bit of a shock to the senses, as we suddenly found ourselves surrounded by traffic lights, honking horns, and speeding automobiles after traveling down quiet Route 66 for some time. Bloomington was our first major urban stopover since arriving on the route, and it took a moment to shake our heads clear of the serenity of having the tarmac to ourselves. We decided to put up at the DoubleTree for a few days and use the time to strike out and experience other small towns within driving distance that were on our bucket list.

It was nice to be off the road. The day had been full, even a little overwhelming, as the route evoked a plethora of emotions, especially in the rainy haziness of the overcast early morning. We were traveling down a highway that had given birth to so much history, history that had given birth to legend. Al Capone, the famous Chicago mobster, once operated up and down the route, passing through tranquil towns to visit his brothels and bootlegging operations. And we would soon be passing through Lincoln country, a land steeped in undeniable narrative. Engaging with townsfolk, we were witnessing the legacy of Route 66 firsthand, and it was impossible not to absorb not only their longing for what once was but also their hope for what will be. They, too, were fighting for their better tomorrow and their American Dream, just as their families did before them. While the towns have the unique benefit of residing along a famous roadway that may hold added opportunities, they still represent small towns across America that do not—towns that also struggle to keep afloat as business and industry across the country has moved or died over the years.

Thembi and Kate took an opportunity for a quick swim at the hotel to refresh their tired bodies, while I grabbed a nap. After a short siesta, we headed out.

———

BLOOMINGTON, A TOWN that spreads out past its own Route 66 city bypass, offers a variety of great restaurants and its fair share of noteworthy attractions. The David Davis Mansion is the grand Victorian-era home of the Illinois senator who was Abraham Lincoln's mentor, and the Prairie Aviation Museum has a good collection of military aircraft that is worth seeing. The first Steak 'n Shake restaurant in the nation was opened in neighboring Normal in 1934. However, perhaps the most noteworthy attraction in Illinois's fifth-most-populated city is the impressive McLean County Museum of History. This venerable building features a variety of exhibits that trace Abraham Lincoln's time as a lawyer in the area, and celebrate the state's Route 66 heritage. We knew we had to see it for ourselves.

Outside of the museum, Kate quickly spotted a bronze statue of Abe himself sitting on a park bench, gazing sideways and smiling. "I need a picture!" she called before thrusting herself down beside the president and gazing affectionately in his direction. The photographs from that day really do look like they are two lovebirds enjoying a romantic afternoon and a heartfelt glance. I'm not sure how I feel about that.

The museum—which is housed in the county's longest-standing courthouse, dating to 1903—is impressive, with a small but fantastic Route 66 gift shop on the bottom floor that offers tons of books and merchandise. Stairs lead up to the awe-inspiring courtroom, with its incredibly ornate floor and ceiling, antique-looking chairs for the audience, and a rather intimidating bench where the judge would have presided. Lincoln practiced law on the Illinois Eighth Judicial Circuit, on this very site, but in a previous courthouse building. The museum reminds visitors of Lincoln's important work as a proponent for the antislavery movement, and of the birth of the Republican Party in the state of Illinois. We didn't know very much about Abraham Lincoln, or life in McLean County at the time, but as we wandered around each exhibit in the building, we became more and more impressed with the work and the man, and marveled at life in the quiet county in bygone years.

"It's pretty impressive, isn't it?" commented a mother of two as she gazed up at the high ceilings in the courtroom. Her eldest little boy was busy running around the spacious room, banging on polished wooden bannisters and jumping up and down on chairs. He was a bit of a menace.

"No, no, Jacob, don't do that, you'll break it!" Obviously exasperated, she looked down at her baby in his stroller, still innocent and, at the moment, sound asleep. "Why can't they just stay this way forever?" she mused, sighing.

"Are you guys from Bloomington?" I asked.

"Well, not really, but my grandparents on my mom's side live here, so we visit them a few times a year. My grandfather passed but my granny still lives nearby. What about you guys?" she asked, tossing her long, dirty-blond hair to the side and out of her eyes. She looked to be in her midthirties.

We explained about our background and that we were driving Route 66. She was impressed and surprised. We were beginning to realize that few Americans, even those living near the old road, actually knew much about it. Even fewer seemed to care. But they were curious, maybe even envious, when they discovered that we were heading west across the United States, and they had lots of questions for us.

"I would love to just get away. I lived in New York for a few years, Syracuse. But that was just after college and we've been in Illinois since before Jacob was born—Jacob, put that down! No, it is not a toy, stop spinning the chair! Jacob!"

Thembi had moved over onto the judge's bench and was preparing to hand out justice when the baby decided to wake up and join his brother in raising hell. The largely empty room with its impossibly high ceiling was the perfect location to magnify the reverb of the child's high-pitched cries.

"I better get these guys out of here. It was nice meeting y'all. Have a safe rest of your trip. You have a ways to go!"

She looked enviously at Thembi, who watched the courtroom drama unfold with interest. "Your little one seems like he will be just fine on such a long trip. I wish—Jacob, please stop running!"

Then, in a flash, they were gone and the room went silent.

"I am so glad we only have one child!" Kate whispered, putting her arm over my shoulder.

After they had departed, Judge Thembi Matthews dispensed his ruling: "You three are banished from this courtroom. Forever!" With the bang of a gavel, the case was closed.

5

FUNKS GROVE PURE Maple Sirup farm is tucked intimately away in a haven of leafy trees, twelve miles south of Bloomington and slightly off Route 66. Providing visitors something a little different from the normal 66 attractions, Funks has been producing and selling delicious maple sirup—their official spelling—in the region since 1891. History has it that Native Americans were the first to produce maple syrup and use it to season their food. Isaac Funk, the founder of what is now famously known as Funks Grove, was a member of the Illinois state senate (and a personal friend to Abraham Lincoln) before settling down to focus on his magnificent forest. Today, still under the care of the rather large Funk family, the grove produces over 1,800 gallons per season.

The air was heavy as we stepped onto the historic soil. Tall, distinctive maples provided shade and comfort from the heat of the day, giving some idea of what the landscape must have looked like 130 years ago, when Funk first arrived on the scene. A cornfield and a barn completed the view, while squirrels scurried to and fro, playing in the nearby brush.

A middle-aged man dressed in a pair of khaki pleated shorts and a collared polo shirt emerged from the tiny wooden store and made his way toward us. "How y'all doing today?" he asked, putting a brown paper bag inside of his blue BMW convertible. "Y'all down here to get some syrup? You driving 66? How far do you plan to go?"

Friendly, conversational, and eager to welcome us to the area's share of the Mother Road, the gentleman identified himself as a cousin to the Funks and waxed lyrical about his family and their long and interesting history in the community, before dashing away down the long, still road.

"I need to run—we're having a bit of a family reunion down in these parts."

A small RV pulled in as he left, carrying two older couples who were themselves doing Route 66 together, but at a much slower pace. "We're planning to take three months for the trip. There is so much to see and, frankly, we have nowhere else that we need to be for now. And I like spending so much time with the old girl," Tony said, chuckling and pulling his embarrassed wife in tight.

"Oh, you just stop that nonsense, mister. Never mind him, he's an old fool, always messing around." After planting a kiss on his cheek, she headed inside with her companion, Alice.

"Don't spend too much, Agnes," he called out. She huffed loudly and responded back, "We'll see! Depends what I find."

Kate followed in behind them.

Raising his camera, Tony's friend, Doug, had a proposition for me. "Do ya wanna trade?"

"Cameras?" I asked, surprised by his offer and a little taken back. I am rather fond of my Canon.

"No," he said, smiling. "I mean, if you take our picture, we'll take yours."

I laughed. "Sure, no problem. Are you guys heading west?" I asked.

"You betcha," Doug answered. "All the way to Mexico. We're heading south to get Tony's teeth fixed."

"Tony's teeth?" I wasn't quite sure how to respond.

"Oh yeah! His smile's been pretty awful for a long time now," said Doug, jabbing Tony playfully in the ribs. "Time to fix those pearly whites. We'll make a new man out of him."

Trying not to sound too shocked, I asked, "So you're driving all the way to Mexico, in an RV, so that Tony can get his smile fixed?"

"Yes, sir," Tony responded excitedly. "And we've been told that these days Mexico is a leading country for dental cosmetic surgery. And I'll save a lot of money to boot!"

I had literally just watched a documentary, before leaving for our trip, on the dangers of getting plastic surgery south of the border. But it reminded me that people travel down Route 66 for all sorts of reasons.

"Can I ask, what made you guys decide to invest your extended holiday on Route 66?" I inquired.

"Well, it's pretty simple," Tony started. "Agnes and I had done the route before, about six years ago, and we were just blown away by all that there was to see, and by the hospitality of the people we met on the route. We were in a smaller vehicle at that time, and only drove to Flagstaff, but it gave both of us a sense of pride, as Americans, to discover how much Route 66 really developed the country, and to meet so many down-to-earth people working every day to keep it alive. We wanted to get back out and really take some time to reengage with the road, and revisit some of the places and people that meant a lot to us during the last trip."

"For us," chimed in Doug, "we're just tagging along!" His laugh was loud and contagious. "You know, us Americans know so little about our own country. We watch too much television and so we think we know what's going on. There's a whole history that few of us know anything about, and kids these days . . . ha! They're being taught very little in school and seem to largely reject much of what our generation stood for. It's a shame, really. It's great that you're exposing your little boy to Route 66. I'm sure that he'll remember this trip forever."

Tony nodded vigorously.

"I hope so. He's really been enjoying the trip so far. He's a huge fan of insects and rocks and minerals, so New Mexico and Arizona will likely be his favorite spots, but we'll see."

I took one last photo of the men as Kate emerged triumphantly from the shop with a brown paper bag in hand. She had grabbed a large glass bottle of syrup. "Why did you get the glass bottle?" I asked. "Isn't the plastic one lighter and easier to pour from?"

"It is, I guess, but I like this one. Doesn't it look pretty?"

The older women had not made their way out of the shop yet and their husbands began to take on worried expressions. "I think we better go and check on our wives." Tony laughed. "We need to make sure that we have enough money left to finish the trip."

We watched as they disappeared into the store, happy, relaxed, and embracing their retirement. It is a position that we all hope to be in one day.

"Dad, come and check this out," Thembi shouted from the edge of the adjacent forest. "Can we go inside and investigate? Look, there is even a walking path."

"Okay, hold on, we're coming," I called. He was already on the move.

Kate took my hand in hers and leaned in to kiss. It was a time of repose and happiness. There we were in the middle of a serene, lush green forest, fresh from Funks with two months' worth of their maple syrup, a curious little boy, and most of the Mother Road still ahead of us. Could things get any better? Thembi led the way along the short but pleasant path that meandered through the shady woods. It was cooler in the forest and Kate commented about needing a sweater. Plastic tubing stretched across the trees, transporting maple syrup to holding containers while dozens of daddy longlegs spiders ran across our path. We listened as birds sang in the thick foliage above.

"Dad, did you know that daddy longlegs aren't even really spiders?" Thembi asked. "They have eight legs, but spiders have two body parts—a cephalothorax and an abdomen—and daddy longlegs have only one body part. And most spiders have eight eyes, but daddy longlegs only have two small eyes mounted on their back."

The natural world has always been fascinating to Thembi, and insects have always been his favorite. Back in Africa, the great outdoors was at his fingertips. It was not unusual to spy a Jackson's chameleon in the garden or a large tortoise lollygagging across our lawn. A simple investigation of our avocado or lemon trees or scratchy grass could expose a wonderment of bug and animal life. There, in the mature forest of Illinois, it was refreshing to step into a familiar world that reminded us of home.

"No, actually, I had no idea," I answered. "But this forest is packed with them. They're everywhere!"

"I'm outta here," said Kate "There are way too many creepy-crawlies for me."

6

THE ROAD WEST of Bloomington along Route 66 is some of the loveliest, most peaceful asphalt in Illinois. The state has well-placed brown Historic Route 66 road signs in strategic locations to keep travelers going in the right direction, leaving drivers free to enjoy the calm, untroubled sojourn through country as old as time. As we maneuvered along, the huge sign for the Dixie Travel Plaza loomed in the sky, announcing its location in tiny McLean. The parking lot was filled with vehicles and intimidating 18-wheelers. It was either a very popular joint or we had arrived at a particularly busy time.

Established by businessman J. P Walters and his son-in-law, John Geske, in 1928, the truck-stop restaurant has been serving happy customers for a very long time. The name Dixie is odd for an Illinois-based restaurant, but the venue was so named to reflect its southern hospitality (it was called both Dixie Truck Stop and Dixie Truckers Home in earlier years). Dixie is considered to be the first real truck stop in Illinois, and most likely one of the first on Route 66.

We slid into a booth near the window and sank down into the well-worn upholstery. "Can you imagine a place like this in Kenya?" Kate whispered. "Local truck drivers would be in heaven."

Dixie is spacious and airy with big windows that gaze out onto the generous parking area. There is a counter with stool seating, and the walls are adorned with midcentury, old-school memorabilia. Road travel in Africa comes with no official rest areas or access to public toilets, let alone a designated travel center for truckers. In America, there is a romanticized notion of the truck driver, and truckers are given a level of respect that is miles apart from their African counterparts. There are no country songs about African truckers, even though they are the backbone of many African economies. Instead, they are generally considered a nuisance and a menace on the highways, blocking traffic and causing accidents. They are often regarded as rough characters with risky, often amoral behavior, who drive too slowly or too quickly, and are best avoided. In the United States, they are very much the salt of the earth and their work seems to be understood by many as essential to the economy.

A plump older gentleman, with gray hair and innumerable creases on his seasoned face, glared at us unflinchingly from an adjacent booth. I couldn't tell if there was a hardness or a curiosity in his eyes. I smiled back, uncomfortably, but he simply looked away and then down at his menu. I wondered if his intent gaze was of the "Hey, there! I am slightly out of my mind and I am so glad that you are here!" deranged variety, or the "I spend way too much time alone and am somewhat socially awkward and a bit lonely" kind.

After ordering, he looked up again and then gawked back in our direction.

"Why is that man staring at us?" Thembi whispered in an uncertain voice.

He was actually starting to creep us out.

After what felt like an eternity, the man finally spoke. His voice was soft and gentle, surprisingly measured. "Where y'all headed?"

I paused before answering. Should we tell him?

"We're driving Route 66 to Santa Monica," I said slowly. I've never been very good at evading questions. I crack immediately.

"Well now, that is quite a trip. Quite a trip, indeed," he said while taking off his tan jacket and adjusting his low-hanging trousers, pulling them up to cover his exposed lower back. A huge set of keys dangled from a loop on his waist, further tugging at his pants each time he shifted in his seat. With a brush of his hair to the side, he settled in and let out a deep sigh.

And so that is how we met Dan, not a traveling serial killer, but a Vietnam vet turned professional bus driver, who, while a little odd, had some interesting stories to share.

"I was a bus driver with a leading company during Katrina, down in New Orleans. That was a bad time. So many people affected, so many lives destroyed . . . it was my job at that point to pick up as many people as possible from New Orleans and drive them to safer locations in Dallas and Houston. I live in St. Louis now, but since my wife died nine years ago, I don't really have any desire to be at home, so I'm on the road a lot."

His life struck me as a lonely one. I could appreciate why, after losing his wife to cancer, he was not crazy about sitting alone in his house—and why he had, as a result, the inner need to connect with others when opportunity allowed. Still, it was taking us some time to get used to how intimate, how open and trusting, people in Middle America could be. Americans on this route appeared to wear their hearts on their sleeves, offering themselves freely and asking for nothing in return but respect and a friendly ear.

"Where are y'all coming from? You don't look like you're from Illinois."

That was an interesting statement. I wondered what people from Illinois looked like, but I didn't ask.

"Do you know Kenya?" I responded.

He stared at me blankly.

"It's a country in East Africa. We—"

Dan jumped in. "Africa! Now there's a place I've never been. What language do y'all speak over there? I see that y'all know a bit of English. That's good. And people over there in Africa know about Route 66? Well, I'll be . . . who woulda thought? So how are y'all finding America?" His questions came rapidly, one after the other without any real pause for us to answer.

Living in Canada since late 2015, we had heard a lot of folks speak unfavorably about their neighbor to the south, but we personally have always viewed America as a land of opportunity and, genuinely, a beacon of tolerance, where we all can find a place to fit in. Kate and I love America and its unique character.

"Well, I don't think too many folks back in Africa know much about Route 66," I said. "But in many ways, American culture, in general, is very similar to our own."

"You'd be surprised by how much influence America has in some parts of Africa," Kate added. "As a matter of fact, American TV and music hugely impacts how kids in Nairobi grow up."

"But the portion sizes in the US have been a bit shocking," Thembi tossed in, as a young waitress delivered a tray of food to the booth behind Dan. "Restaurants here serve huge amounts of food."

Chuckling, Dan replied, "Yes, indeed, young man. We do like to eat in the US. But some people are just gluttons. There is a lot of waste here. But you look like you could use a little meat on your bones. You're just a stick."

Thembi smiled shyly.

As though on cue, the waitress arrived with Dan's order, an overflowing plate of mashed potatoes, requisite biscuits and gravy, and a gigantic turkey sandwich. We were amazed. Dan, however, was not satisfied. "Can I get some more biscuits?"

"Sure, darlin', I'll be right back." The waitress barely batted an eye.

"What was I sayin'?" Dan asked, digging in. A large glob of gravy rested on the corner of his mouth. Couldn't he feel it? Should we say something? Thembi began to speak and I squeezed his leg. He hushed. Mercifully, Dan suddenly sneezed and wiped his nose, inadvertently removing the gravy as he did so. "Oh yeah, Route 66. I haven't actually done the whole route myself, but I intend to one day," he said. "I'm just not sure when I'll be able to find the time. My driving keeps me on the road a lot. But I get to meet new people all the time, and I like that."

When our food arrived, the conversation took a pause, giving us a good opportunity to take in the place. Dixie's decor is 66 to the core, with aged adverts for brands like Ted's Root Beer, Coca-Cola, and Tootsie Rolls covering the walls and lit emblems of Sinclair, Fire-Chief Gasoline, Phillips 66, and Mobil decorating the wooden partitions between cozy blue-and-wine-colored booths. Dixie is a celebration of all things '50s and vintage.

Dan noticed that we were having a hard time finishing our meals, and laughed. "You guys barely ate a thing. Not much of an appetite in Africa?"

"We're not really used to being served so much food," said Kate.

When Dan ordered a large piece of apple pie, Thembi's eyes grew big, but he knew better than to say anything. Dan finished every last bite, belching to show his satisfaction. Thembi giggled.

Standing to leave, he held out his hand, offering a firm grip and some kind words. "Y'all travel well and take good care. You got a lot of road ahead of you, but I bet you'll have some real stories to tell when it's done."

As I watched him walk out the door, I was struck by the reality that we will most likely never see Dan again. Roaming down Route 66 and across America, we had already encountered dozens of friendly, interesting, kind people, most, if not all, of whom we would never meet again. Life is funny in that way, how we come and go in and out of each other's lives, if only for an instant, and yet still seem to leave an impression, and, if we are lucky, an impact.

———

"THERE IT IS!" Thembi exclaimed, pointing. In front of us stood the next Muffler Man giant that we had on our must-see list. Down in the tiny town of Atlanta, Illinois, population under 1,700, stands a true testimony to American history and ingenuity. With a height of nineteen feet, slightly smaller than Gemini, and holding a hot dog, rather than a rocket, the Paul Bunyon (spelled with an "o" to avoid copyright issues) giant is a sight to behold, with his royal-blue pants, bright-red (and slightly too tight) shirt, and huge black shoes. And this little town is the perfect place for him to reside. But he did not always call Atlanta home.

Originally, back in 1966, "Tall Paul" was located on the roof of Bunyon's Hot Dogs on Route 66 in Cicero, Illinois. But soon he was relocated to the front of the venue so that children would be able to see him properly and appreciate him. They liked to climb on his feet. When Bunyon's closed, the giant was put up for auction. Atlanta made the successful bid in 2003 and the smiling Muffler Man found a brand-new home. Long may he remain.

Across the street from the giant were the Palms Grill Cafe and the Memories: Route 66 Museum, both perfect additions to the streetscape. Atlanta is very much a one-street town, with a quaint little library that serves as a serene, safe hangout for local kids on the weekends. The town was quiet and empty; not much happened while we were there, but we loved the simple, relaxed atmosphere of Atlanta, and have added it to our list of favorite places to spend some time on Route 66.

We decided to grab a slice of pie at Palms and spent the next hour gazing at the tourists as, one after the other, they arrived and marveled at the historic advertising gimmick that is still pulling people off the highway.

"Can we get two hamburgers, with onion rings and two Cokes, please?" asked a customer who had taken a seat near us, along with his companion. "But we're in a rush—we're on our way to St. Louis and we're behind schedule."

"Are y'all driving Route 66?" she asked, jotting down their order.

"Yes, but we only have one day for Illinois," the man responded with a German accent. "So we want to finish here quickly and make sure that we see Springfield and the museum in Litchfield before it gets too late." She didn't seem fazed. We were.

"Excuse me," I said, leaning in their direction. "Are you guys trying to get to St. Louis today? When did you start your trip?"

The two men spoke to each other in German. The quieter traveler did not seem to know much English.

"We arrived in Chicago last night and will do Illinois in one day. We were told that there is not really much worth seeing so are trying to get out west quickly. We only have two weeks to get to Los Angeles."

He must have seen my eyes go wide. "Why, how long are you taking?" he countered.

"We're moving a bit slower across the country," I responded.

"Yes, but how long here in Illinois?"

Kate and I looked at each other. "One week," I said as he took a gulp of soda.

Choking, he coughed up soda on to his chin and translated for his companion, whose eyes also grew big.

"Wow, that is a lot of time. Are there that many things to see here?"

We chatted about the history and the gas stations, the museums, giants, vintage vehicles, and all that the beginning of the Mother Road has to offer. He seemed disappointed that he and his fellow traveler wouldn't get to experience it all this time around, but after polishing off their meal and gearing up to hit the road again, he stopped and looked at us.

"I think that we will slow down on our way south and try to see what else there is to take in."

For a great many travelers, domestic and international, the Midwest represents the ordinary, the expected, but the West is where the trip really starts to come alive. From our experience, by that point, Illinois had more to offer than we had ever anticipated or hoped.

7

ROAD TRIPS ARE always filled with expectation, not to mention the unexpected, but more than anything, driving for long distances gives travelers time to fill—lots and lots of time. Dropping south through Illinois, the 122-mile stretch to Staunton gave us (or I should say, gave Kate) a good opportunity to catch up on some Mother Road reading. On her lap were several handy guidebooks, crowding her already-limited space. But she didn't mind.

"Did you know that there was a book called the *Green Book* that came out in 1936?"

"The *Green Book*? No, what was it?"

"Apparently, black road travelers were not allowed to spend the night in a lot of towns along Route 66 during the '30s up to the '60s. There was even a name for it: sundown towns. All blacks had to be out of town before dark or risk being arrested, or worse. Can you imagine?"

Those were indeed difficult times, and discrimination and blatant racism were present across many parts of the country, not just along America's Main Street. Most people don't know this side of the history of 66, but the route was not always carefree and "live and let live" in its nature. In early 1930, according to a 2016 article in the *Atlantic* by Candacy Taylor, forty-four out of eighty-nine counties along Route 66 were considered "sundown towns."

First produced in 1936 by Victor Hugo Green, a New York postal carrier, the Green Book was originally titled *The Negro Motorist Green Book* and initially focused on the New York area. However, the book became hugely popular, and the following year, a second (revised) edition was released that included other places within the United States. The new edition came out with a simplified name: the *Green Book*.

"Check this out," Kate continued, sharing a disturbing piece of information that she had read. "During the '50s, Esso was one of the only franchised gas stations available to blacks. That is crazy. All of these stations along Route 66, and only Esso was open to taking black money?" Kate was astounded. "Black travelers even had to carry buckets in their trunks, as many whites-only establishments did not allow them access to the toilet."

"That is unbelievable," I answered. "I had no idea there was so much black road travel in the '40s and '50s. We haven't seen a lot of black representation so far on the route, or even on any of the old promotional items."

"Yeah, we haven't," Kate said, nose still deep in her book.

"So is the guide still in any form of production?"

"No, it was discontinued after the passing of the Civil Rights Act in 1964. I always thought that race issues in the US were focused in the Deep South. It kind of makes Africa seem ahead in at least one area," she added.

Since the end of the colonial period, race in Africa has never really been a big issue—outside of South Africa and Zimbabwe, that is. In Africa, tribalism often plays a much uglier role in prejudice and discrimination. But being a minority in Kenya, I can certainly appreciate the reality of being made to feel different and an outsider; however, I was never barred from going where I wanted, when I wanted. Traveling across Route 66, my black wife, mixed-race child, and I had experienced nothing but kindness and hospitality thus far, but it was sobering to realize that the reception may have been quite different fifty years ago.

———

UP AHEAD, THE sky was dark and overcast again. The promise of more rain hung in the air.

"I thought that we had left the bad weather behind." Kate sighed.

"Maybe it's only an isolated spot," I responded. "The forecast calls for sunny skies as we head south." In the distance, the clouds were looking a little cataclysmic.

"What are you guys talking about?" Thembi asked, closing his book on little-known facts about insects and reptiles. "Not rain again! By the way, where are we going now?"

"We're going to look for a place to stop up ahead," Kate answered. "How are we doing on gas?" she asked.

"Good. We're fine," I said. We were down to half a tank.

"Do you think we'll make it, or should we fill up when next possible?"

Kate has a deep paranoia of a vehicle running out of gas. When the gauge reaches a quarter empty, her anxiety begins to build.

"We'll be fine. We have plenty of fuel and Illinois has lots of towns to stop in."

"Okay, but if we break down on the side of the highway, you're the one going for gas."

And with those encouraging words and the serene towns of Lincoln and Broadwell behind us, the clouds closed in and brought with them a violent deluge. The road, mostly empty, vanished, and I braked quickly and switched on my hazard lights. All I could see was a wall of water. It was an incredibly heavy downpour that created zero visibility, but we kept going, slowly. I was afraid to pull off the road and potentially get hit from behind by someone not aware of our stationary vehicle.

Outside, the atmosphere became dismal again, and Route 66 took on a less romantic, more downtrodden, glum feel. It's amazing how much the weather frames our perception of places and events and affects our mood.

"Look, it seems to be getting brighter up ahead," Kate noted, a trace of hope in her words. "Don't miss the turnoff. It's coming up."

"I won't! I see it," I said defensively. It was the third time she had mentioned it. I was about to tell her to relax and stop worrying when, without warning, I drove straight past our exit. She was silent but I could feel a slight grin developing on her face.

Dan was somewhere far down the road by now, but once again I sensed a pair of eyes burrowing into me. I refused to look in her direction. I turned back around and gently backtracked toward the entrance to town. Kate patted my leg and shook her head and huffed. "You!"

As we entered the town of Elkhart for lunch, the wind and rain blew past.

THERE WAS SOMETHING curious about the very idea of a man opening up his home to dozens of bunnies, but with the Mother Road, nothing surprised us anymore; we were acclimatizing quickly. Anything was possible, and even the strangest of ideas could find a home. Highways like Route 66 are very much the petri dish of America.

"Do you really want to stop here?" I asked Kate.

"Of course! Why not? When I was young, we had a pet rabbit named Tweety."

"Tweety?" Thembi asked, poking fun at his mom.

"Yes, Tweety, and he was very friendly!" She knew that he was having a go at her. "He used to bite us when we tried to pick him up and constantly tried to run away, but otherwise he was a great pet."

"What happened to him?" Thembi asked.

"He managed to get out of his cage one day and our dog, Nyuki [Kiswahili for 'bee'], killed him," Kate answered. "But he was nice while we had him."

Thembi and I looked at each other with a grin. After such a tragic story, how could we refuse? And so in we went to the compound.

A large beige van was parked out front of what looked like an old filling station, next to some restored Olympic gas pumps. Hearty laughter was erupting from inside the small structure, so we decided to explore the assortment of oddities in the front yard in order to allow the visitors their time with Rich and the live rabbits, while we had the exterior to ourselves. A neat row of VW Rabbits buried nose down in the soil was rusting away in the sun, a shout-out to the more famous Cadillac Ranch in Amarillo, Texas. To the side of the building was an enormous eight-foot-tall rabbit, complete with stairs. While the creature was smiling, there was something ominous about it. Maybe it was the numerous gravestones beside it, each bearing the name of a dead rabbit. Okay, yep, that was definitely a bit unusual.

As we loitered around some old vintage motel signs that rested, as if discarded, on the well-trimmed lawn, the visitors stepped out of the building and into the sunlight, obviously elated with their stop.

"I really love this place," a gent with a clipped English accent noted. "Especially getting to touch the bunnies."

"That fat one in the back seemed to really like you!" reassured a woman with a pixie cut and pink highlights, as she straightened out her pale-pink "Kicks on 66" T-shirt and adjusted an enormous handbag that rather resembled a suitcase. On her head, a mauve "Route 66 Rocks" visor protected her eyes from the sun, and a stack of Mother Road postcards filled her hand.

Climbing into their vehicle and returning to the hunt for the perfect 66 adventure, the group made a right turn from the compound and headed west, back down the Mother Road.

"Come in, come in," exclaimed a man as we gently pushed the door open and peered inside. Dark hair peppered with slight gray framed a round face, while rimmed glasses shielded expressive, intelligent eyes. The man exuded a jovial disposition. "Where are you people from? Africa? Wow, I'm not sure I've had too many people come in here from Africa. Maybe South Africa. So you must be doing Route 66? Hello, young man, do you want to say hello to the bunnies?"

Located forty-five minutes from the Missouri border and the historic Chain of Rocks Bridge, Henry's Ra66it Ranch was much smaller than we expected. It was more of a shop than a ranch, crammed full of Route 66 memorabilia and perhaps half a dozen rabbits in individual cages. But it immediately gave off a positive vibe, as did its proprietor, Rich Henry.

Traveling down the Mother Road in 1995, Rich noticed a lack of visitors' centers on Route 66. Realizing that this needed to change, he immediately set to work, opening one in his hometown of Staunton. In recent times, there has been an explosion of visitors' centers and souvenir shops on the route, but back in '95, the Ra66it Ranch, which actually started out as Henry's Old Route 66 Emporium, was at the forefront. But why rabbits? Well, the Henrys' daughter, Emily, it seems, had received a pair of lovable rabbits, but was unaware of their propensity to multiply. Soon, to everyone's dismay, there were many bunnies. But being on Route 66, this was not a problem. In fact, it gave the Henry family an answer to the puzzle they were trying to solve: What would the nature of the attraction be? And so, as they say, the rest is history and the Ra66it Ranch was born. And grow it did. At one point, the ranch had a whopping forty-nine rabbits.

"After seeing the quirky way Juan at the Snow Cap operated, I felt this rabbit ranch thing, with both the bunnies and the VW Rabbit cars, would be something to catch people's curiosity. And it has, and has them coming back for more, once they've been here once. Besides, who doesn't love a furry, cuddly bunny?" Rich explained. (Delgadillo's Snow Cap is a kitschy eatery in Seligman, Arizona, that has become a major roadside attraction known for its food pranks.)

"Are those real graves beside the big rabbit in the yard?" I asked.

"Yes, eventually the area there with the big eight-foot-tall bunny will be made into a formal memorial park called the Tale of Ears."

Okay, that did sound a bit eccentric, at least to me, but it was obvious how much Rich loves Route 66, and how much attention he has dedicated to his rabbits.

The ranch has even had celebrity bunnies. "Big Red was the man who succeeded Montana as the official counter greeter of Route 66 travelers. Like the rest, he was a bunny from the shelter of the House Rabbit Society of Missouri in St. Louis. He had a special demeanor about him, like no other. He would lie on the counter waiting for travelers to come in and take notice of him. Then he autographed postcards for the people when asked to do so. His time here was special and his memory and legacy continues on like Montana and the others."

As we listened to him share his thoughts on modern-day Route 66, Rich's soft voice and gentle persona made him instantly likeable. He is one of those people you root for, regardless of how long or well you know them. As he told us about the multitude of bunnies that have passed through his care, it was hard not to visualize Rich in the host role on a 1980s children's television show, sitting in a cozy armchair, fostering a love of long-eared mammals with a small group of well-behaved kids sitting crossed-legged at his feet . Picture Mister Rogers with a fat, lovable rabbit on his lap. There is a real congeniality in Rich that, mixed with his enthusiasm for his furry friends and Route 66, created an instant rapport.

America's Main Street survives because of passionate individuals like Rich Henry, people who have spent their entire lives nurturing the route, which in turn takes care of them too.

8

ON THE OUTSKIRTS of St. Louis, near the forested town of Eureka, sits a different face of Route 66, a darker, more sinister visage. Originally known as Lawler Ford Road, the nondescript, unmaintained route has been dubbed Zombie Road since at least the 1950s. Built in order to open up access to the Meramec River and the railroad tracks, the once-scenic road has experienced a substantial share of death and is reported to be haunted. Tales of a flaming car driving along the road, the appearance of the ghost of a man hit by a train during the 1970s, and the hair-raising screams of an old woman are just a few of the more popular stories passed down from generation to generation. However, it is believed that it is the spirit of Della Hamilton McCullough, perhaps more than any other, that still haunts the road. Killed in 1876 when she was struck by a train car, McCullough is said to wander the road, translucent and alone, forever attached to the tragic location where her life was lost.

Whatever the truth, we are not the type of travelers to detour in search of ghouls and ghosts. In our world of coastal Africa, spirits and apparitions are all too familiar, and few people have an interest in seeking them out. That detour was a hard pass for us as a bleak drizzle enhanced the spooky history.

The *Route 66: EZ66 Guide for Travelers* offered multiple options for motorists to navigate the various Route 66 alignments once in St. Louis, but for some reason, we found ourselves lost in an area of town that did not sound familiar. St. Louis is a big city, full of people and cars, and with a lot of summer construction, normally flowing roads were closed, and multiple lanes unexpectedly turned into single ones. Motorists were noticeably confused and frustrated. And they knew their city! But somehow, we managed to follow the road signs and found our way out of the urban tangle.

Once we had left the hectic streets of St. Louis and the surrounding suburbs behind, we found ourselves grateful to be back on Route 66—we actually do love St. Louis, with its vibrant history and welcoming feel, but we were a bit flustered with the constant traffic and endless construction that day. Missouri is rightfully famous for its forested wilderness, rolling green hills, and abundant rivers and lakes. There was an earthy feel from the moment we left big-city St. Louis and its concrete buildings and crowds, though straight out of St. Louis, the road does not lead back to a quiet two-lane route but rather a very fast-moving highway (but at least it was moving). We generally enjoy the outdoors, but that day the incessant drizzle we had entered did not help enhance the energy in the car. We were all quiet as we headed south.

We passed through the tiny town of Pacific, an easy-to-miss destination best known for its scenic lime bluffs. That day they were hard to enjoy due to the thick fog blanketing the highway. As we continued on, an old motel sign waited up ahead, missing an "e" in the title—an empty spot where the letter once lived—and there were auction signs everywhere, advertising an upcoming event. A quite dilapidated Gardenway Motel loomed on the left, its once-proud sign close to crashing down on the wet concrete.

The weather was making us lethargic. Sleepy. We didn't know exactly where we were—maybe Villa Ridge? Small trailers rested on the right-hand side of the road, beside an abandoned brown-brick building. Up ahead, also on the right, was the Sunset Motel. We wanted to pull over and take some pictures of the faded sign and V-shaped building, but traffic had built up behind us and we had become a magnet for tailgaters. It was too dangerous to try to stop, so we made a mental note to visit another time. American flags decorated every other house, their proud fabric lying limp in the moist air. A group of motorcycles overtook the long line of vehicles to our rear, gradually making their way to the front of the convoy. They were the variety of bikes with the huge, cushiony seats that make riders look more like they're sitting on a living room couch than on a bike. The last rider in the line waved to us and stuck a thumb in the air. Perhaps our meandering was too much for our fellow road users, or perhaps they were sparked on by the motorcyclists, but one by one, the vehicles behind us pulled out and pushed ahead, disappearing around a bend in the curvy road. Soon, we were all alone again.

"What's that?" asked Kate a few miles later, motioning ahead. There was a huge flea market taking place on the right, just off the highway. The sign indicated that it was the Great American Flea Market, and it was buzzing. The lot was full of cars and pickup trucks, and an adjacent trailer park was alive with onlookers watching the day's activities. Soon, signs for Meramec Caverns began to appear. Meramec Caverns is the largest system of caves in Missouri, running 4.6 miles long through the Ozarks and visited by over 150,000 people a year. There had been indications of the destination back in Illinois, but now that we were in Missouri, billboards advertising the attraction were beginning to pop up in rapid succession. It was a cool throwback to old-school advertising campaigns: "Meramec Caverns Ice Cream," "Meramec Caverns in 12 Miles," and then a sign with an outlaw hiding his face—we could just see his shifty eyes—advertising the Jesse James Wax Museum up ahead (exit 230). Farther down the road, behind a billboard on the left, was an old, broken-down white house that had been totally taken over by the forest. It was almost hidden, crumbling in real time as the earth reclaimed it. The treetops were covered in thick, heavy spiderwebs. Thembi was amazed. "Can you imagine the size of those spiders?" he commented.

Route 66 crisscrosses I-44 continuously in some parts of Missouri.

It can get confusing at times to stick to the Mother Road as you cross over or under the interstate numerous times. After another few miles, we slowed down and got over onto the south frontage road, driving past a run-down trailer court. A dozen teenagers were sitting around on lawn chairs, gabbing. Two boys were playing basketball with a single improvised hoop that they'd set up. Their court was a field of scraggly, thorny grass and stone. It was a depressing scene in a dreary area.

Another Meramec Caverns sign came into sight, this time with a magician showcasing the Caverns. "Ta-da!!" The road continued to rise and fall as we gradually made our way west and tried to escape the dull weather and oddly overpowering greenery and forest.

———

"CAN WE GO and see the Jesse James Wax Museum?" Thembi pleaded. "I want to see if they'll have any of his guns on display."

"I don't know, guys," I responded slowly, looking up at the washed-out, dated sign. "I'm not too sure that this is going to be worth our time. It actually looks a bit sketchy."

"Why don't you just go inside and take a look?" suggested Kate. "If it's good, just come back out and get us. It would be nice to be out of the vehicle for a bit." Kate had a look of determination on her face, and I knew not to protest.

Inside, the venue was crammed with toy guns and an assortment of black-and-white photographs and Route 66 and Old West memorabilia. Unlike the museums in Illinois, this one was pretty small and rather run-of-the-mill. There was no "pop," but the place itself did generate a weird feeling of stepping back a few decades (not to the Old West, but to the 1980s). After a quick chat with the manager and a look around, I fig-ured that it was worth a visit, since we were already there. The tour began with a VHS tape—totally '80s in quality and feel—whose crackly sound underscored the vintage vibe in the place, further transporting visitors out of the twenty-first century. Alone on the tour, we sat on wooden benches, oddly alert to any noises or sudden movement behind us. The room was dimly lit, save for the glow of the box television. It was an unusual place and a little bit eerie.

"Can we walk around now and see the museum? I think I've seen enough of the film," asked Thembi, after watching the grainy documentary for ten minutes.

So had we.

Around the corner began a short, but well-sculpted wax-figure display. Scenes from the James household depicted life as it may have been for the frontier family, with Jesse's mother hard at work at her sewing machine. Other scenes included Rudy Turilli, son-in-law to Lester Benton Dill, the original proprietor of the famous Meramec Caverns, interviewing a very aged James from his hospital bed, as well as a great dummy of Cousin Zeke. Turilli was the driving force behind this memorial to the life of Jesse James.

According to Turilli's theory, James, wanted by the law, did not truly die in 1882 but rather, in an effort to evade capture, faked his own death and changed his name to J. Frank Dalton. The man who was killed was said to be Charles Bigelow. The celebrated outlaw then went on to live a full life, passing away in Texas in 1952. The museum celebrates the gunslinger and this angle, showcasing his life and the world that he once roamed and promoting the idea that he didn't die until the 1950s.

The museum housed an excellent collection of antique guns, along with the umbrella and bathtub of Jesse's brother, Frank James. It was a simple establishment with an ambience that was retro to the extreme—not overly grandiose in what it offered, but perfect for what it was setting out to do. Thembi stayed locked on the gun collection for some time, amazed with the weapons of yesteryear and awestruck that this cowboy legend may have indeed once used some of the firearms himself.

Who's to say whether Jesse James was indeed killed by Robert Ford in 1882 or if, as J. Frank Dalton claimed, he changed his name and sought out a quiet life far from the limelight? But in 1995, forensic scientists found James's 1882 grave, dug it up, and tested the DNA, the results of which showed, with 99.7 percent certainty, that the remains belonged to the gunslinger. We may never truly know, but I personally prefer to believe that he escaped assassination and lived out his days peacefully in Texas. It's just a more romantic notion.

9

"WOW!" SAID THEMBI, pointing in shock at a telephone pole in front of a run-down white, wooden house whose paint had seen better days. "They nailed him right to the pole!" Someone had shot an arrow through the head of a large brown teddy bear, pinning him to the wood. His right eye was missing, and all of the rain made him look ragged and sad, abandoned to rot in the elements.

"Why would they do that?" Thembi asked, concerned.

"They must have thought it would be amusing," Kate responded.

"I don't see how that is very funny," said Thembi. Kate and I looked at each other but said no more. It was a quiet drive, with this long, sweeping, tree-lined section of Route 66 void of busy traffic as it climbed charming hills and followed a shaded path through Oak Grove Village, Sullivan, and Bourbon (with its famous titular water tower).

Passing through these small communities, it became clear that eastern Missouri has experienced some undeniable poverty, and many people have had a hard go of it. The densely forested drive was characterized by a myriad of mobile-home parks, crumbling houses, boarded-up businesses, and a general sense of despair. Despite the overwhelming wealth that we had witnessed in the larger towns and cities, it was obvious that parts of the country, such as this one, had been left behind. This was particularly evident on the final stretch of the day as we drove toward Cuba, where we saw many seemingly abandoned homes, their front yards replete with a miscellany of junk: piles of scrap lumber and metal, cars up on blocks, kids' toys scattered everywhere, the occasional disemboweled washing machine, and yes, a teddy bear pegged to a pole. The gloomy weather, the jarring signs of people's misfortune on Route 66, and the fatigue of being on the road had put a damper on our otherwise jovial travel mood and we were all quite glad when we pulled into the driveway of the Wagon Wheel Motel in Cuba, Missouri.

The woman behind the counter seemed a little flustered when we checked in. She was multitasking and had her hands a bit full.

"Just a second, please," she said, holding the phone away from her mouth. She was busy taking a booking for a future visitor and the caller had a number of questions about the motel and the rooms. While I waited, I took a look around.

The office at the motel doubles as a boutique, filled with lovely clothes and designs and an assortment of Route 66 books, plaques, and paraphernalia. It had a homey feel, like a cozy bookshop of sorts. But I was tired after fighting rain on the way down from St. Louis, and we were ready to take a break from the wet road. We were anxious to get our key, check into our room, and put our feet up.

Built in 1935 and owned by Robert and Margaret Martin, the venue was first known as the Wagon Wheel Cabins, Cafe, and Station. A 1939 edition of the AAA travel directory described the venue as "one of the finest courts in the state." It was later bought by John and Winifred Mathis in 1947 and christened the Wagon Wheel Motel. Today, the Wagon Wheel is owned by Iowa native Connie Echols, and has been rightly added to the National Register of Historic Places.

"Sorry about that," said the woman, finished with her call. "Welcome to Cuba and the historic Wagon Wheel. You guys are traveling 66, right? Have you gone up the road yet to see the murals?" This was how we first met Connie, not only the Wagon Wheel's unflappable proprietor but also the town's fiercest supporter.

The murals that Connie was speaking of were championed by Viva Cuba, a local beautification group. In 2001, Peoples Bank commemorated its one hundredth birthday by painting a mural on its building, depicting its very first cashier and longtime president, A. J. Barnett. This led to eleven additional murals being commissioned throughout the town depicting Cuba's history, from the area's Civil War history to its very first Model T automobile and a surprise visit from famed aviator Amelia

Earhart in 1928. These murals have given the small town its trademark signature and its moniker, Route 66 Mural City.

"We haven't yet, but we're going to take a stroll around when the weather clears up. From what we've seen so far, you have a lovely town."

"Yes, I think so!" she responded with a smile.

We were assigned cottage 11, a simple but comfortable room that was earthy and reminiscent of architecture in the highlands of colonial Kenya. The motel cottages were made from Ozark sandstone, with steeply pitched roofs, decorative trimming around the windows, and wooden doors. The hardwood floors spoke of the natural building preferences during less industrial times. In Africa, natural resources are still commonly used, while in the modern, cost-saving world of the Western Hemisphere, stone and real wood have become expensive and untrendy.

I have a bad back and was a little anxious about the bed that I would be assigned. When on the road, this is generally my top concern, other than safety, when selecting accommodations. But I soon discovered that the beds at the Wagon Wheel were comfortable, with just the right amount of firmness. These would do just fine.

"It's Sunday, town will be quiet. We should walk around for a bit and check out the downtown area," Kate suggested, reaching for her camera. But as we prepared to leave, the sky thundered angrily and it started to rain again, hard, snuffing out any opportunity of seeing Cuba that day.

Outside, a truck pulled in, the slamming of doors stirring our interest. We went to the window to spy. A silver-bearded man and a teenage boy with blue hair grabbed their luggage and rushed into the neighboring cottage to avoid the downpour. Their plates indicated that they came from Illinois. A little while later, I watched as the man rushed up to the office, darting through the incessant precipitation. He returned after a few moments, and the pair shifted their bags to a cottage a few doors down.

That is so odd. Why would they do that? we wondered. Could they hear us through the wall? We couldn't hear them.

The rain kept us trapped in our room for most of the afternoon, but that was fine by us. While Thembi gravitated toward the iPad to play a game, Kate and I took the time to catch up on some news, and I had to work on some final revisions for an article I was writing.

A few hours passed, and the rain finally stopped, but the heavy clouds in the sky hastened the night's darkness and the lighting of the Wagon Wheel's classic neon sign. The grassy lawn was soggy, well hydrated with the Missouri downpour, but luckily, the Wagon Wheel has gravel roads around the cottages that manage the wet weather well, providing safe passage for foot travelers. I could see a few people taking photographs of the sign already, including the father-son pair from Illinois.

"Come on, Thembi, put your shoes on, we're going outside to take some pictures and get a good look at the Wagon Wheel sign."

He yawned, threw his legs over the bed, and sat up. "Good idea," he said. "I need to stretch and want to get out of this room."

Like a shot, he was up and out the door, rushing headfirst into someone's picture as he had done numerous times on the trip, prompting a chuckle from the Illinois dad. "You guys are in cottage 11, right?"

"We are," I answered. "You guys were beside us but moved. Were we too loud?"

"Oh no, not at all. But the place isn't full tonight and for some reason Connie put us right beside you guys. We like our space." That made sense to us.

"So, what brings you guys down to Cuba?"

"Oh, sorry, right, I'm Don, and this is my son, Timothy." We shook hands and went through the normal pleasantries.

"We're driving down to Arizona. Timothy is starting a great geology program in Flagstaff. I'm driving him down and then his mom and sister will fly down to meet us there and we'll drive back together. You guys?"

We told them our story and then answered their questions about Africa.

Timothy had little to say, standing transfixed by the flashing neon and the deafening song of crickets that exploded in the night. Don nudged him and the soon-to-be college student startled back to life and grinned at his father. They appeared on the verge of beginning a new stage in the parent-child journey.

"Well, we better call it a night," Don said, ruffling his fingers lovingly through his son's hair. "We have a long drive tomorrow and we're hoping to make it to Oklahoma City."

We smiled, appreciating the close bond between father and son. Thembi put his hand on my shoulder and leaned into me. When they were gone, we stood alone on the quiet street, with the constant blinking and humming of the hypnotic neon sign and the chirping of the nocturnal life. Like at the Gemini Giant in Wilmington, there was a deep sensation of standing in the middle of history and being transported back to another period in time. How many travelers had passed the Wagon Wheel along this unassuming stretch of road? How many motorists had the motel sheltered and cared for over the last eighty years? Our trip had taken on a spiritual element and no one felt the need to speak—that is, until Thembi finally broke the silence.

"Dad?"

"Yes, Dadu?" I asked, using a nickname that I'd had for him since he was born. I sensed that he, too, was deeply moved by the experience.

"Why was that boy's hair blue?"

10

BY MORNING, THE sky had cleared, and the day looked promising. Thembi was up and dressed, playing outside on the dewy lawn, and Kate was busy reorganizing our bags. I needed coffee. In the motel's lobby, Connie offered guests complimentary caffeine, even though each room already came with its own machine and supplies. But I was eager to hear her story, so I strolled up to the office to share a cup of java.

When Connie took ownership of the motel in 2009, the venue was in a serious state of decline and rooms were being rented at a throwaway price. Life was difficult in Cuba and the town needed the Wagon Wheel desperately, just as Connie needed a fresh start. But refurbishing the motel proved to be very expensive and difficult—it needed new plumbing, wiring, bedding, and modern amenities, just to start—and labor was, and still is, undependable at best.

"Buying the Wagon Wheel was a spur-of-the-moment decision. I had always liked the cute stone buildings and was tired of the floral business, but I knew very little about Route 66 at the time and only began to see the history after meeting a few people and witnessing the support they were giving to the restoration (of the motel). The hardest part of taking over the Wagon Wheel was the constant need to tell people that rooms were no longer eleven dollars a night! People had no money and nowhere to go, and some individuals got downright mad because the motel was being restored and was no longer the old, disreputable Wagon Wheel. Also, the restoration problems seemed to multiply daily."

Connie's husband had hemophilia and passed away in 1993, leaving her alone after twenty-seven years of marriage. Yet, through laser-sharp focus and some true grit, Connie Echols has managed to create and maintain one of the best venues on Route 66. Today, the Wagon Wheel boasts of being the oldest continuously operated motel on the Mother Road.

"My favorite part of owning this motel is the wonderful people we meet from all over the world. Billy Connolly visited us from England for several days while filming—he was very funny—and the Oak Ridge Boys have stayed three times. We get so many interesting people passing through."

—

WALKING AROUND CUBA, we started to notice the vivid, true-to-life wall paintings that were neatly spread out around the quaint downtown, and we excitedly competed to see who could spot the most the fastest. Thembi, of course, was enthralled with such a competition and rushed ahead, ducking down side streets and around corners. Unsurprisingly, he won.

An odd-looking building with bright-green and -yellow walls and a multicolored pattern of green, red, and yellow on the roof caught our attention. Right on Route 66, within walking distance from the Wagon Wheel, the FourWay restaurant resembled something from a children's fairy tale—the building looked like it was pulled directly from the pages of *Hansel and Gretel*. We walked over and sat at one of the outdoor tables facing the four-way stop on the street, eager to catch a glimpse of an average day in Cuba.

A young waitress came to our table to take our drink order. "Have you been working here long?" Kate asked her as Thembi perused the menu.

"Not too long. I was attending Southeast Missouri State but I've come down to help my mom. She runs the café now."

"Oh, this is your place?" Kate responded.

The girl nodded, smiling warmly at Thembi. "It *is* ours! It's been a lot of work, but my mom is just so passionate about it that FourWay seems to be working. Where are you guys staying? Down at the Wagon Wheel? That's by far the best place in town. We like to send people Connie's way whenever possible."

"So have you guys been very busy? Has the place been picking up this season?" I asked.

"We have! Not as busy as we would like, but we're trying. My mom and I were here from early yesterday morning until around eight in the evening. Things were insane. But then other days, it's quiet."

She was young and pretty, with long brown hair and wide, friendly eyes. "Excuse me for a moment," she said as she headed over to greet a family of four who had just arrived and taken a seat. It was encouraging to see younger people invested in the route. So much of what we had seen thus far had been managed by retiree volunteers. We were amazed by how many people selflessly invested their time and lives into the preservation of the route, but what America's Main Street really needed was a jolt of youthful exuberance and energy. It would do the Mother Road good to have some fresh blood.

Originally constructed in 1932 by Paul T. Carr, the FourWay was initially a fueling and repair station under the banner of Phillips 66—hence, we found out later, the distinctive cottage-style architecture—and then later the Standard Oil Company. The business would later be purchased by Bill and Lynn Wallis in 1968 and transformed into a Mobil station. At the time of our visit, the FourWay was serving up food and drink, welcoming visitors and locals. Like so many locations on America's highway, the building had a fascinating and diverse story to share.

The four-way stop stayed busy as we sat there and I couldn't help but wonder if the vehicles heading west were on their own American road trip and if the ones moving east were on their way home. There is a mystery when traveling down a well-worn route. It is easy to be curious about who you are sharing the road with: where are they from and where are they going? We finished our drinks and moseyed off to explore some more.

———

THAT EVENING, AFTER an early meal of chicken and ribs at Missouri Hick Bar-B-Que, another Route 66 favorite, located right next door to the Wagon Wheel, Kate and I reclined on lawn chairs in front of our Tudor-style stone cottage while Thembi played Minecraft on the iPad in the room. Darkness had fallen and the Wagon Wheel sign was switched on once again, casting its warm glow into the night.

We watched as a small group of recreational bikers checked into the motel. They parked their bikes to the rear of our cottage and busily carried their gear to their rooms. This became an increasingly common sight on the trip: small or large groups of motorcycle enthusiasts who were taking to the road to experience a summer on Route 66. There is even a company out of Chicago that organizes large-scale European motorcycle trips across the route for their clients, while company vehicles trail behind with their luggage. It is a big and expensive business.

One of the ladies from this biking group, a tall, blond woman with short hair, high cheekbones, and refined features, came over to where we were seated and introduced herself. "Hi! I'm Mary. How are you guys doing tonight? So what's your story?" Just like that. No small talk. Little hesitation.

Introductions done, Mary invited us to join them for some drinks and snacks. One of the best things about a road trip on 66 is getting to meet other travelers and being afforded the opportunity to hear their stories. We eagerly obliged and joined the foursome under a large, leafy tree in the garden. The group, who had been close friends for a very long time, was from Chicago and had ventured down to Cuba, specifically to the Wagon Wheel, to enjoy the open road together as couples.

"So you guys are doing the whole route? Like, all the way to LA and back?" asked David, a sarcastic, intelligent, highly gregarious, and slightly overweight water engineer who was enjoying his first time in Cuba.

"We are! All the way," Kate responded. They were impressed.

"And what do you think so far? I mean, how are you guys finding America?" David asked.

But before Kate or I could answer, David's wife, a high school teacher named Annie, interjected. "Well, we just discovered that not far from here is the location of a terrible massacre that was inflicted on the Native American people, and it was done by the US government. We are just so ashamed of our history sometimes, and not sure at moments like these how proud we are to be Americans." It was obvious from the shaking in her soft voice that she was deeply moved by the discovery.

"That really is a tragedy, for sure," I said, thinking that perhaps she was referring to the Trail of Tears, which did run through parts of Missouri. "But honestly, we love America. Americans are intrinsically hopeful. No matter how many times they get knocked down, they keep getting up. You have an amazing country filled with tenacious people and unlimited opportunities. People aren't perfect, but anything is possible here. That really does make America unique."

"It's true," Kate added. "America doesn't have a blemish-free past, but who does? History is a great teacher, and just like with South Africa and apartheid, horrible periods in your history don't need to define you. We may not be Americans, but it seems to me that there is a great deal more that unites Americans of all backgrounds than divides them."

The foursome looked intently at us, speechless. Had we offended them?

"It is so encouraging to hear non-Americans speak about the United States like that," David finally responded, glancing over to the others. Mary was staring down at the ground in silence, as was Annie. "We get so used to denigrating the country and our values and history that it's uplifting to hear someone else's positive view of our nation." The others nodded and for an instant it felt good to have encouraged them. The United States was going through so much political and social turbulence at that moment, and Chicago must have been a real hotbed for debate. But out there in rural Missouri, on Route 66, none of that mattered, not really, and for that moment, everyone treated each other with dignity and respect.

Annie spoke up again. "You guys must be experiencing the highway in a unique way as a mixed couple with a little boy? Have you experienced much racism?"

Kate and I looked at each other. Up until we discovered the *Green Book* and its necessary use, it hadn't entered our minds that we could potentially experience discrimination while traveling. Outside of Kenya, we've never really had any problems. Back home, mixed-raced couples are often viewed with suspicion. Many people assume that the African is pursuing financial gain and that the Caucasian is looking for a sexual companion. Today, there are an increasing number of interracial couples and, outside of smaller or rural communities, it is not such a big deal—but Kate and I, coming from very touristy Mombasa, where vacation relationships are common, have had to deal with our fair share of ignorance over the years.

Kate responded, "No, none at all. We've found people to be very friendly and welcoming. We don't really see ourselves as black and white. We're just a family on the road."

That seemed to shock Annie. Her eyes grew wide and she sat up straight in her chair.

"We have a lot of problems with racism in our country," Annie said. "So I'm glad that you guys haven't encountered any real harassment."

"We know that America has a complicated history, but so far, we've been very welcomed and treated well by everyone that we've met," said Kate. "We've had a great trip thus far."

I nodded and watched the flames of the fire flicker.

The group became suddenly quiet, lost in their thoughts.

Kate and I love talking politics. In Kenya, politics are a part of most conversations. We are fascinated by how people view and comprehend the world. We are equally baffled by how one statement or action can receive such visceral and opposite responses. Over our time in North America, both Kate and I, and sadly even a very young Thembi, have learned to hold our voice and opinions until we better understand how they will be interpreted and received.

In many ways, it seems, there are two Americas. The big-city, high-flying, ultramodern, politically correct one where people tend to be incredibly concerned with what others think about how *they* think, and where ambitious people dwell due to industry and opportunity, endeavoring to climb the ladder of career success. And then there are places like Cuba—small-town or rural America, where people care more about their reputation than about any business acumen or any of the isms that define big-city America. Their priorities are rather to be honest, kind, fair, and hardworking. It is fascinating to compare the two and realize that much of what either version of America wholeheartedly stands for, the other side largely rejects.

After a drink or two more, we retired for the evening, and our new friends headed off to their rooms. Our minds were racing with everything that we had been hearing and witnessing. America is such a complicated place. So much in America is extreme in nature, including religious and social differences. Brothers stop speaking to one another, parents and children find themselves at immoveable loggerheads, marriages break apart, best friends unfriend each other on social media . . . and all because of a difference of opinion. In America, it seems that so much is bathed in deep, overwhelming emotion, which has the capacity to really divide communities and negatively impact relationships. Kenya, in comparison, seems so much simpler. People are diverse, but there is much more commonality than division. Most people believe in God—Muslim or Christian—and to define yourself as an atheist would result in many people thinking you are mad. There are forty-three native tribes in the country, along with local whites, Arabs, and Indians, each with their own respective traditions, history, and language. Yet somehow, core beliefs unite Kenyans, and hot-button issues of race and gender are not nearly as divisive and incendiary as they are in America. Even how we define identity is different.

"It's fascinating to me," Kate said, back in the room. "Here in America, a mixed-race person is generally considered to be black. Look at Barack Obama or Halle Berry, for example. Neither one of them are actually black, they are half-white and half-black, equal measure, but publicly considered black. It's confusing. How can people disregard half of a person's ethnicity and identity?"

In contrast, throughout East Africa, most mixed-race people would be viewed as white, especially outside of the big cities—again, a reality that is completely opposite to that of North America—even though, in fact, they are neither white nor black. They are a beautiful blend of both races and perhaps signify a more common future.

"But I wonder," Kate continued, "if Obama were to define himself openly as a white man, how would Americans react? I'm not so sure he would find a lot of support from blacks or whites. So why is it acceptable as a mixed-race person over here to consider yourself black, but not white? Why would it be deemed inappropriate to do so?" Those are good questions. How does America heal and unite after such a difficult past?

Thembi was already asleep and snoring sweetly, his angelic face at peace in his dreams. Those complicated, emotion-filled issues did not need to trouble his young life at that point.

EARLY THE NEXT morning, the bikers were gone, and we were back on the road, heading west through sleepy Fanning, a minute town just outside Cuba. On the right loomed something pretty hard to miss. Back in 2008, recognizing that he needed a unique angle to pull motorists off Route 66 in order to entice them to visit his archery and feed store, Danny Sanazaro decided to construct a monster of a rocking chair—the biggest on the planet, actually. At one time, the Route 66 Red Rocker was certified by Guinness World Records as the largest rocking chair in the world. It was an impressive forty-two feet and four inches high. But because this is America, someone had to try to outdo the ridiculous honor and build an even bigger chair. Now the largest chair in the world is in Casey, Illinois, and the record to beat is a gigantic fifty-six feet and one inch. That is a bloody big seat. As we stared up into the heavens to the top of the rocker in Fanning, a freight train rumbled by across the road, heading east. It seemed endlessly long as it roared past. It was the first train we had seen on Route 66 and Thembi was thrilled.

The sun was out and the drive through the towns of Rosati and St. James, known for their wineries and roadside grape stands, was a pleasant surprise. We crossed over I-44 once again and found ourselves in the university town of Rolla, home of the first nuclear reactor in Missouri, a much smaller replica of Stonehenge, and the Totem Pole Trading Post, with its fantastic huge sign. We continued on into Pulaski County and stumbled onto one of the most unique spots in Missouri: Hooker Cut. This section of Route 66 was created when road engineers, on behalf of the federal government, literally cut their way through the rocky hills and forest that stood in the path of progress, and created the first four-lane portion of 66. The goal was to ease traffic congestion and facilitate the movement of troops and military equipment out west. It took them from 1941 to 1945 to complete the project, which was considered an engineering marvel of its time. Today, it is still a captivating sight to behold.

A bad accident came into view on the eastbound side of the highway, and we slowed down to take a look. A red sedan had been smacked hard on the passenger side and had its rear passenger door and bumper totally ripped off. The vehicle was facing westward, having been spun around in the ordeal. Debris was scattered on the side of the highway, and a bewildered family of four stood off to the edge of the road, staring into the deep forest. A man in a short-sleeved blue polo shirt and jeans, likely the father, kicked the back of the vehicle, clearly upset. But at least they were all still alive. Up ahead, flashing lights were headed in their direction. A mile up the road, on our side of the highway, the body of a big rig was lying on its side, its wheels no longer spinning. The driver was nowhere in sight. It was a cryptic scene that we were glad to leave behind.

Dropping down toward the idyllic Big Piney River, we spotted a long row of motorcycles lined up outside a simple inn, where burley motorcyclists jostled at the entrance, beers in hand. German tongues shouted over loud music while the bikers aggressively roughhoused with each other. They were jubilant and reveling in their moment. Although curious, the scene was a little intimidating so we decided to continue on, and crossed the Devil's Elbow bridge, an original 1923 truss bridge, named after a particularly difficult bend in the serene waterway. The morning had been pleasant, and we'd enjoyed the more upbeat face of Missouri. Sunshine and some open road really did make all the difference.

11

"WHAT IS THAT?" quipped my startled son, suddenly sitting up and taking notice of the unlikely stopover that had emerged from the leafy forest, as though from thin air.

Before us was a wooden water tower with the words "Uranus, Missouri," painted across it, announcing the curiously titled roadside destination of Uranus. Small-town Cuba, only fifty miles east, now felt a world away. The large, spacious parking area was mostly empty, creating a bizarre, apocalyptic sensation, like we had stumbled upon a long-abandoned roadside attraction. On one side of the property was a row of Old West–style storefronts, with tongue-in-cheek callouts greeting visitors. The pool hall's facetious signs read, "Everyone has fun in Uranus" and "The more balls in Uranus, the more fun for everyone." Big Louie's Burlesque Saloon boasted, "Live on stage: Show girls, 24 beautiful girls and 1 ugly one," and the Fudge Factory bragged (somewhat concerningly), "The best fudge comes from Uranus." It was a fun, unexpected stop that pulled us away from the rhythm of the drive. Luckily, we enjoy such experiences and gamely explored the oasis of oddity.

Next to the faux town, another building caught our eye—not that the huge man-eating dinosaurs, real-life retired double-decker London bus, and broken-down police vehicles with convict skeletons inside had not—and we made our way over. Outside, a hand-carved black bear stood tall on his hind legs, welcoming visitors as they approached. In front of him was a warning: "Please do not feed the bear." As we entered and the bell on the door rang loudly, a pair of friendly teenage girls behind the counter called out in unison, "Welcome to Uranus!" They had been well trained.

There were aisles of candy on sale throughout the store, with special luxuries like Lik-m-Aid and Big League Chew, treats that we had not seen since our childhoods in the early 1980s. Unusual choices such as lollipops with dead scorpions or ants in the center filled the shelves, and mysterious or deformed creatures hidden inside glass boxes lined the back wall. The store had clearly taken a note from the Ripley's Believe It or Not! playbook. It fit Route 66 perfectly.

"Wow, Dad, check this out," Thembi said excitedly, taking my hand to lead me toward a wooden Indian with a lollipop headdress. "It almost looks real, doesn't it?"

"Welcome to Uranus!" screeched the girls again as a new set of customers walked in.

I spotted Kate at the end of the candy counter eyeing some fudge and chocolate-covered cashews. "These look delicious," she whispered. "Let's get some."

"Welcome to Uranus," squealed the girls as the door swung open a third time. Kate and I looked at each other with suppressed smiles, trying not to laugh. Thembi was entranced with some superlong pieces of licorice, and I could already recognize the plea in his mind before it left his mouth.

"No."

"What do you mean 'no'? I didn't even ask anything, Dad."

"Okay, sorry, buddy."

"Dad, can I get some of this licorice?"

"No."

Thembi sighed.

The door chimed again as two middle-aged women walked in.

"Welcome to Uranus!" shrieked the girls.

———

MOVING ON THROUGH the Show-Me State, we passed the historic Munger Moss Motel in Lebanon, with its fantastic, larger-than-life sign. From Lebanon, Route 66 took us away from the super slab again, past old picturesque barns, loads of neatly stacked hay bales, and remnants of dilapidated buildings. Then the road began the roller-coaster effect that Missouri Route 66 is famous for, where the road takes travelers on an up-and-down, curve-after-curve stretch along the hills of the Ozarks. It carried us through small historic towns that were still surviving—Phillipsburg (with the "world's largest candy store"), Conway, Niangua, Marshfield, and Strafford—before crossing into Greene County's bustling Springfield, known as the Queen City of the Ozarks. While in Missouri, we had traveled down Highway Z and Highway ZZ, gone from Highway C to Highway CC—and even to Highway oo. Route 66 takes on many names across the Show-Me State.

Our goal had generally been to steer clear of larger towns as much as possible, but Springfield was one that we could not afford to miss. It was home to the Best Western Route 66 Rail Haven, a motor-court motel that we were eager to experience. I was beginning to enjoy motor courts much more. I loved the convenience and safety of parking the vehicle right in front of our room and not needing to haul our luggage in and out of hotel lobbies. And at Rail Haven, there really was so much enjoyable history to soak in.

Built in 1938 in an apple grove, just twelve years after historic Route 66 was commissioned, the Rail Haven was celebrated for the comfy experience it provided weary motorists as they made their way slowly across the state. Consisting originally of only eight handsome sandstone cottages, the venue became part of the Best Western chain in 1948, but has maintained its luminous neon and Route 66 charm. Even though the rooms have been remodeled and updated with modern amenities, the management has continued to pay homage to its unique historic past, with black-and-white photographs on the walls showing the past and present Rail Haven, and colorfully painted Route 66 images on their room keys. It was a nice touch.

Springfield is a busy town. Home to 164,000 residents, the town is chock-full of 66 mementos and attractions, including the Calaboose (old city jail), Bud's Tire & Wheel, and the Route 66 Car Museum—but the first one on our list was the quintessential Route 66 dining experience of Steak 'n Shake. It was only seven miles away from the motel, and with its original tile floor, stainless steel counter, and kitchen cookline visible to customers, the diner had been maintained to perfectly resemble 1950s reality.

"Welcome to Steak 'n Shake, can I get you guys some drinks?" sang our friendly waiter after we'd settled at a table.

Without a moment of indecisiveness, Thembi was prepared, "Can I please have a very thick chocolate-mint milkshake?"

"Would you like whip cream and a cherry on it?"

Pausing, as though there were any doubt, he replied, "Sure, why not?" We are generally quite careful about the amount of sugar Thembi consumes, but when on the road . . .

The place was packed. Everyone seemed to be out. There was a loud ringing in the air as dozens of people conversed freely and kitchen staff battled to keep up with the incoming orders. We really liked this place right from the start. It had character.

Food came and empty plates were cleared with great speed, and we were once again amazed at the gigantic food portions and correspondingly gigantic appetites of Americans. It was just so shocking to see so much food consumed with little to no concern. We knew that obesity was a growing epidemic in America, but as the trip went on, we were starting to understand why. Fun fact: More than a third of Americans are considered obese. That is a pretty significant number.

Our waiter passed by and noticed us taking in the room. "Where y'all from?" he asked with a smile. He was a young, skinny black man with a heavy southern accent.

"Well, we're down from Canada, but originally come from Africa," I said.

"Even you? But you're white."

"True, I am white," I said. There was no denying that. "But yep, even me. There are lots of different races that call Africa home."

He looked at me suspiciously for a moment, sizing up my response. Then he quickly turned and scanned the room and frowned.

"Do people eat a lot over there like they do here?" he asked. He must have noticed our interest in the size of the portions being consumed.

"Some people do," Kate said. "We have a lot of weight-related issues in Africa too."

"Yeah, but not like us here, I bet. Anyway, aren't most people pretty poor over there? Y'all don't have these types of restaurants, do you?"

"We do!" Kate answered. "We have a lot of fast-food spots, but most are South African chains, and I don't think we have any 'diners' like this, certainly not in Kenya." The fact that South African restaurant brands have highly influenced the Kenyan market was lost on the waiter, as it would be on most Americans. But in Kenya, it is a big issue that has a strong cultural impact. South Africa was the first African country on the continent to really embrace Western music, fashion, entertainment, and culinary culture, among other things. This was later imported into Kenya.

The waiter simply shook his head, asked if we wanted anything else, and cleared our milkshake glasses and Thembi's plate. He had left most of his fries and half of his hamburger. The shake, unsurprisingly, filled him up. We spent the rest of our time at Steak 'n Shake dreaming, discussing whether a '50s diner of this style would succeed in the Kenyan market—it seemed unlikely—and people watching.

Done with our meal, we ventured downtown to check out Park Central Square, where legendary cowboy and frontiersman Wild Bill Hickok shot and killed cowboy Davis Tutt on July 21, 1865. It is rumored that the gunfight and initial fallout was the result of a dispute over women. Hickok had reportedly fathered a child out of wedlock with Tutt's sister, while Tutt is said to have had eyes for one of Hickok's love interests, Susanna Moore. Either way, the relationship between the two men soured and they were not on good terms. At one point during this dispute, Hickok was involved in a game of cards while Tutt stood nearby, inserting himself into the game and aiding the other players, even lending them money as the need arose. Seeing that he could not goad Hickok into a fight or affect his card game, Tutt reminded Hickok of a debt that he owed him. There was a dispute over the amount and Tutt grabbed Hickok's watch off the card table and announced that he would retain it until the debt was repaid. Hickok was furious, but outgunned. He let it go.

The next day, Tutt continued to provoke an increasingly irritated Hickok. When the two men showed up at the square at six in the evening, Hickok clearly warned Tutt, "Dave, here I am. Don't you come across here with that watch." To do so would be a humiliation that Hickok could not allow, as he planned on remaining in Springfield. As they faced each other, Tutt is said to have gone for his gun first, but Hickok was faster, and his bullet hit Tutt in the left side of his chest, shattering his ribs.

According to historians, Tutt hollered, "Boys, I'm killed!" before running into the street and collapsing. Hickok was charged with murder.

Hickok's trial lasted only three days, and, in the end, he was acquitted when the jury believed his story of self-defense. The Old West is full of such fascinating tales.

"Do you remember that episode of *Legends & Lies* about Wild Bill, Dad?" inquired Thembi. He stood still, looking straight ahead at the area where the event is said to have taken place, his young mind turning history over and over.

The square was a lively hub of activity. People sat on concrete steps that led down to the central plaza on the square, enjoying the warm summer evening, while others stood in front of a large limestone fountain to have their picture taken. A sculpture by Aristedes Demetrious decorated the grounds, and a huge historic sign loomed in the sky announcing the History Museum on the Square, the city's amazing Route 66 museum. Route 66 goes completely around the square, making it impossible for Mother Road travelers to avoid. There was an air of energy and glee as laughter arose from an adjacent café, where young people sat and chatted.

"Let's get out of here and grab something to drink and take it back to the motel," suggested Kate.

Glenstone Avenue is a very busy street, and like most bigger city streets, it has a good and a dodgy section. It runs straight through the city and is home to countless stores and shops, businesses and restaurants. And it is where the Rail Haven is located, so we decided to pull into a nearby convenience store to grab supplies for the night and replenish our junk-food stock. I ran inside and left Thembi and Kate in the comfort of the vehicle. Outside, a scruffy, homeless-looking black man with tangled, dreadlocked hair and an unshaven, scarred face approached our car. His T-shirt was torn and, though once white, soiled beyond recognition. He was missing a shoe and his eyes were wild. I had the keys and the windows were down. Kate was trapped.

I hurried the cashier along in order to get back outside, but the man was clearly hostile and getting worked up. "This is my town. If I want your money, you damn well better give it to me!" I heard him shout, standing with his head looking inside of the vehicle. The cashier barely took notice. How do people in larger towns get so accustomed to such behavior?

Seeing me step out of the store, the vagrant quickly walked off, stumbling down the sidewalk, screaming threats back at us, a torn plastic bag and a faded jerrican in his hands. I stood at the front of the vehicle for a moment and watched him go.

Kate was not a happy camper.

"Are you okay?" I asked, concerned.

Clearly annoyed and terribly insulted, Kate shook her head. "He kept calling me Whoopi Goldberg! Now I really need a drink."

It was an August night and a balmy summer mood filled the air. The sky glowed in the distance as the remnants of a stunning sunset turned fluffy white clouds into gorgeous hues of deep red and burnt orange. Back at the Rail Haven, we sat by the outdoor swimming pool and enjoyed the darkness as it descended. Traffic passed intermittently on the street and a delightful breeze began to pick up. Relaxed and without care, Whoopi and I passed the evening in contentment as we watched nocturnal Springfield come alive beneath the gleaming vintage neon of the Rail Haven.

12

ROUTE 66 FROM Springfield is interstate free and became even prettier as we left the city and wound through some of the most curious locations in the state. It felt good to be back on the road and on the move after a few days out of the car. Putting miles under the tires. We made a quick stop in Halltown—population 176—and peeped inside the long-closed Whitehall Mercantile. The historic building was constructed in 1900 and has had many incarnations throughout its life. Most recently, the structure was an antique shop for thirty-five years before finally closing in 2016. During its heyday, little Halltown was often referred to as the Antique Capital of the US. Now the Missouri town receives very few visitors and is known as somewhat of a ghost town. Across the road, some barefoot young men dressed in overalls (but shirtless) looked suspiciously over at us as they worked under the hood of a '70s muscle car.

We cruised through another roller-coaster section of the old road, laughing as our stomachs sank with each rise and drop of the land. It was a serene route, flanked by rolling green fields, picturesque old barns, innumerable churches, and huge billboards inscribed with verses from the Bible. Then after some time, up on the horizon, a curious sight came into view. We had arrived at Gary's Gay Parita Sinclair gas station in Paris Springs Junction—yet another destination that we had no idea existed before arriving at its welcoming gates.

As soon as we walked in, we were enthusiastically welcomed by George, co-owner of this historic attraction, and before we knew it, we had launched into a fascinating conversation with him.

First started by Fred and Gay Mason in 1930, the Gay Parita station met the needs of travelers as they passed by in droves, providing them with trusted Sinclair gas and a variety of homemade sandwiches prepared personally by Gay. The pair saw the potential for further expansion, so they added on a shop and a service area where motorists could get their tires repaired or oil changed. The station operated successfully for over twenty years, until Gay's death in 1953. Fred continued to run the business, but after a fire destroyed it in 1955, he did not rebuild Gay Parita.

The site was then purchased around 2003 by Gary Turner, a long-haul truck driver from Missouri, who eventually built the nonfunctional replica to bring back the station's original shine. In fact, what he managed to do was build a time machine that transports visitors back to the 1940s, complete with country atmosphere. It was a fantastic feat, a true slice of Americana delivered in one tiny capsule. Sadly, Turner died in 2015, and his wife, Lena, followed shortly after. The station then became silent and idle for some time. However, his daughter Barbara has since relocated from South Carolina and, with her partner, George, set about making the attraction better than ever.

A roadside stop that certainly received our stamp of approval, with its classic Sinclair signs, antique Ford automobiles, and tastefully cluttered yard and shop, Gay Parita is a photographer's playground. I was eyeing an old newspaper article on the attraction when I heard an alarming shout from Kate. I rushed to her aid and found her holding her side with a stitch, embarrassed. Sheepishly, she pointed to what had startled her: a pair of legs jutting out from underneath an old automobile. The remnants of an unfortunate mechanic, it seemed. "They look so real!" she exclaimed. "Thembi, come and see this!" she called, laughing.

As we were looking things over, an older couple walked through the gate. Tall in stature, wearing a pair of khaki shorts and a short-sleeved polo shirt, the man called out in sing-song English, "G'day! This is quite a place, isn't it? Even better than what we seen online." He turned back toward the road and used his key to remotely lock the doors of a red Mustang.

"Are y'all from Australia?" asked George, rising to greet them. "There's some complimentary tea and coffee over there if you want, and we have some water if you'd prefer. Please help yourself."

"Thank you! You really have something here, mate. Look at those cars and all of the great Route 66 stuff. I reckon that this must have taken some time to pull together."

George was patient and took the time to recount the whole story of Gary and Lena, again. He was used to receiving visitors and had committed his time to carrying on the efforts of Barbara's parents. Although a transplant from South Carolina, he had become a true believer in the magic of Route 66.

The Australian couple had rented their car in Chicago and planned to drive the entire route, then return the vehicle in Los Angeles before flying north to Seattle.

"Hugh, Hugh, look at this—come and see these gas pumps. This is just as I pictured it. Take my picture, darling." The Australians had found their notion of America.

Gary Turner himself is somewhat of an icon on the road now. His warmth and enthusiasm for Route 66 and travelers is legendary, and those whom he left behind still wax lyrical about his hospitality, generosity, and ability to talk your ear off.

Back in the car after another half hour at Gary's, we left the Australians, a young Spanish couple, and two gents from Springfield at the station, each absorbing their own Mother Road experience.

Up the peaceful road and over a stunning 1926 through-truss bridge, we crossed the picturesque Johnson Creek and passed into the nearby silent ghost town of Spencer, a small, charming place that was once an active center. Now it sleeps in the bittersweet embrace of reminiscence. The road that leads past the town was one of the loveliest, but loneliest, on the Missouri stretch of the route, its edges adorned with wide patches of beautiful black-eyed Susans, local wildflowers with dark-brown centers and a mild scent. We decided to spend some time in the quietness, absorbing the mood and memories of Spencer. So much of Route 66 offers an opportunity to ingest what once was, to savor the taste of towns and places that few people will ever even know exist.

We were lost in the moment, navigating the diverse Show-Me state portion of 66, when the all-too-familiar dinging sound of a nearly empty gas tank woke us from our reverie. We needed fuel. This made me happy, as I had discovered a new favorite gas station. First admired almost two weeks earlier, back in Wilmington, Illinois, and then again and again as we progressed on the route, the happy, grinning brontosaurus of the Sinclair filling stations had won me over. I was now committed to the dinosaur and decided to only fill the tank at a Sinclair station when possible. Luckily, the familiar sign was smiling warmly at me just over the horizon.

The wide-open parking lot of the station seemed to stretch on forever, an impression reinforced by the fact that ours was the only vehicle there. But just when things looked a bit forlorn, I gazed up and the smiling dinosaur reminded me that all was well in the middle of nowhere. Just then, a huge semitruck pulled into the other side of the station and screeched to a halt, the big rig letting off a giant sigh as the driver shut off the engine. Dressed in impossibly tight jeans, decorative cowboy boots, a black T-shirt that boasted "We Do It Better in Texas," and a white cowboy hat, he walked around his truck, kicking his tires, moving in a slow, methodical manner. When he saw all was good with the rig, he strode past us and went inside, but not before looking back over his shoulder. "Howdy, folks," he said as he stroked his thick mustache. Thembi's eyes followed him, awestruck.

"Is that a real cowboy?" Thembi asked, obviously impressed.

"I don't know," Kate responded, looking to me.

I wasn't sure if I had ever met an actual cowboy. "He certainly dresses the part," I said.

Bona fide cowboy or not, Thembi stared at him in amazement.

"You should get a cowboy hat, Hun," Kate said to me, putting her arm across my shoulders.

"I don't think so," I said.

"Why not? You'd look so cool!"

I knew that she was poking fun at me. Our sense of humor is thankfully one of the things that we have in common.

"My head's too big."

"Then we'll get you a really big hat."

"Please get in the car," I said, laughing and shaking my head.

"Is Dad getting a cowboy hat?" Thembi asked, excited.

Tank full and ready to roll, we crossed out of the Sinclair station and back onto the old highway.

13

IT HAD BEEN a long, eventful day, and we were taking up residence at the quirky Boots Court Motel in Carthage, Missouri. Like the Wagon Wheel, this motel holds a wonderful history, and its improbable story, restored architecture, and vivid-green wraparound neon attract travelers from far and wide. Built in 1939 by Kansas native Arthur Boots, the property was originally scheduled for demolition in the early 2000s but was rescued by Debye Harvey and Priscilla Bledsaw, two sisters from Illinois who cared enormously for the vintage motel and have invested heavily into refurbishing the venue back to its 1940s state.

How the pair found themselves owners of a classic motel on the Mother Road is itself an interesting story. They were originally not even thinking about buying a venue; the opportunity just kind of fell onto their laps. As a matter of fact, the sisters didn't even know how nationally and internationally famous the venue was at the time, but they really liked the way it looked with its Streamline Moderne style. It is certainly a unique design. In fact, since the 1995 demolition of the Coral Court Motel in St. Louis, it may be the only one of its kind still existing on Route 66.

Debye and Priscilla had first driven the Mother Road in 2006. That is actually how the pair came to know about Boots Court (Boots Motel, at the time). When the ladies first met the motel, it was in a very sad state of disrepair. It had been neglected and was run-down. They began to ponder saving it.

After some research and negotiation, the sisters found themselves the new owners of the iconic property. Almost immediately, they set to work to restore the motel to its former glory, and the rest is history.

Now we were actually there ourselves and happy to be in Carthage. Debbie Dee, the Boots onsite manager, had checked us in and was enthusiastically telling me about the motel, its history, and recent developments when a young lady shyly walked through the screen door. She looked awkward and uncertain, constantly glancing nervously back outside toward a man waiting in an idling black sedan.

"Good evening!" Debbie said in an upbeat tone. "Can I help you with a room?"

The girl brushed scruffy, long brown hair out of her face and pushed it behind her ears. "What does it cost to stay here?" she whispered, gazing down as she scratched her forearm aggressively and pulled her worn maroon jacket down over her hand, as though to hide her marked skin.

"I can get you a rate of sixty-six dollars. Does that work for you?"

Staring at the floor, the girl fidgeted slightly before fleeing out the door. "Oh, okay, thank you."

Back into the night, she quickly climbed into the vehicle and pushed on into the Carthage evening.

"I guess she thought your rate was too high," I commented, locking eyes with Debbie, who was looking up the road and watching the vehicle disappear. I was struck by how many interesting, even unsavory, characters Debbie must meet running a motel on America's Main Street. Route 66 and the road's renaissance has been formed around a romantic search for America, but all along the journey, travelers will come face-to-face with other aspects of the nation too. Route 66 is a living, breathing highway that caters to folks, of all stations in life and, unlike Disney's Cars Land, the Mother Road is not always bright, shiny, and pretty.

"I guess so," she said, frowning. But then she snapped back into a smile and picked up the conversation we had begun a moment before.

A world traveler herself, Debbie has always had Africa on her bucket list. When she discovered that we were from Kenya, she excitedly shared her childhood dreams of visiting the Mother Continent. There was a lot to chat about, but we were all very tired and wanted nothing more than to unpack for the day and kick back. Kate and Thembi were waiting out in the vehicle. Debbie could see that my energy levels were dangerously low, and after kindly showing us to our room—a short stroll down a quiet driveway—bid us a good evening. There would be ample time to catch up in the morning.

But sleep suddenly disappeared now that we could breathe easy after a long day, so we left Thembi in the room, safe in his bed, and stepped outside to get some evening air. In the darkness of the night, we sat on flimsy plastic chairs—there was only one other guest checked in—and listened to the sounds of southwestern Missouri. The air was warm, but a periodic cool breeze blew in from the east, sending a chill through our thin T-shirts. Kate went into the room to get a light sweater. The bright-red neon sign at the front of the motel called to motorists, its large vintage font blending perfectly into the relative silence. The slogan below, "Radio in Every Room," was a shout back to the original selling point of Boots Court. And, true to the advert, each room came furnished—not with the requisite flat-screen television of modern-day hospitality but with a boxy Crosley Traveler 1940s reproduction radio. When we had arrived earlier, our radio was tuned smartly to the sounds of an era of yesteryear. The almost eerie glow of the green neon that wrapped around the building demanded a photograph. But no matter the beauty of the picture, Boots Court at night creates an otherworldliness that can only be understood by being there, by bathing in the neon and its constant purr.

As I soaked in the moment, a vehicle pulled into the parking lot and made its way slowly back toward the rooms, and us. It was a black 1955 Chevy Bel Air with orange flames painted on the sides, and an Arizona plate. With its rumbling engine, the car made quite an entrance, interrupting the tranquility of the night. Two men jumped out and started to pull their bags from the trunk.

"Good evening!" said the driver. "We hope that we haven't disturbed your night. We went out to drive around Carthage and show off the Bel Air. You guys just check in today?"

I told them a little bit about our trip and plans for the way west, admiring the car.

"I'm Phillip, and this is my dad, Kyle. We're up from Arizona. Just driving across America really. We wanted to see some of the country."

Kyle yawned and waved good night, excusing himself to get ready for bed. Kate was still in the room. She must have been talking with Thembi, although he should have been asleep by then.

"Can I ask a big favor?" Phillip asked, noticing my camera. "I've been trying to get a picture of the Bel Air at each of the motels that we've been at, but I just never seem to be able to get a good picture. Would you mind?"

"Sure, no problem. Just drive up to the road and we can shoot you under the Boots sign."

He was thrilled and jumped back into the car. The engine began to hum loudly again.

Out front, the road was empty; we were alone under the green glow. I took some pictures that he liked and agreed to email them over to him.

"So what made you and your dad decide to do this trip? Are you married?" I asked.

"I was. We were married for over twenty years actually. I thought we were happy, but then one day I turned around and she wanted out. It's been hard, but it is amicable. I work with the police in Arizona as a watch commander, with Information and Intelligence. My ex-wife is actually the one who paid for the Bel Air. I received money with the divorce settlement, and she encouraged me to buy the vehicle. So I bought it, fixed it up—really, only the body is original on her. I replaced pretty much everything else. And now here we are."

"How far are you going?" I asked.

"We're heading to Springfield tomorrow, and then we'll turn around and head west again. Where to, who knows? But I'm enjoying the time with my dad. He's getting older, in his midseventies now. Route 66 is amazing and a great way to clear the mind. It's been a real joy for him, and me too, getting to hear his stories and memories from when he was much younger. He used to drive the highway back in the day, and this trip has been very nostalgic."

We stood together for a few moments without saying a word, just staring at the vintage automobile in front of Boots Court, basking in the glimmering green and envisioning what it must have been like during the road's heyday. It is easy to drift off in thought along the ribbon of highway when the quiet hours of the day commence.

"Well, I better go inside and check on my dad. I really appreciate your help with the shots. If you're ever in Phoenix, make sure to look me up." Handing me his email, he carefully swung the car around the side of the building and made his way down to the rooms. I listened as doors opened and closed and knew that they were tucked in for the evening.

As I stood alone, my back to the once-busy street, I could see Debbie on her computer in the front office, a solitary presence working into the late hours. There was something melancholy about her lone figure in the largeness of the dark night. It was an uncanny feeling being in an unfamiliar town, in the middle of a recently busy intersection—Route 66 meets the Jefferson Highway here—and being by myself, as though no one else existed. I suddenly felt vulnerable in the black stillness, in the middle of the empty street, in the heart of Middle America, seemingly far away from the faux safety of the little motel. The world had disappeared. There was only Debbie and I, each of us alone in the company of our contemplation. A dog barked down the block as a car stopped for a red light at the corner on Jefferson before evaporating into the night. Under the peculiar illumination of the neon sign, the air was calm and, other than the light breeze, mute once again.

14

"YOU NEED TO go to Red Oak II! There's nowhere quite like it," Debbie Dee told us the next morning, unfolding a large Carthage tourist map across the office counter. The day was gorgeous, with a pure, blue sky void of clouds. It was going to be a hot one. A cyclist pedaled past the motel, decked out in tight-fitting, luminous spandex, ringing her twangy bell and hollering "Cyclist coming through!" as last night's lifeless intersection once again buzzed with traffic heading in all directions.

Herself a native of Illinois, Debbie came to Carthage to visit her friends and help run Boots Court, and then simply fell in love with the town and the venue. Now Debbie was a wealth of information and enthusiasm, greeting every would-be guest with the hospitality they deserve.

Turning to the map, she guided us through Carthage and toward the offbeat, but picturesque, quasi village of Red Oak II, the brainchild of artist Lowell Davis, who grew up in the "real" Red Oak, Missouri, about eighteen miles northwest of the "new" Red Oak II. Often referred to as the Norman Rockwell of Rural Art, Davis had a passion for simpler days (something that becomes obvious when strolling the grounds of Red Oak II).

Frustratingly lost for over an hour, we passed in and out of Carthage a bunch of times before we finally found the road to the elusive attraction. There were other vehicles in the lot when we pulled in, but not many, and for the most part, we appeared to have the "town" to ourselves as we entered into the mind and unusual vision of Lowell Davis.

The village is peculiar, to say the least, decorated with a Phillips 66 petrol station, an old schoolhouse, a typical 1950s diner, a town hall, a quaint jailhouse, a blacksmith, a fully stocked Red Oak General Store, and numerous private homes. The Red Oak General Store was actually once run by Davis's father and is where he learned how to sculpt and paint. Most of the buildings were moved from the original Red Oak site and rehoused in the new development. Situated along the property are a good many of Davis's sculptures and old vehicles, each with their own history to tell. Walking through Red Oak II is like visiting a land that time forgot. There is a bizarre sense of being in a town that simply ceased to exist one day, as though the residents had just pulled up stakes and disappeared.

"Dad, he's coming back again," Thembi said, concerned.

"Stand beside me. He is attracted to you because you're smaller than he is. He's a bit of a bully."

A full-grown resident deer had begun to follow us around, intent on building a close friendship, or perhaps he just wanted to get rid of us. However, rather than being a sweet-natured Bambi, the fellow had become a nuisance, using his antlers and hooves to push Thembi around.

"Keep walking, guys, and maybe he'll go away." But he did not. He followed closely behind. We picked up our pace, cautiously keeping an eye on him. We passed others on the path, but for some reason, he decided to hang out with us, and no matter what direction we took, he remained hot on our heels, stopping periodically to munch on well-cared-for flower beds before trotting back up to us.

Rounding a corner, we were surprised to see a petite lady busily watering the grass on her front lawn, a scene that was slightly weird, as though she were living in the middle of an established suburb and not a roadside attraction that had been re-created to look like a vintage movie set.

We waved hello and continued to explore, stopping periodically to enjoy colorful displays and off-the-wall art creations. The sun began to beat down stronger, and we suddenly realized that the deer had thankfully moved on. At the foot of some steps at a nearby building, another shape moved through the bushes, slithering slowly into the shade.

"Dad!" Thembi shouted. "It's a snake. A big one!"

We walked over—Thembi ran—to carefully take a look. A huge black rat snake was stretched out, sunning itself in the warmth of the day. His skin glistened, and he seemed unbothered. Thembi was in heaven. We stayed with the snake for a half hour, until it finally slithered away, perhaps on the hunt—perhaps to find some solitude. Regardless, Kate and I were glad to see it go.

"Do you guys want to go to the drive-in tonight?" Kate asked. "We can call and see what is playing this evening."

It sounded like a great plan, but after speaking with the theater, we were disappointed to discover that the film we wanted to see would not start until much later into the summer night. It would be long past our bedtime.

Some distance down the path, a commotion was taking place. A group of people were shouting and stomping their feet, their voices betraying fear. They were obviously frazzled and upset—desperately trying to shoo away a deer.

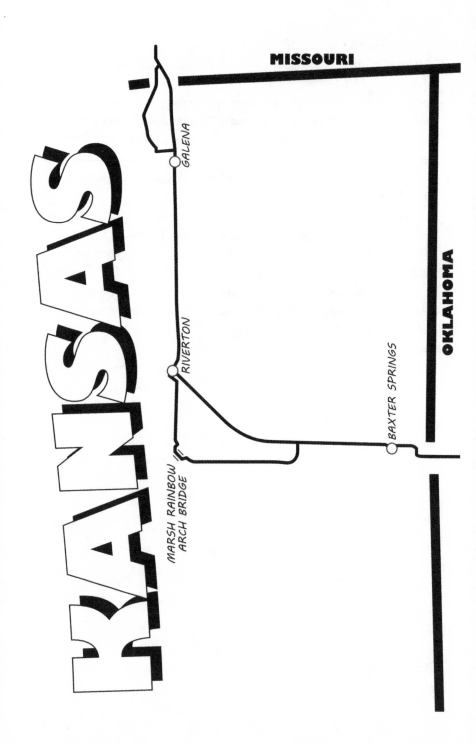

15

ROUTE 66 CAN be difficult to navigate, even at the best of times, but we had a secret weapon. We were using the detailed directions and insanely accurate guidance of the *Route 66: EZ66 Guide for Travelers*. And we needed it as we made our way through energetic Joplin and traversed the corner of Missouri, crossing into southeastern Kansas. With only thirteen miles of 66 to its fame, Kansas is making the most of them.

The *EZ66 Guide* told us to look for a sign that read "Old 66 Next Right" after crossing Malang Road in Joplin. We found it, took the sharp right turn, and stumbled onto an older section of 66, crossing the state line out of Missouri and into Galena, Kansas—and smack-dab into goofy but lovable Tow Mater, the fan-favorite character in Pixar's hit *Cars*. Before us rested two old tow trucks, each with a set of wide eyes and a pair of ridiculously large buckteeth.

The trucks, along with a replica of Red, the terribly trepidatious but dependable red fire engine from *Cars*, stood guard over Cars on the Route, a former Kan-O-Tex Service Station turned café that welcomes guests into the friendly mining town of Galena. Across the road rests what was once an infamous bordello, where, legend has it, a murderous madam, Ma Staffleback, and three accomplices killed and robbed at least fifty patrons who visited the brothel in search of a little affection. Staffleback, her two sons, and husband were charged in 1897 with murdering Frank Galbraith, a miner, and dumping his body into a nearby mineshaft. All were convicted. In recent years, some historians have debunked the manor's sordid past, suggesting that this history is not accurate. Who's to say, for sure? What is certain is that it does add to the intrigue of the small town.

The day was hot and humid, and even though it was only midmorning, the piercing Kansas sun was already wide awake and streaming down. Silence filled the air and the quiet café seemed to tremble in the heat. There was a stillness—no people, no vehicles, no insects, no birds, just a void of sound. For a few minutes, it felt like we were lost to time. But then, out of nowhere, a young attractive couple appeared around the side of the building, bursting with enthusiasm and gazing with childlike amazement at the modest but striking yellow, red, and white café. With their entry, it was like a bubble burst and we joined the modern world once again.

"Excuse me, but can you . . . " He turned to his pretty wife and posed a question in sing-song Italian.

" . . . take our picture?" she picked up his sentence. "That is correct, no? You take our picture?" She enunciated each word carefully.

"Yes, sure!" I said. They made a handsome pair and we worked out that they were on their honeymoon—a peculiar choice for a romantic tribute to the start of a life together, perhaps.

"Very . . . very nice," he added, stretching out his arm to reference the café and its surroundings. The woman reached down and gently grasped his hand.

We smiled and nodded. Love is infectious, especially new love. Kate moved in closer and wrapped her arm around my waist as we watched Thembi admiring the *Cars* replicas.

"Are you going to drive all the way to California?" I asked.

A blank look crossed their faces.

"California? Will you drive to California?"

After a brief pause, he laughed and answered, "Ah, California! Yes, yes, we drive to ocean. Then we stop. I want to give try to surfing."

There is an exuberance, almost an innocence, to the way that international travelers seem to embrace road travel in America. It is unabashedly giddy in some respects and, for us, contagious and refreshing. Unlike many more "seasoned" vacationers motoring across the United States, foreign visitors have a very different interpretation of what America is and of all that it still has to offer. For many Americans, long drives, especially with children, can be tantamount to torture. The sight of a giant tacky dinosaur is only of vague interest and driving over two thousand miles to visit a museum or experience a historic roadside motel would be an inconceivable waste of time. But for those traveling all the way around the world to hit the open road, everything represents a new adventure and an opportunity to truly embrace life.

We like it.

———

"ARE YOU GUYS getting hungry?" asked Thembi. "Can we stop for a snack?"

Our stash of juice boxes and bottled waters, miniature Kit Kat bars, Snickers, and Lays potato chips had sadly run out. We needed to make a new food run when we next got gas. But for now, we decided to pull in at an iconic local store in the area—the Old Riverton Store (dating back to 1925). Inside, the shelves were cluttered with basic food items and touristy Route 66–focused souvenirs, and there was a sensation of crowdedness, even though we were the only people in the store. It was a tight space. Thembi joked with the older man behind the counter.

"Are you in high school?" the man asked our wide-eyed little boy.

"No, I'm going into grade four," Thembi responded politely, giggling.

"You look much older. Are you sure you're really only in the fourth grade? You look like you're married." His antics cracked Thembi up. Outside, Thembi suggested that Kansans are welcoming. "These people are really nice and so talkative. I like it here."

The sun splashed its rays down onto the grassy lawn and the myriad of flowers that decorated the store's surroundings. A teenage girl, perhaps seventeen years old, was busy admiring the plants. Making eye contact with us, she smiled and said hello. We took the opportunity to ask her about the area and about herself. She surprised us with her directness and candor.

"Y'all aren't from around here, are you?" she asked. From an observational perspective, I'm never sure if that statement is meant as a good thing or a bad thing.

"No, we are driving Route 66, all the way to Santa Monica," I answered.

"Wow, that is so cool," she said. "I've met a lot of people who are doing

Route 66. I would love to do that someday. As I bet you've seen, there's not much to see or do locally."

"And you? Do you live in this area?" Kate asked.

"I do! I live just up the road, maybe a fifteen-minute drive. I live with my grandma. Actually, she practically raised me." This is how we met Claire.

"Oh, where are your parents?" Kate asked.

"My mom and dad were both really bad into drugs. My dad managed to kick it a couple of years back and he is doing all right now. But my mom, she never really managed to get clean. There was a time when we were all together—but I was young then—and my mom convinced my dad that she was no longer taking, because he was trying to stay clean, but then he discovered that she was still getting high. She left soon after that."

Claire's gaze dropped to the ground for a second but then shot back up to us.

We were aware of the rampant drug-addiction problem in small-town America, but it is one thing to watch a documentary on television and another entirely to sit with someone and listen to their very personal, raw story.

"Are drugs a big problem in this area?" I asked. "Do you have a lot of drug use at school?"

"Oh yeah! Almost everyone I know does drugs. Not *every*one, but most people. I've never done them. I know that addiction runs in my family and I don't want to take any chances. I want to finish twelfth grade and then go to school and become a nurse. I just want to stay focused and help my brother and sister."

"Oh, you have siblings?" Kate inquired.

"I have one brother and one sister, but they didn't have it as easy as me. I mean, my life hasn't been easy, but at least my grandmother took me in. My siblings went into the foster system and my brother—he's the youngest—he's been in several homes. I know that they have both been abused and the state officials have had to move them a few times."

Her eyes drifted again as she spoke about her siblings. They were sad and lonely, filled with a sense of desperation. It was heart wrenching to learn of the plight of others as we passed through idyllic little towns in Middle America. On the surface, everyone is friendly and welcoming, and family values and relationships are firmly intact. They go to church every Sunday, and on the surface, people care deeply about one another. You would guess it's the perfect place to raise children. But underneath it all bubbles something—anything but the American dream.

"Do you want to stay in this area?" I asked. "Or are you open to working in larger towns or cities in Missouri or Oklahoma?"

"I wouldn't mind getting over to Springfield, Missouri, or maybe Joplin. That's not too far from here. But I need to stay near my brother and sister and make sure they turn out all right. My dad does try to help, but my mom doesn't really bother with any of us. I really wish that she did more." She looked down, rubbing her arm nervously.

We chatted with Claire for another half hour and then let her get on her way. She had to get home to help her grandmother with some family errands. As we drove off, we watched as she made a right-hand turn down a long, straight, quiet country road. Her future was uncertain, but her determination to rise above the misfortune and bad family circumstances that she'd had thrust on her was commendable, and, even in her difficult situation, she displayed something that in itself is truly American—a hope for and commitment to a brighter future.

———

UP THE ROAD, just beyond the Old Riverton Store, rests the Marsh Rainbow Arch Bridge, one of the last of its kind in America. It was built in 1923 and named after James Barney Marsh, the architect who designed the then-ultramodern structures. Crossing over Brush Creek, the arched bridge was placed on the National Register of Historic Places in 1983 due to its historic significance on Route 66, and is now protected from destruction. The bridge has been vandalized with graffiti numerous times over the years, but when we visited, it was painted white and appeared to be back to its former glory.

Feet planted firmly at the edge of the structure, we stopped and listened, careful to observe the sounds of the thick forest beside us and the gurgle of the tranquil, muddy-brown water below. A meadowlark landed on the guardrail, shaking its feathers in the heat of the sunlight, just as a loud splash rang out. Both the bird and I turned quickly to see what had disturbed our serenity. It was Thembi. He was engaging in some stone tossing over the edge and appeared quite proud of himself. "That was a good one!" he beamed, his little legs running to collect some more stones.

The roadway leading up to the bridge is branded tastefully in a number of 66 shields, guiding pedestrians toward the crossing. We walked slowly across the bridge, stopping to take in the quietude that is available in this little forgotten part of the United States.

"Dad, why would they want to tear down these bridges?" Thembi asked, rightfully confused.

"To build bigger, wider, stronger ones. Not everyone appreciates history or sees the value in preserving it."

There were once seventy arch bridges built across the Midwest, with most in Kansas, but now only thirty-five remain. This is the only one remaining on Route 66.

He was pensive for a moment, his little mind pondering my answer.

Just then, a black two-door Honda pulled around the bend, edging its way toward the bridge and then cautiously across. A woman dressed in casual blue jeans and a black Aerosmith T-shirt hopped out, took a few pictures, and then got back in and drove off with her traveling companion. They had gotten their photograph. They can say that they were there. We had already witnessed so much hit-and-run photography on the highway—it struck us as a real waste of a magical journey.

The world moves at sonic speed these days, and people have little time for atmosphere and introspection. But on the Mother Road, like so many other historic two-lane highways in America, time can once again become a friend, if you let it.

16

LESS THAN FIVE miles up the road, past the Field of Dreams baseball field, we passed into one of the prettiest towns on 66. The wide, empty streets created an Old West feel that was amplified by its typical American Main Street architecture and decor, with striking murals painted on the sides of the town's long-standing buildings. Baxter Springs has seen an eventful past. The town was named after John Baxter, an enterprising individual who settled in the area in the mid-1800s, but was killed in a gunfight in 1859, dying before Baxter Springs took on his name. Four years later, another bloody event took place that further defined the small town's reputation. Confederate raiders, led by the infamous William Quantrill, attacked and killed a modest force of Union soldiers who were set up just outside of town. Only a small number of troops survived. The massacre still remains in the hearts of local residents. By 1870, Baxter Springs had grown into Kansas's first cow town, due to the large number of longhorn cattle that Texas ranchers were transporting across the area.

I paused in the middle of the sidewalk to take in the surroundings. Thembi and Kate were ahead of me, stopping to peek into the wide store-front windows. The main road was void of life, save for the odd passing vehicle and some activity inside one of the shops that made up Military Avenue. The sun warmed our skin, bathing us in the aura of midcentury America.

Angels on the Route café was the next stop on our list. The location had a great history that dates back to the 1860s as John M. Cooper's Dry Goods and Clothing Store, next as Reedy's Pharmacy for a half century, and then as a café—it had taken off once again when Alan and Cheri

McCamey took over management on October 1, 2015. There were no lights on and the mural advertising the restaurant was faded, reminiscent of a bygone time. At first, we thought the café was closed—a natural reaction, as over the years many once-great businesses have closed as travelers simply pass by on the interstate.

"Let's just walk down the street and take a look around," suggested Kate. And so we did, observing all the quaint, endearing 66 memorabilia and traditional brick architecture. Baxter Springs has a long and intriguing history, with rumors suggesting that the town was robbed twice by notorious outlaws Bonnie and Clyde, and that Jesse James and his gang passed through in 1876, robbing the Crowell Bank.

"Wait," said Kate. "Back there, that is Cafe on the Route. We're looking for . . . "

"Angels on the Route," interrupted Thembi, pointing to a large sign on the right. True enough, we had been admiring the wrong café. Angels was very much open, its huge colorful banner screamed from above the entrance. The word "café" was painted in big, bold black letters across a white background, while just below the vintage wording, the café advertised their claim to fame: sandwiches, desserts, pies. A patriotic Americana pleated bunting hung below it all, further proof that we were in the Midwest.

"Welcome to Angels on the Route," called out a smiling gent from behind the counter. "Sit wherever you'd like."

The venue was simple and cozy, a welcome change to the 66 dining experience of tasty, but often greasy, fare. Don't get me wrong, we love diners, but I don't eat hamburgers and the opportunity to enjoy some fresh food—delicious homemade soup and sandwiches—and a great shake in a homey environment was just too good to miss. The next few hours passed fast in animated conversation with Alan and Cheri, learning about the venue, the town, and the two of them.

Cheri shared their story: "Alan and I were childhood friends in the area and college sweethearts. Our families were close. During college, we considered marriage but ended up choosing different routes: Alan settled in Indianapolis, and I settled in Wichita, Kansas. Some years ago, my stepfather became ill with cancer, and I moved back home to help. We lost him the following January, which was very difficult, but during this time I became reconnected to Alan, and having both gone through divorces after thirty years of marriage, we were ready for a new start and finally got together, at last. We were married in February 2015 and are happy, with eight children between us and five grandchildren." Her cheerfulness bubbled out of her, with an undeniable natural warmth and kindness.

"Wow, that is a big family. But how did you guys find yourselves here, opening a café?" Kate asked.

"We came to the opportunity of taking over Angels on the Route through a friend," Cheri explained. "Since we both love people, and our gifts, skills, and experience are in hospitality and the service industry, we felt like the café was a perfect fit. I love food, cooking, and creating, and love how people respond to banqueting. They become themselves with food. We get to be a part of hundreds of dreams and bucket lists from travelers who have planned for years to travel Route 66 or take that long-planned-for vacation. We literally meet people from every continent and hundreds of cities and villages." Cheri's eyes sparkled with enthusiasm as she spoke, her face lighting up.

As we talked, a guitar player—whose cousin was apparently a lead member of the popular group Rascal Flatts—strummed his instrument in the corner near the entrance of the café, banging out hit song after hit song. Thembi was enamored. He had recently started learning to play the guitar and was excited to watch a live musician. "Do you know 'Take Me Home, Country Roads' by John Denver?" Thembi called out during a short break. The older entertainer was impressed. "Why, yes I do, young man. And I'll play it if you come up here and help me sing it."

Thembi flashed a look to us and we nodded. "Go ahead."

It is times like these, out on the road, away from our creature comforts and all that we know, that truly create life-defining memories. That afternoon, we got to know two of the sweetest people on America's Main Street, and Thembi sung his heart out. In a short period of time, we were no longer strangers from very different worlds. We were new friends with a great deal in common. We were connected. And it was all in that tiny corner of Kansas, along Route 66.

Gemini Giant, Wilmington, IL. Photo By Brennen Matthews.

Standard Oil Gas Station, Odell, IL. Photo By David J. Schwartz.

Illinois Route 66 Hall of Fame & Museum, Pontiac, IL. Photo By David J. Schwartz.

Red brick road, Auburn, IL. Photo By David J. Schwartz.

Hot and cold water towers, St. Clair, MO. Photo By David J. Schwartz.

Motorcycles heading west past the Wagon Wheel Motel, Cuba, MO.
Photo By David J. Schwartz.

Gary's Gay Parita Sinclair, Paris Springs Junction, MO. Photo By David J. Schwartz.

Boots Court Motel, Carthage, MO. Photo By David J. Schwartz.

66 Drive-In Theatre, Carthage, MO. Photo By David J. Schwartz.

Cars on the Route, Galena, KS. Photo By David J. Schwartz.

Dairy King, Commerce, OK. Photo By Marshall Hawkins.

Ed Galloway's Totem Pole Park, Foyil, OK. Photo By David J. Schwartz.

Blue Whale, Catoosa, OK. Photo By David J. Schwartz.

Pops 66, Arcadia, OK. Photo By David J. Schwartz.

Round Barn, Arcadia, OK. Photo By Marshall Hawkins.

Rock Cafe, Stroud, OK. Photo By Marshall Hawkins.

Part 2

The Great Push West

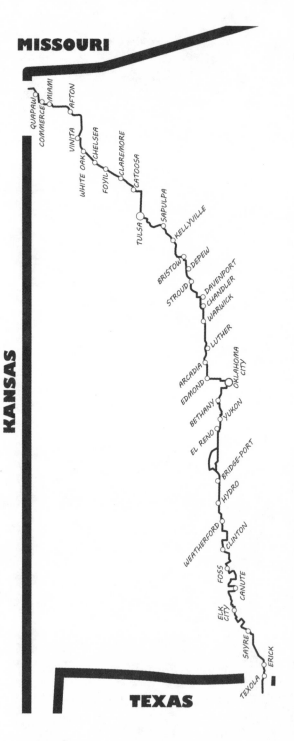

MISSOURI

KANSAS

TEXAS

QUAPAW
COMMERCE
MIAMI
AFTON
VINITA
WHITE OAK
CHELSEA
FOYIL
CLAREMORE
CATOOSA
TULSA
SAPULPA
KELLYVILLE
BRISTOW
DEPEW
STROUD
DAVENPORT
CHANDLER
WARWICK
LUTHER
ARCADIA
EDMOND
OKLAHOMA CITY
BETHANY
EL RENO
YUKON
BRIDGE-PORT
HYDRO
WEATHERFORD
CLINTON
FOSS
CANUTE
ELK CITY
SAYRE
ERICK
TEXOLA

17

THERE IS A story told by Michael Wallis about a young farmer from western Oklahoma, whom he met while researching his 1990 book, who,
during the Great Depression, lived and farmed on what would become
Route 66. The man remembered the laying of the concrete, the crude
machinery, and the men, many of them migrants, who stopped along
the nascent road to get a job. "Every night," Michael told me, "he'd get
his young wife and they'd take a wind-up Victrola phonograph and some
other young couples, and they would go out to the new highway, turn
on the music, and dance on the fresh road, and they did this all the way
across western Oklahoma, until the new road went into Texas. They
danced on the Mother Road." Those people are now long gone, leaving
only a fading and distant memory of their time on earth, but their hard
work and dreams developed the Midwest, establishing the very concrete
vein that was transporting us west.

Oklahoma has always held romantic notions for me. The very feel of
the land and its frontier heritage and history bring it alive. Oklahoma is a
country that has generally been understated, but it has drawn searchers
seeking a better life for more than two centuries. The Cheyenne, Comanche, Osage, and Pawnee tribes migrated into the region in the early 1800s
and by around 1890, Europeans followed. Striking out into the unknown
carries with it an undeniable romance, but in the mid-nineteenth century, Euro-Americans who ventured to Oklahoma and the lands beyond
were generally not in search of a grand adventure but were rather retreating from a less-than-desirable certainty. What was contained in the safety
of the towns and cities they ventured from was simply not worth staying

for and what awaited them beyond the mysterious frontier, though uncertain and likely dangerous, promised rare opportunity. These men and women who lived during a poetic period in history gambled with their futures and went on to form a captivating, vital part of the American imagination. Their exploits have become things of legends and their accomplishments heralded. Today, there are few unconquered swathes of land left, and the often assumed simplicity and romance of that time period neglects to account for the failure that followed a great many of those hopeful travelers. It is this reality that intrigues me. These folks, who toiled and charted the path and are now long gone, paved the way for people like you and me to traverse America. As we motored into Oklahoma, down historic Route 66, these were the thoughts that flooded my mind.

The sky was cobalt when we drove through the small farming town of Quapaw and straight into Commerce, where we parked across from the famed Dairy King. As we started to cross the road toward the café, a middle-aged couple in a white pickup truck pulled in beside us. Quick to say hello from inside their vehicle, they shut off the engine.

"It's getting pretty hot out today, isn't it?" said the man, wiping his creased brow. He was casually dressed in a black T-shirt and had tanned skin painted with age spots. His wife, a heavier-set woman, wore a cream-colored tank top and wide-rimmed sunglasses. She was studying a thin, well-worn booklet.

"Y'all live in Commerce or around these parts?" he asked. When we explained that we were driving Route 66, his enthusiasm was evident. "Kim, did ya hear that? These nice folks are driving all the way to Los Angeles."

"Oh, wow, that's a wonderful trip. So you're going all the way?"

We nodded and smiled. "Yep, right till the beach," I said.

After suggesting some key places we should not miss in Oklahoma, especially in their hometown of Vinita, Terry, a retired train builder, explained that the couple was trying to find Angels on the Route in Baxter Springs. They had heard good things and wanted to grab lunch after antique hunting all morning. "We actually spend most of our days now just driving around and visiting auctions and antique shops."

"Do you guys keep everything you purchase, then?" Kate asked.

"Oh dear, heavens no," Kim answered. "It's a business. We find unexpected treasures and then resell them at other auctions or online. There's a lot of money in it, and you never know what you'll discover. It's really exciting, actually. I used to be in real estate, but then that grew tiring and now I get to travel all over the place and find the most wonderful things." This fit with our experience so far on the trip. Every small town seemed to have at least one cluttered, colorful antique shop. Antiquing is a big business in the States, but little heard of in Kenya.

The scorching sun was now beating down on us and we tried to extract ourselves from the conversation. They seemed like a lovely couple, if a bit odd—but we were keen to get into the Dairy King and out of the humidity. Seeing our body language, Terry switched gears in the discussion. "Are you believers, by any chance?" Normally, this would have seemed out of left field—but not there in the heartland.

"Yes, we are," I answered. "We are both Christians." Up in Canada, no one had ever asked us about our faith. It is actually a topic that makes a lot of Toronto residents a bit uncomfortable.

"That's great to hear," he said. "But what do you know about the original sin that happened in the Garden of Eden?" We were totally caught off guard. Then it hit me. We had stumbled upon some fanatics.

"You know, most people, including Christians, don't realize that the first sin was not Adam and Eve eating from the forbidden tree and disobeying God's command. No, it was Eve having sex with the devil in the garden." His eyes were serious and fiery. We had accidentally fallen into a subject that Terry and Kim obviously had deeply held beliefs about. "The devil seduced the woman," he clarified, "and they had forbidden intercourse. It may have happened many times, actually. We cannot know. But Cain—y'all have heard of Cain and Abel, Eve's sons? Cain was the offspring of Satan and was not Adam's biological son at all."

"Right," I said, nodding. Oh boy. "That is definitely something to think about."

Kate looked at me, touched my shoulder, and said her goodbyes to Kim and Terry. "It is getting really hot out here, so I am just going to take Thembi into the café. Nice to meet you both." Then she was gone, leaving me to fend for myself to break free from what quickly developed into a weirder and weirder conversation. I envy her ability to simply walk away from a discussion that does not interest her. I, however, usually feel guilty and am afraid of causing offense—so I end up trapped.

The next twenty minutes was consumed by Terry educating me on the logic behind his theology, with intermittent additions from Kim. As a Christian, I appreciate faith as part of one's life and seriously respect Bible-focused doctrine. But Kate and I are conservative Christians and do not stray very far from Scripture and literal interpretation. I needed to get away from this wacky discourse, so I tried to slowly move away from the truck—but every time I got a distance away, his voice rose to follow me. Finally, almost out of mercy, Terry saw that I was getting restless and allowed me to break free.

"You must be getting bored of us jabbering on. But give it some thought, and you'll see that the logic is sound."

"I sure will! It was fantastic to meet you both. And we wish you guys huge success with the rest of your trip and treasure hunt."

"Enjoy the road, young man, and take care of that handsome little boy of yours. He seems to have a great deal of curiosity. Make sure to keep stoking that. You are on the right road for it. You know . . . " Oh crud, he was beginning to start up again.

"Okay then," I slightly hollered, my voice increasing in volume as I ran across the street. I was committed to not letting them trap me in more conversation.

Inside, Kate and Thembi had already ordered a treat.

Once a Marathon Petroleum Company gas station, the idyllic little café resembles a life-size dollhouse, with its red, gabled roof and flat canopy over the area where the gas pumps once functioned. Frequented for its ice cream and burgers, the café's most recent claim to fame has become its cookies, shaped in the form of the Route 66 shield.

"I make these myself," shared owner Charles Duboise (who runs the place with his mother, Treva.) "People come from all around the world for our cookies." I found it a bit unlikely that international visitors intentionally make their way to this little corner of Oklahoma just to experience a cookie, but according to Charles, customers have come from

Tahiti, India, South Africa, and the Caribbean. "I even get orders and have sent cookies as far away as Europe." Duboise had a patent hanging on the wall to prove ownership of his design.

The Duboise family had been in Commerce for over one hundred years. Pulling out a photo album, Charles excitedly flipped through faded pictures, evidence of how the store and the surrounding town once looked. Much had changed. As we were talking, a heavyset man tapped me on the shoulder. "Have you tried their hamburgers?" he asked. "People come from far and wide for a burger from here."

"Sorry, just the cookies for me. I don't eat red meat," I answered. There was silence as the men looked at each other slightly puzzled. It appeared to be a concept that was foreign to them. We had not met many non-beef-eaters on 66 yet (let alone vegetarians).

Kate and Thembi, sensing a long conversation about to ensue, fled the shop to check out a remodeled green-and-red Conoco gas station across the street. (Perhaps you are noticing a trend by now?) I heard Thembi laughing as they admired the vintage design, and then he ran away from his mom, resisting having his picture taken. The heat of the day was intense at that point, and I noticed that he was not wearing his hat. I politely excused myself and, some extra cookies in hand, headed back out to join my family.

Other than the Route 66 cookies at Dairy King, Commerce has another claim to fame: this small town was once the home of baseball legend Mickey Mantle. As a boy, Mantle liked to spend his free time practicing at bat with his father and grandfather—one of them pitched right-handed, the other left-handed. This trained young Mickey how to switch-hit from an early age, a skill that did well for him as his career advanced and he moved into the major leagues, becoming one of the most talented players with the New York Yankees during the 1950s and '60s. Mantle retired with more than 536 home runs under his belt. Mantle's home on South Quincy Street still stands today, only a few hundred yards off famed Route 66. There is also a nine-foot-tall bronze statue at Commerce High School celebrating this local hometown hero.

18

OKLAHOMA IS A beautiful state, open and spacious, the proud owner of 432 lovely miles of America's Main Street. Driving past seemingly never-ending fields of neatly baled hay and fat grazing cows, the Sooner State was more expansive than any other we'd encountered thus far on the trip. The deep-blue, cloudless sky was perfect for the day's movement, and it felt good to be free of Missouri's thick forest. But in Oklahoma, things can change quickly: Route 66 runs right through "Tornado Alley," and the sky can turn at any moment, so we kept a close eye on the weather forecast. Oklahoma's section of 66 is a journey through time, not just miles. We experienced historic towns like Miami (pronounced "Miamuh"), Afton (a cool little ghost town), and Vinita (home of Clanton's Cafe, with their huge EAT sign and famous fried calf testicles), towns that sprang up more than a century and a quarter ago over wide-open plains once ruled by Native tribes and roamed by huge herds of bison. Across the wind-swept prairie, there was a strong sense of being in the heart of America, the gateway for where the real West begins.

The road unraveled into a straight line now, through beautiful, mani-cured fields and scenic, regal forests. Dozens of chestnut-brown horses grazed contentedly on soft summer grass, and a huge Hay for Sale sign stood at the end of a long, nondescript gravel street. The Route 66 signs were again brown with white writing, and old, rusting vintage vehicles began to pop up from time to time, likely having been parked for an eter-nity on the side of the old highway.

As we approached Chelsea, we saw two hitchhikers—a man and a woman, maybe in their early twenties—on the side of the road. Dressed in frumpy pajamas and donning a look of desperation, they were both disheveled and terribly sunburned. They appeared to have spent a lot of time waiting for a lift. That day, we could not be of assistance, but they hardly seemed bothered and made little effort to flag us down. They sat slumped against a wooden signpost, looking bored and strangely at home in their hopelessness. The landscape then changed again, slightly, and turned into rolling hills. We passed ponds and barns and lots of unexpected barbed-wire fences, water towers, and concrete silos. The roadside was littered with roadkill—possums, mainly.

We didn't stay long in Chelsea but did check out the now-dilapidated Chelsea Motel, which has become a great old relic, and then headed down a pretty little forested loop to see the 1926-constructed Pryor Creek Bridge. The water below the bridge was shallow, filled with playful turtles. Big ones, small ones, all swimming and frolicking in the sunshine. I was taking advantage of the thick foliage around the bridge to relieve myself of the many bottles of water I had drunk throughout the morning when I heard an urgent warning from Kate.

"Brennen, there's a police car coming!" she said, alarmed.

I scrambled to finish my business and zip up my jeans when the grinding of gravel under tires rose in the air.

An officer exited his cruiser and headed over to us, an expression of curiosity in his eyes.

"How are you folks doing today? Where are you visiting from?" he asked, having noticed our foreign plate.

Thembi stopped tossing stones from the bridge and turned to watch the officer.

"We're down from Toronto. We're on our way to California and driving Route 66," I answered.

He stared at me for a few seconds with a serious expression across his face. Then he removed his hat and wiped his brow.

"That's a pretty big trip. How are you guys enjoying Oklahoma so far?"

We shared some of our experiences and told him about our time on the road. He quietly listened, nodding.

"Okay, folks, there's not a problem. I just wanted to make sure that you didn't need any assistance, but it seems like you have everything under control." He turned to Thembi and said, "Young man, you have a very big journey ahead of you. Make sure that you pay attention and take it all in."

"Thank you, I am!" Thembi responded with a big smile. This seemed to delight the officer and he quickly climbed back into his cruiser and, driving past us, headed back out onto the two-lane highway. We remained at the bridge for a little longer, relaxing in the shade of the trees and listening as the river gurgled, before returning to the well-worn pavement ourselves.

Up ahead, we spotted what we were looking for—a humble, easy-to-miss sign that led us toward Ed Galloway's Totem Pole Park just outside of Foyil. The Mother Road offers a lot of odd and uncommon attractions, and Ed's was one on our to-visit list.

A retired manual-arts teacher, Galloway taught for over twenty years in Sand Springs, Oklahoma, before shifting gears and moving to a small farm near Foyil. Interested in Native American traditions and art, Galloway set to work building his first totem pole—a project that would require six tons of steel, twenty-eight tons of cement, and one hundred tons of rock and sand, and would, in the end, stand ninety-eight feet in the air. It was completed in 1948. The park now consists of eleven totem poles and a gift shop, comfortably spread out over fourteen acres.

Galloway lived at the park until his death from cancer in 1962. After his passing, the park fell into a sad state of disrepair until the Rogers County Historical Society acquired it in 1989 and, along with the Kansas Grassroots Art Association, began a very effective restoration process.

Sitting on the soft summer grass, we gaily observed our surroundings. It was quiet, even whimsical. Birds were chirping, bees were buzzing, and a warm breeze was blowing by, rustling the foliage of nearby trees. There was a calm, a soothing stillness. The totems were aged, but still colorful, speaking of a different era, each carving offering a story of its own. Here, only three and a half miles off Route 66, there was a sensation of having entered another dimension.

"This is one big country," Kate noted, as we watched Thembi play around the totem poles. He was standing at the edge of the tallest one, looking straight up into the heavens, amazed at the height. "I mean, we have driven over a thousand miles and passed through so many different places, and we are not even close to being halfway down Route 66, let alone really seeing the country," she added, duly impressed.

"True, we could have crossed Kenya twice by now." I laughed. "And there is so much diversity." That is one thing that I have always loved about America. The country has sandy beaches and wide-open plains, tropical islands, the bayous in the South, deserts in the Southwest, and the Arctic tundra in the North. There are just so many options here for how a person can choose to live their life.

Traveling through most African countries, save perhaps South Africa, can be very monotonous. Most small towns are very similar to the next: rural, dusty, rough roads, with little to no notable infrastructure or amenities. In East Africa, few small towns would even boast of a decent coffee shop or place for lodging. A road trip in Africa is, for the most part, about getting from point A to point B. In America, the interstate and all of its amenities are always around the corner, and on highways like Route 66, the rural towns are what make the journey so special and memorable. Driving through the different states is like visiting a collection of micro-countries, each with its own identity and personality. The vastness of the country is overpowering, yet profoundly inspiring, and the possibilities of discovery limitless.

"Dad, don't move," Thembi cautioned, the sound of wonder in his voice. "A roadrunner is walking right beside you." Rushing past my feet, the distinctive little bird appeared to be looking for lunch, barely concerned with our presence, but careful nonetheless. "Look at the crest on his head, Dad. See how it is solid black against the brown and white stripes on the rest of his body? This is a greater roadrunner. Imagine, they can nest on cactus!" We watched it as it mowed around the open grass, darting between the totem poles, before taking flight. Up until that point, I had no idea that the roadrunner was even a real bird. I always thought that the iconic *Looney Tunes* animal was made up!

A lone woman arrived at the park with an enormous, furry, chocolate-brown dog, the canine eagerly looking for a good place to leave his mark. He pulled her powerfully as she desperately tried to hold on to his long leash. Waving hello, she was not paying attention to the ground and tripped over something on the grass, accidentally releasing her hold as she attempted to right herself from falling. The dog darted toward some long grass and disappeared for a few moments before returning notably calmer. She was not impressed and rushed him back to their forest-green Subaru Outback. Muttering obscenities, seemingly at the dog, she peeled out, filling the dry air with dust.

We were alone again.

We were privileged to pass the day in the shadow of a man's simple, yet elaborate, vision. Galloway's remarkable musings were literally all around us, once again reminding us of a time long before our own modern age of instant communication and immediate gratification. For a moment, we were lost in the euphoria of his imagination.

———

CONTINUING WEST, WE were building up an appetite, and chocolate bars and bottles of warm water weren't doing the trick. We stopped in the picturesque town of Claremore, with its J. M. Davis Arms and Historical Museum and super-charming Main Street, and sought out lunch. As usual, we scoured the area to find the quaintest, most traditional-looking venue possible. This practice often resulted in a great, home-cooked meal in a friendly, tranquil environment. Other times, we seemed to stumble into a café that time forgot. Our luck that day in Claremore brought us an interesting encounter.

As we took a seat in a worn-out booth beside the window, five waitresses milled about near the kitchen, each staring in our direction, but no one actually came over to take our order. Finally, after enough waving that we were almost taking off in flight, one of the pack broke free.

"Can I get you something, dear?"

"Do you have cappuccino?" Kate asked.

"No."

"Caffe latte?"

"No."

"Please say that you have espresso!"

"No, we only have regular coffee. None of the fancy stuff."

"Okay, that sounds good."

As we waited, I noticed a picture hanging on the wall above the tables, of one particular local dreamer who traipsed along Route 66 in its early days before making good on a national scale. Born in 1879 to a Cherokee family in Oologah, Oklahoma, some fifteen miles northwest of 66, beloved actor and writer Will Rogers grew up in Claremore, traveling the road many times and moving along it wherever fame took him. The highest-paid Hollywood actor of the 1930s, he starred in more than seventy movies, both silents and talkies, wrote six best-selling books, and penned thousands of daily newspaper columns. A box-office sensation, thespian, vaudevillian, social commentator, and modern philosopher, Rogers adamantly promoted the Mother Road and the opportunities that it opened for millions. Folksy and jolly, the small-town cowboy turned nation's most beloved performer could regularly be spotted along the route. The actor was tragically killed in a plane crash in 1935, at just fifty-six years old. Grieving, many people began calling Route 66 the Will Rogers road. In 1952, the U.S. 66 Highway Association officially dedicated the legendary road to the storied man, continuing his memory with the Will Rogers Highway moniker.

Our server, a middle-aged woman dressed in a traditional and unflattering 1950s waitress uniform, seemed to have stepped out of the past herself as she sashayed around the restaurant, chatting casually to the few other customers while continually returning to hold down the order counter with her colleagues. The atmosphere was a bit unreal, with elevator music softly setting the mood, creating a weird *Twilight Zone* vibe. Coffee pot firmly in hand, she finally returned. "Where y'all from?" she asked.

"We're actually from Africa, but we currently live in Toronto, up in Canada."

"Ah, I visited Toronto. We had a moose convention there a year ago."

"I'm sorry, a what?" I asked.

"A moose convention." This seemed to excite her. Now we were in her wheelhouse.

"As in the animal?"

"Yes, sir," she said, beaming. "It was very well attended."

19

OUR AMAZEMENT WITH the big Blue Whale of Catoosa was interrupted by a bevy of motorcycle-driving tourists noisily invading our otherwise tranquil space. Loud and intrusive, and perhaps totally oblivious, they made their way down into the belly of the giant whale and began to snap away with their cameras.

"Can you take our picture?" asked a gent in his early thirties with a thick German accent. The way that he phrased it seemed not so much a request as a demand, as he thrust his phone in my face. Standing arm in arm with his pal, they smiled and frowned, looked amazed, and then appeared stunned. I clicked away on his iPhone until they seemed to tire of posing.

"I'm sure you'll find something good in there," I said, smiling and handing back his device. They simply took the phone and walked off without a thank-you.

A heavyset man in his later years had driven into the lot and taken a seat at one of the concrete tables that dot the grounds in front of the pond. Dressed in dark-blue trousers held up firmly by bright-red suspenders—contrasted by a faded gray T-shirt that stretched over his pronounced belly—he was an arresting figure. I couldn't help myself and struck up a conversation.

Glenn was seventy-two years old and a very successful retired businessman. A longtime resident of the area, he spent a lot of his time in the shade of the bur oak trees, interacting with visitors and reminiscing with them about the birth of the Blue Whale and other stories of Route 66. This was his local coffee shop.

"I like to come over here when I have time and just chat with people.

I take pictures for them when they ask. I like to help," he explained as his eyes constantly scanned the area.

"Have you ever driven Route 66 yourself?" I asked. He had.

"I first rode 66 when I was eight years old. I did it with my parents and can remember most of that trip. Things were certainly not easy back then, especially in the desert. But I've done it twice since, once on a motorbike. I saved the desert driving until nightfall due to the heat. I drove for hours in the pitch blackness."

"You drove your motorcycle in the Mojave at night, in the dark?" I asked. "Weren't you concerned about crashing into animals crossing the road?"

"Nah, I just took my time. It's a whole different world out there at night. But it sure was dark."

I began to wonder what Thembi would remember about the trip that we were on. Would he carry the experiences with him as he got older? What impact would crossing America via its most famous two-lane highway have on him? He was already starting to forget aspects of his life in Kenya.

"Look at that." Glenn pointed. A couple with their two young children were skipping pebbles on the surface of the water. Their youngest, maybe five years old, was over the moon with glee.

"I see new faces here every day and am really happy that people are welcome to visit the whale again," he said. "There was a time when the family had closed the whole place off."

It always astounds me how creative and industrious some people can be when opportunity calls for it.

It was the early 1970s, and Hugh Davis, then director of the Tulsa Zoo and owner of a small alligator farm just off Route 66, had a big day approaching. He decided to surprise his wife, Zelta, for their wedding anniversary. He knew that she loved whales, so what better gift to give her than an eighty-foot-long, sky-blue sperm whale, right? Only in America.

Initially enjoyed only by Davis, Zelta, and their two children, the joyful whale with the toothy grin had, by the mid-1970s, become the famous centerpiece of the couple's new attraction, Nature's Acres. The venue also boasted a wooden replica of Noah's Ark, a handful of large concrete mushrooms, and a trading post located across the highway that was run by Davis's Native American brother-in-law. Davis enlarged the spring-fed pond for use as a swimming hole, and the big Blue Whale quickly developed into a beloved Route 66 icon. As the couple advanced in age and it became difficult to continue to take care of the attraction, it slipped into disrepair, with Nature's Acres finally closing in 1988. Hugh Davis died in 1990, and Zelta followed in 2001.

For a decade, ole Blue sat neglected and crumbling. But love for the whale runs deep, and well-wishers tenderly tried to patch him up and restore his faded appearance to its former glory.

The heat of the day was intense—Oklahoma skies are often cloudless and pure blue in the summer, allowing the fierce midwestern sun to paint the dusty earth with its burning rays—but a heavy breeze suddenly blew through the treetops above us, ruffling leaves and raining down dirt and debris. I instinctually closed my eyes and threw my arms over my head. Glenn didn't seem to even notice. Pieces of twigs and leaves rested on top of his hair.

"I better be heading out. The missus and I have an event to go to tonight and my wife doesn't want me to be late. I'll never hear the end of it if I am." He laughed.

He walked slowly up the slight incline toward the parking lot, nodding politely to visitors as he went.

As Glenn pulled away, followed by the gaggle of motorcycles, Kate and I spent a few moments in solitude with the Blue Whale, looking through a Davis-family photo album available on one of the picnic tables. Inside were dozens of vintage photographs from the 1970s that depicted a happy time, when friends and family merrily splashed and played with the big blue concrete mammal. He still had the same goofy grin, but it was impossible not to feel a little nostalgic for what was obviously a very special era in Catoosa.

"Just look at this, will ya?" said a dark-haired beauty, possibly in her late fifties. She was talking to her husband, or maybe to us; I wasn't sure, as she seemed to be sharing her thoughts aloud generally. "Now that is a real piece of Americana. And he looks so happy."

I turned my gaze to the mouth of the whale, where Thembi stood feeding the turtles and fish. The day was passing slowly but had been filled with amazing discoveries and conversations. I was emotionally, or perhaps intellectually, exhausted, feeling really burned out. Too many conversations, maybe. When on the move, it is easy to get tired from endless stimulation, and sometimes all you want to do is rest in your silence and thoughts.

"Your little boy is so precious," said the lady, approaching us with an outstretched hand, who we later learned was Daisy Clemens. "He sure is an inquisitive little fella," her husband, Fred, added. "He was able to tell us the species of fish and turtles gobbling up his boxes of Rice Krispies cereal. I would never have even thought that marine life would eat cereal. But there ya go."

The couple came from Indiana and had jumped onto 66 in Lincoln, Illinois. They had managed to traverse a good bit of the country and now found themselves unexpectedly in Catoosa.

"We just love Americana," Daisy said. "I'm a retired schoolteacher, and Fred here, he does estate management. Mainly for larger farms and large-scale landholdings. But he grew up on a farm, so it's natural for him. Me, I miss my kids, but I love having the freedom to hit the road now that they are grown, and discover places like this. Us Americans know so little about our own country. The tourists come from afar just to travel and see things like this—can you imagine? But us, we ignore what's right in our own backyard." Fred nodded in agreement.

"We were told that we would see mostly international tourists on the road," Kate said, "but we've met a ton of Americans too. Maybe word is getting out and people are curious about America's past, about being on the road."

"It's possible," replied Daisy. "We're gonna take as much of Route 66 as we can to Tucumcari, New Mexico. I don't think we'll make it all the way to Albuquerque, though. Maybe another time."

"After that we need to head to Oregon to see our children," Fred chimed in. "They're both living there with their own families now. We'll take the train from New Mexico. At least, that's the plan. We're in a rental car for this leg of the trip."

"Do you think you'll try to do the whole route in the future?" I asked. "Or is this trip a bucket-list opportunity?"

Fred's face grew serious and his eyes narrowed. He suddenly looked sad. "I'm going through a sort of midlife crisis at this point in time. I'm in my sixties and I just look at life and it all seems to be behind me. It really has passed too fast. Where did the time go? When did the kids grow up? When did we get old? Traveling Route 66 and any of these two-lane highways reminds me of how things were when I was a young man." With these words, he teared up a little. It was an uncomfortable moment, and Kate and I both looked down at the ground. Daisy put her arm around him and squeezed him tight.

"I'm sorry about that," he said. "I don't mean to get blubbery. And you folks are young, so you still have a long way to go yet. And that little boy of yours is guaranteed to keep you young. But you're doing the right thing bringing him out to explore the country now. I've been hoping to get out on the road with my own kids now that they're grown. But everyone's schedules are always too busy or in conflict to get us all together." He frowned.

It's an old story, told by Harry Chapin via his hit song "Cat's in the Cradle." Children are always demanding the time of their parents, who seem to have little to give, but then when the kids get older and the parents desire more intimate time and connection, the children, in turn, are too busy to invest the hours.

Thembi lumbered toward us, climbing a gentle incline from the water's edge. He hugged me warmly and then walked toward the little gift shop that was closed, peering in the windows. Daisy and Fred announced that they needed to get a move on, and we walked them to the parking lot. On their dash was a fat, well-worn road trip book that they were excited to introduce when Fred noticed me eyeing it.

"We use this all the time," he said. "It's a bit tattered, but it has helped guide us to many places all over the country. You really should get a copy!"

I made an assurance that I would, which seemed to make them happy, and wished them a fond farewell.

They pulled out of the gravel parking area and turned right, heading west toward the welcoming embrace of Tulsa.

We passed another hour there in Catoosa, lost in reverie and conversation. In the warmth of the late-summer afternoon, I was struck by the privilege that we had been given to sit in the silence of the past. Hugh and Zelta Davis are now long gone, but their blue whale, often forgotten over the years, still endures, calling travelers from all corners of the globe to come and take a pause from the madness of today and soak up some nostalgia of yesteryear.

20

BYPASSING THE BIG city of Tulsa, we whizzed through Sapulpa, past its old buildings, colorful wall murals, and Rock Creek Bridge, enjoying the old section of 66 that passed in front of us before stopping for supper at the Rock Cafe in tiny Stroud. It was still early evening, so their neon sign had not been turned on, but we immediately saw that the venue was unique. The exterior of the building was built from large stones and the entranceway was carpeted with old tire bits. We were warmly greeted when we walked in, and, as had generally been the case since we first set foot on Route 66, conversation with strangers ensued. Posters of the Pixar film *Cars* covered the walls and small toy figurines of the characters were displayed throughout the restaurant.

"You really need to talk to Dawn," insisted our waitress when she discovered that I was a writer. She was referring to the owner of the café, Dawn Welch.

"That would be great," I said, excitedly. "Can you ask her to come over? We'd love to meet her."

"Sorry, no can do. She's out of town traveling at the moment."

"Oh," I responded, disappointed.

"Have y'all seen the movie *Cars*? You have? Okay then, do y'all remember the character Sally? You do? Okay then, so, Dawn is actually Sally! That's right—Pixar modeled the Sally Carrera character after Dawn. Okay then, do y'all wanna see some news clippings?"

Thembi was enthralled. He was a big fan of the movie—we all were—and was loving the bright posters and newspaper clippings that covered the café walls. The character that was modeled after Dawn was the intelligent, high-flying, big-city-lawyer Porsche, who had given up the fast life to enjoy a slower pace in a small town. Sally was also the love interest of the movie's main character, Lightning McQueen.

According to John Lasseter, the film's cowriter and director, the concept for the movie was born after his own road trip across a portion of the United States—some of which was on Route 66—with his wife and five kids in 2000. Upon his return to work, he contacted Route 66 expert Michael Wallis, who subsequently took eleven animators from Pixar on two different road trips along the route. Traveling in white Cadillacs, they soaked up the scenery and history of America's iconic highway as they went along, taking in every possible detail of the Mother Road for the film. The result was the myriad of colorful characters that fill the fictional town of Radiator Springs.

And like the film, both Dawn and the café came out of unconventional beginnings.

Construction of the Rock Cafe began in 1936, smack-dab in the middle of the Great Depression, which was a gutsy move for any businessman. Confident in his endeavor, Roy Rieves pushed ahead, using mostly local materials to build the café's unique stone exterior and carrying out most of the work himself, with the aid of hired youth. Rieves was able to procure sandstone, at a fair price, left over from construction of the Route 66 roadway, which was built in Stroud in 1926. A lucky break.

The café opened its doors in August 1939 and became a busy local stop for the Greyhound bus company during World War II, but the café's signature neon signage was not installed until the late 1940s. At one point during 1959, the café was so popular that it operated twenty-four hours a day, drawing people from far and wide. However, as with most businesses located on Oklahoma's Route 66, visitor numbers began to decline with the construction of I-44. With the formal decommissioning of Route 66 in 1985, the famous highway became Oklahoma State Highway 66 and is still the road that leads to the Rock, as the café is known locally. By then, the business was in a state of disrepair and about to be torn down, until local businessman Ed Smalley mercifully purchased the property in order to save it from being leveled. Smalley had himself worked at the café as a boy, even meeting his future wife, a Rock Cafe waitress, at the historical venue. He wanted to ensure its protection and preservation.

As a young girl, Dawn grew up in Yukon, Oklahoma, the eldest of four children, working and saving enough money to buy a motorcycle. Putting away hard-earned coins received from babysitting and work at a local pizza parlor, she managed to purchase the bike at the young age of fourteen, and still has it to this day. After high school, Dawn rushed off to Florida to join the cruise-ship industry, desperate to travel and see more of the world, which she did. In six years, she had saved enough to follow another dream, that of opening a restaurant in Costa Rica—which she wanted to call the Yellow Submarine Shop, named after the famous Beatles album—but fate would lead her on a different path.

One day in 1993, while Dawn was rollerblading down Stroud's Main Street—which was actually Route 66, though she did not realize it at the time—an older man in a Chevy pickup truck pulled up beside her and asked if she was the girl from the cruise ship who wanted to start a restaurant in Costa Rica. The fellow was none other than Ed Smalley, owner of the Rock. Dawn was only twenty-four at the time, but the wizened Route 66 business owner was able to talk her into delaying her move to Central America for a year—a year in which she agreed to lease the café for a twelve-month trial period and see how it went. That was twenty-nine years ago.

Focused on restoring the venue's legend and potentially buying and selling the business down the line so that she could relocate to tropical Costa Rica, Dawn forged ahead, diving headlong into operating her eatery. But something unexpected happened. As Dawn interacted with a myriad of tourists from faraway Europe and learned about Route 66 and people's passion for the fabled highway, she came into her element and simply carried on. Costa Rica would have to wait.

Some years later, in 1999, tragedy struck the small town of Stroud when a tornado ripped through a local mall, destroying a number of local businesses. The Rock Cafe's sign was damaged, but thankfully the building itself was left intact. However, with the local economy now in distress, the café's earnings were also painfully affected. But that was not to last, as the café continued to receive an influx of international Route 66 visitors, enabling it to stay afloat. In 2001, the Rock Cafe was honored by being listed on the National Register of Historic Places, a distinction that allowed it to apply for much-needed grants and loans that would contribute to repairing the neon and completing other restorations.

In May 2008, disaster struck again, this time in the form of a fire that burned down the entire café. Only the heavy grill was left intact. At eleven at night, on the last day of her children's school year, Dawn's phone rang with the news and she rushed to the scene, where she stood with what seemed to be the entire community and watched as the café burned to the ground. They were helpless to do anything to stop it. Devastated, but not one to be held down for long, Dawn set a plan in motion to clear the debris and rebuild the café. Dawn is a fighter. Sometime after our visit to the café, she and I spoke about the incident and Dawn made her position clear. "Never in my life has walking away been an option." It would take a year, but on May 29, 2009, the Rock Cafe opened its doors once again.

It was a fascinating story and we would have loved to stick around longer, but we had something farther up the road that we were dying to see.

21

AN ENORMOUS SODA bottle rising sixty-six feet high into the sky, complete with a fat drinking straw, stood before us. There was a certain buzz in the air, anticipation for dusk, when the lighting of the bottle would take place and the large, stark white symbol would suddenly transform into a brilliant, multicolored monument to soda pop. We were in Arcadia and on our way to Oklahoma City for the night. It had been a long and exhilarating day, filled with quintessential Mother Road attractions and a host of interesting people and their tales. Now we had arrived at Pops 66 to witness the bottle for ourselves before making the final dash—twenty-nine miles away—to Oklahoma City.

Established in Arcadia in August 2007, Pops is a truly unique restaurant that serves a basic but eclectic menu with more than seven hundred flavors of soda pop. The enormous glass windows are filled with various offerings, from the traditional Coca-Cola and Sprite to the less traditional Dog Drool, Dr. Brown's Cream Soda, Earp's Sarsaparilla, and Dublin Dr. Pepper. Plus, they offer all of the Route 66 options like root beer, cream soda, and orange soda, as well as the political varieties of Hillary Hooch (classified flavor), Donald's Populist Soda Pop Poll, and Hillary's Liberal Soda Pop Poll. There are bacon-flavored and peanut butter–resembling options, Beefdrinker's Teriyaki Beef Jerky Soda, and Lester's Fixins Ranch Dressing Soda. Yep, there is something for everyone, no matter how bizarre your taste.

Inside was packed. Outside was packed. The place was humming and as people left, more arrived in their wake. But somehow the crowd made the energy more pleasant, like we were all experiencing something together and were waiting on a major unveiling. We made our way toward the rear terrace, where tables and chairs were set out facing a huge grassy backyard. A girls' sports team took a few tables nearby and excitedly celebrated their teammate's birthday.

As a somewhat recent addition to the attractions on Route 66, Pops is an unexpected sight on the historic route. The highly modern architecture, the floor-to-ceiling glass walls, and the colorful assortment of drinks brings a welcome fresh energy to the more iconic places on the road. We finished our sodas and made our way to the front of the building to await the lighting of the giant neon pop bottle. Thembi, tired of being cooped up in the vehicle, was a ball of energy, and Kate and I were fighting the fatigue of a long day.

An older, white-haired lady with black, full-rimmed glasses, carrying a small dog in her arms, walked over and stood beside us. "This is very exciting waiting for the bottle to light up, isn't it?" she asked. She was almost giddy. "My daughter and I are heading to Tulsa to see my sister, and we accidentally discovered this place. I would never have known. We only got off the interstate to sleep in Oklahoma City and someone told us about this enormous bottle."

"But Tulsa is only a few hours away from here using Route 66," Kate said. "Why don't you guys jump on 66 tomorrow and spend a bit more time seeing the road? There are lots of great places like Pops on that stretch."

The older lady's eyes lit up and a grin spread across her face. "That's a great idea. Let me suggest that to my daughter." We stood silently for a few minutes, and then a heavyset woman in jeans and a charcoal tank top sauntered over and gently put her hand on the lady's shoulder. She turned and smiled.

"These nice people have suggested that we can drive to Tulsa on Route 66 tomorrow. It's not very far from here and sounds a lot more interesting than the busy highway," the older woman offered.

"Mom, Route 66 will take too long and we really need to get to Tulsa early. Maybe another time." Although the mom tried to put up an argument, her daughter was not interested, and the decision was made. "We don't have time for the back road." Interstate, uninterrupted speed, and boring generic it was to be. The mom turned to Kate and winked. "I'll see if I can talk her into it," she whispered.

"The bottle is taking a long time to light up," someone complained from behind. "When will they turn it on?"

"Actually, it's always on. They never turn it off," said a young photographer setting up his tripod and camera. "The light of the bottle just isn't seen until it's dark enough for the LED lights to be effective." There was a murmur of comprehension from the crowd.

The sun burned low on the horizon as it slowly set, ushering in the night. Another brilliant Oklahoma day was ending. Suddenly, the sky was ablaze with light and the soda bottle came alive. Standing in the middle of Oklahoma on that warm summer night with my family and a gigantic full moon that painted the impossibly clear sky, the moment was unforgettable.

22

I WAS STILL trying to figure out why a round barn was such a popular attraction when I heard Thembi call to me from atop a grassy hill. "Smile, Dad, it's your turn to be in a picture." We had bought him a camera for his seventh birthday, and during the trip he was making good use of it. The big Arcadia Round Barn was closed the prior evening, so we had to backtrack to the pretty town that morning in order to see it for ourselves. It was worth it. But what a difference daytime makes—Arcadia looked completely different. It was no longer an enchanting little town under the glow of a magical full moon; it was now a peaceful, welcoming tiny village.

Constructed in 1898 by William Harrison "Big Bill" and Myra Eva Odor, the Arcadia Round Barn has the privilege of being the most famous barn on Route 66. In fact, it is so well known that it holds the distinction of being the most photographed landmark on the Mother Road. This struck me as a bit odd. It's perfectly nice, but there are certainly many other more "photogenic" places. Its earthy-red hue and the simple fact of its enormity make it attractive, but I was not sure why it is so special. The barn was built in its circular shape in the hope that tornadoes would dance around the structure and move on, rather than destroy it. However, there is no actual scientific evidence that the shape of a barn can protect it from twisters.

Over the years and with several ownership changes, the barn fell into disrepair due to neglect and wear and tear. Finally, in June 1988, the intricately designed roof fell in, slumping like an egg soufflé. Soon after the roof collapsed, a retired local building contractor named Luther Robison pulled together a team of volunteers and set to work restoring the once-majestic roof to its original elaborate design. It took them four years.

The upper level of the barn was empty that day. I had expected something, anything, but it was bare—a large empty space with a clean wooden floor and a powerful echo effect. The domed roof, however, was breathtaking. It was made with overlapping planks, and, in an amazing testament to the workmanship, there were no supporting beams whatsoever in the center. In some ways, it reminded me of the neatly woven thatched roofs of coastal Kenya.

"Let's go down the stairs to the gift shop. I want to look around," suggested Kate.

"Okay, but let's just look, please. We can't buy stuff everywhere we go," I pleaded.

The shop was filled with old knickknacks and Route 66 memorabilia. There were informative posters around the entrance that told the story of the Round Barn and vintage pictures that offered a glimpse of an old-time Arcadia. As is my usual tradition when visiting a gift shop, I left Kate and Thembi to take their time looking around and ventured over to the counter to strike up a conversation with the gent manning it—a tall, slim man with a friendly face, who looked like a cowboy. Could there be a better person to represent the Round Barn? Looking up from the magazine he was reading, the Oklahoman not only looked the part but spoke with a mesmerizing drawl.

"Can I help you find anything? Y'all driving 66?" he inquired.

"We are indeed, all the way to California," I answered.

"Well now, that is a great trip. What do you think about everything you've seen so far?" he asked, his eyes seeming to soften. He appeared sincerely interested and curious about our experience beyond Arcadia. Time and again during our crossing in Oklahoma, we were in awe of the genuine, kind nature and down-to-earth character of these Middle American folk. It was a place that we could call home.

I answered his questions briefly but was more interested in him. "How is it that you've ended up here on Route 66 at the Round Barn?" I asked.

"I grew up in Tulsa, close to Route 66," he explained. "Tulsa was home to Cyrus Avery, the man credited as the Father of Route 66. I went to high school with his granddaughter, Joyce Avery. We didn't run in the same circles in high school, but I knew who she was because she was a good guitar player and singer and played in some school assemblies. Folk music, that kind of stuff. I didn't really know anything about her connection to 66 at the time. When I was very young, in the '50s, my family would drive Route 66 to western Oklahoma to visit my grandparents' farm. I was well acquainted with the road at an early age."

A retired employee of the Federal Aviation Administration, he now volunteered his time at the Round Barn, investing back into the route he had grown up with. "My favorite part of volunteering is meeting and talking to people from all over the US and all over the world. People who come here doing Route 66 are on an adventure, and they're usually easy to talk to. I learn a lot."

"Have you ever driven the full route yourself?" I asked.

"In 2001, I rode 66 on my motorcycle," he replied. "It was great, I met so many good people along the way. The occasion was my youngest daughter graduating from navy basic training at the Naval Station Great Lakes outside Chicago. I went from there to visit her older sister in California, all on Route 66. Greatest trip of my life. When I hit Needles, it was a hundred and nine degrees. Then I had to ride through the Mojave Desert, and it only got worse. It was a real scorcher. The route, like everything else, has of course changed over the years. Some of the landmark buildings I was able to see in 2001 are gone now. And some towns along the route have done more for preservation than others. Generally, towns have awakened to the economic benefits of preservation, but in some instances, they go too far, embellish too much, and make photo ops that are not true to the road."

"I've seen a lot of pro-Republican signs on lawns across Missouri and Oklahoma. Can I ask, are you a conservative?"

Laughing, he scratched his head. "I am not. But you're right, this is a largely Republican state. People around here can be a bit conservative. It can get a bit tough being a Democrat in Oklahoma, or any of the neighboring states, for that matter. But that's what's wonderful about volunteering at the Round Barn and National Cowboy and Western Heritage Museum in Oklahoma City. When people visit these places, politics takes the hind seat."

With liberal politics in Chicago (the beginning of the route) and in Los Angeles (the end of the route) and mostly conservative politics in between; it is impossible to ignore the wonderful diversity that makes America what it has always been. Bantering with my new friend, I was reminded that beyond political views or religious beliefs, we really are all so much more similar than different, and that the more we can focus on our humanity and drown out the hyper-negativity that extreme perspectives throw at us, the better off our world will be.

23

WARM WIND SWEPT through our open windows as we cruised quickly into El Reno, a small town twenty-five miles west of Oklahoma City. Historical buildings and remnants of a prosperous time dotted the downtown area, and the placid city surprised us with its charm. El Reno actually came into being shortly after the 1889 land runs and was named for its proximity to nearby Fort Reno. We walked its empty streets and admired its architecture, but one miniscule building caught our eye almost immediately with its chocolate-brown exterior and faded red overhang. It looked gaudy, like a hole-in-the-wall dive, but something drew us to it. The large sign on the overhang announced that the venue was Sid's Diner.

Opened in 1990 and named after the proprietor's father, this joint has a great reputation both in town and with Route 66 enthusiasts, but as a non-red-meat-eater, I was a little concerned about what I was going to order. Inside the small, crowded establishment were a handful of tables and a counter where patrons could sit and enjoy their meal.

"What can I do you for?" asked a lady behind the cash register after she had finished with a bunch of paying customers.

"Do you guys have anything besides hamburgers?" I asked, having had time to study the menu while standing in line, but not seeing any actual non-beef options.

"We have cheeseburgers," she replied.

"Umm, what about anything that is not beef?"

She stared at me blankly. Okay, maybe she needed some suggestions.

"What about chicken burgers?"

"No, we have no chicken burgers." But she wanted to be helpful. "We have french fries." Her eyes narrowed and she looked past me and at the queue behind.

I stepped aside to let Kate and Thembi order the specialty: a grilled-onion burger. This is actually a local favorite in the area and people come specifically to Sid's to grab one of these unforgettable burgers. The grill in front of the counter was packed with sliced onions and sizzling patties. The smell of onions and meat permeated the small room, making the thin atmosphere a little stifling. I fled to the fresh air outside. Kate and Thembi soon followed with their food. We sat there for forty-five minutes observing the locals as they came and went, bags of food in hand, laughing as they left. El Reno was a happy town with a very positive aura. Thembi said very little as he consumed his meal, only stopping to wipe grease from his mouth and comment on how delicious it was. I guess that almost three decades of regular customers can't be wrong. But I was getting desperate for a salad.

Not far from the diner is the Canadian County Historical Society Museum. Nearby, travelers can catch a glimpse of the long-closed El Reno Hotel, an original venue that was built in 1892 by J. M. Kemp and moved in 1984 to the museum compound. Adjacent to the museum stands the Rock Island Caboose, a retired train caboose built in 1971, in service for nine years on the Rock Island Line, and then donated to the museum by Union Pacific. The neat little compound was home to a host of other really enjoyable pieces of the past in El Reno, but the heat of the day was once again becoming fierce, forcing us to cut our time outside short. A squeaky screen door betrayed our attempt at a quiet entrance as we went in and took a look around.

A white-haired lady was seated behind a counter, sifting through papers and old brochures. She studied us from behind her glasses but waited for us to approach the counter. "Can I help you with anything?" she asked.

"Yes," said Kate. "Is there any entry fee or do you take donations?"

"It's free to enter the museum," she answered, "but all donations of course help. We're a nonprofit." She then launched into an introduction of the museum's history and items that are housed there, and shared a little bit about the town itself. Directly across from her, a thin, aged man with a weathered face and tired but alert eyes sat listening. I walked over to say hello and ask about his role with the museum.

"I'm a volunteer," he said. "I don't work every day, mind you, but I do come in a few days a week. Do you like trains? Does your little boy? We have a lot of great railroad memorabilia and even have a real train set that runs along the top of the wall near the ceiling."

With a step around the desk from where he was seated, he made his way toward the back of the building. We followed.

There were fliers and photographs, documents and books everywhere. The collection was impressive and a little overwhelming. Suddenly a whistle blew. With the flick of a switch, a miniature train began to circle the room, chugging away as it traveled. The old man seemed to delight in showing off his train and let the replica circumnavigate the chamber four or five times before we politely suggested that we would love to continue to look around.

"Do you live in El Reno?" I asked as we walked back toward the front.

"Yes, sir, I am from the area."

"You must have seen a lot of changes over the years?"

"Yes, sir! I am heading toward ninety years old now but grew up on a farm attending a one-room schoolhouse. Things were very different in those days."

"I bet they were," I replied.

Museums along Route 66 are packed with history, not only in the objects on display, but in the very people manning the door. We stayed talking with him for maybe twenty minutes, listening to stories of his time in Korea and of the horrors that he was forced to witness. The lady behind the counter was ready to leave and she was his lift, so we politely released him from the conversation and said goodbye to the wonderful volunteers at the Canadian County Historical Society Museum.

We then motored to Hydro and made a quick stop at the preserved site of Lucille's Service Station, named after its proprietor, Lucille Hamons. Hamons is often affectionately referred to as the Mother of the Mother Road. She operated the station from 1941 until 2000, when she passed away. The attraction was placed on the National Register of Historic Places in 1997. We then made a much-anticipated stop at the incredible Oklahoma Route 66 Museum in Clinton, and then popped over to photograph the ornate Glancy Motel sign. Clinton is a great little Route 66 town with a 66-themed minigolf course that tempted us to stay and play a round, but we were on the clock. We continued west, past Foss and straight into Elk City.

24

ON THE WESTERN outskirts of Elk City, we decided to pull into a large and busy gas station to fill up our tank. We were running a little low, at half a tank, and Kate was concerned. A mellow wind was blowing, pushing some newly cut blades of grass onto my sandals. They tickled my toes.

"Do you have a bathroom inside?" I asked the young man behind the counter. He was busy with a line of customers.

"Yep, just in the back there. Follow that hall," he said, pointing.

The washroom was straight ahead and down a long, shadowed corridor, cut off from the sunlight streaming into the front of the store. To my left sat four rough-looking men, each shirtless, hairless, and heavily tattooed across their backs, arms, torsos, heads, and faces. They looked at me with intense aggression, their eyes menacing and cold. The scene was frightening. I lightly smiled and looked straight ahead, making my way to the loo. I was not sure, but they looked like they belonged to a gang, and as I stood in front of the urinal, I hoped deeply that the bathroom door would not open.

Finished, I started to head back to the main area, trying to look as casual as possible, when one of the men, seemingly the youngest—he looked perhaps seventeen or eighteen years old—stood up to meet me. His unflinching gaze was angry and intense, and I could feel him watching me as I quickly walked past him and made my way back to the counter. I heard them speaking with each other in hushed tones but I didn't look back.

"You have some seriously sketchy-looking characters back there," I said to the attendant.

"Yeah, they are. We get guys like that every day. They've just been released from jail and are on parole. They come here to wait for their bus. There's a big prison up the road in Sayre."

"You're kidding!" I responded, shocked. Why would convicts be allowed to loiter in a public place? Certainly, that can't be good for business?

"Oh yeah," he answered. "Yesterday, a bunch of them got into a bad fight out back and we still have bloodstains that we haven't been able to wash off the pavement. It can get crazy here."

I laughed nervously. It was such an unexpected reality to discover in well-mannered Oklahoma.

"Have any customers ever been attacked?" I asked.

"We had a young guy come for a job interview a few days ago, and he left his key in the car. We do that sometimes in these parts." He paused for effect. "They stole it."

Eyes straight ahead, I fled back to the safety of the sunshine. Kate had finished filling the tank and was washing her hands with disinfectant.

"Let me run in and use the bathroom too while we're here."

"I don't think you want to go in there," I cautioned, explaining what I had just encountered.

Kate's face dropped. "No way! Okay, yeah, let's get out of here. We're a bit late anyhow, we want to get to the museum before it closes."

Traffic was busy as we doubled back and eased into Elk City along urban 66. The road was a bit congested, but after we passed some construction, it began to flow pretty quickly, and we were soon in front of a gigantic smiling kachina doll and a huge Route 66 sign for the National Route 66 Museum. The museum had been highly recommended, and we were looking forward to exploring it.

The museum was part of a larger complex, made up of several other historical buildings, that had quite an interesting origin story. In 1963, leaders of the Western Oklahoma Historical Society, with support from the town's mayor and council, hatched a plan. They wanted to relocate an old Victorian mansion the city had purchased that same year, with the dream of turning it into a grand museum. Unfortunately, their proposal was declined by the state for fear that the two-story structure was too big to move due to the town's low-hanging power lines. But this group of Oklahomans was not to be deterred. The following morning, residents of Elk City were surprised to find that the house had "miraculously" appeared on the corner of 2717 West Third Street. It was a mystery how it got there, and the state was powerless to investigate the crime. Five years later, in 1968, starting with that old Victorian house, Elk City opened the Old Town Museum, a collection of historic structures that included a small schoolhouse, a newspaper office, two funeral parlors, and other buildings. It would be two decades later, in 1998, that the expansive museum complex would go on to include its most popular attraction: the National Route 66 Museum.

Inside, the museum housed brightly painted wall motifs depicting key stops on the route in all eight states, along with vintage cars, trucks, and the like, each educating visitors on the beauty and the hardships of the Mother Road's history. There were even recorded personal accounts, vividly recounting travel during the height of the historic route. It was a modest but well-done tribute to Route 66, well worth the time and small fee.

The outdoor museum complex spread placidly across grassy earth, shaded by leafy trees and bright, blooming flowers. It consisted of replica structures built to resemble the main street of a small town . . . as it used to be. We passed by the country doctor's office, where we peeked through the windows to see the antique instruments of the day; Paul Jones Drug; the livery stable; the opera house; the Rock Bluff School; the memorial chapel; and, of course, a watering hole. There was an enormous amount to see and experience.

As I meandered toward the gift shop, taken by the diversity found in this small corner of western Oklahoma, a slightly built black gentleman, who had been landscaping the expansive grounds, intercepted me. "Hey, man, how you doing?" he asked, with a twinkle in his eye. Extending his hand, he had dried blades of cut grass covering his palm, held firm by a lake of glistening sweat. I stopped and said hello.

"I'm Calvin," he stated as if he were answering a question. He appeared innocuous enough, but it still felt odd to have my thoughts intruded on by a stranger.

"Nice to meet you. It's a lovely day to be working outdoors," I replied. Calvin didn't seem so sure. He regarded me with curiosity and then gazed around as though in search of something.

"So where y'all from? You locals from here?"

"No, we're actually from Kenya."

"For reeaaal?" he asked, dragging out his pronunciation. "Whach y'all doing down here? You're driving Route 66! Is that still a road?"

I seemed to have made a quick friend.

I explained that it is indeed and that 85 percent is still drivable. Then I pointed out that Route 66 actually runs right out front, past the museum, so he uses it every day himself. This amazed him for a moment.

"Ya know, I ain't even really meant to be working here. They done got me for drunk driving, but see, I wasn't even really drivin'. It was some sort of entrapment. I was at a store, a public store, and happened to be passed out behind the wheel with an open bottle in my hand. Sure, the car was runnin', but I was asleep and not driving."

"But you had been driving, right?" Now I was curious.

"Of course, that's how I got to the store. But listen here. They got my buddy for the same thing and gave him five years. Imagine, five years! So I guess I'm lucky that I only have two months of community service, but it is still wrong, wrong. Ya know what I'm sayin'?"

I nodded. "But was this your first offense?"

"Nah, man! I got arrested before. A few times."

"Can I ask for what?"

"Drunk driving."

"Drunk driving?" I paused. "So you can sort of see where the judge is coming from, right?"

"I don't know, man. Personally, I think it's an injustice. The system has done me wrong. I was asleep at the time."

In the distance, other workers labored away, making the pristine compound the lovely attraction it is.

Out of the corner of my eye, I could see Kate motioning to me, waving me toward the parking lot. Thembi was chasing after a butterfly, and his antics had caught my attention.

"Well, Calvin, it was a pleasure to meet you. I hope that you get to enjoy this beautiful day." I bade him farewell and headed toward the exit.

I sensed Calvin walking behind me. "Hey, man, listen, scuse me, scuse me. Sorry to bother you, I know you need to get going, but let me ask you. Y'all got a lot of pretty women over there in Africa?"

25

THEY SAY THAT everything is bigger in Texas. The sky is enormous, blue, and engulfing, the food portions are more than generous, the history is diverse and fascinating, and the state itself is the second largest in America. We loved the Texas vibe from the very start.

The mood in the car was upbeat and expectant as we admired the endless wind turbines that emerged along the landscape in the eastern Panhandle. To our left, just above the turbines, three odd-shaped airplanes—maybe military—were engaged in some unconventional tactical flying, almost alien in nature, and the highway was our own. Captivated with the gargantuan, slow-spinning turbines and the maneuvering aircraft, we could not help feeling as though we were an involuntary part of a sci-fi film. We were off the grid.

There are a lot of "There it is!" moments on a Route 66 trip. Our first in Texas was the Tower Conoco Station and U-Drop Inn Cafe in Shamrock. Truly iconic, the once-popular fuel station plus restaurant stands out dramatically on the landscape. The structure is unique on the route and unquestionably striking in its art deco architectural design. By contrast, the road running west into town and toward the station was dotted with ordinary, run-of-the-mill motels and small, run-down buildings. It was a pleasant-enough entry into Shamrock, but not very different from the dozens of other little towns we had passed through over the previous weeks.

Shamrock may sound like an unusual name for a town in Texas, but as with so much in the West, immigrant influence was involved. In 1890, an Irish sheep rancher named George Nickel applied to open a post office at his dugout home, six miles north of where present-day Shamrock sits. Nickel suggested the name Shamrock, as he believed that it represented good fortune. However, good luck did not appear to be on his side. Shortly after receiving approval to open the post office, his house mysteriously burned down. But the name did stick, and another local resident's home would become the official post office in the new Texan town of Shamrock.

There was no traffic on the road, and I hit the first set of lights and turned right without a thought. We had arrived.

"Honey, I think there is a police car following us," warned Kate.

I looked up into the rearview mirror and, sure enough, there was an unhappy lawman shadowing me in a large black pickup truck. He was glaring at me and ever so slightly shaking his head.

I have never been in trouble with the "law," but I always get nervous around any form of law enforcement. Even mall cops get me jumpy. As such, my response to such situations is not always logical.

As we pulled into the parking lot behind the station, I quickly jumped out of my vehicle and blithely approached the sheriff's truck from the passenger side. "Howdy, Sheriff, did I do something wrong?" I asked.

I know: Who the hell says "howdy"? But hey, I was feeling local.

He looked a bit surprised at my ambitious response. "Well, hey there, buckaroo," he said. "Why, I couldn't help notice that you were driving pretty darn poorly and were intent on causing a ve-hic-ular accident in my town."

Okay, he didn't actually say that, but that's what I heard in my head when he stepped out of his truck. What he actually said was "You didn't stop properly at that there light over yonder. You just rolled straight on through." There was a grimace across his face, suggesting he was too polite to end his statement with the likely sentiment of "dumbass."

I turned around to take a look. I wasn't so sure that he was right, but it made no sense to argue. I grinned sheepishly, hoping that he would look over and see Thembi waving.

"We have a lot of accidents at that spot. You need to be more careful."

His words floated through the air and landed on the ground at my feet. I was distracted. He was wearing a real-life cowboy hat, and a long-barreled shotgun rested beside his seat. His mustache was awesome, somewhat reminiscent of Tombstone's illustrious Wyatt Earp in his older years, and his crisp, white, button-down shirt was tight at the collar. He was the real deal.

"I'm really sorry, Sheriff. I thought that I had made a complete stop. It won't happen again." I honestly did think that I stopped back there but didn't need a fine. I'd personally been quite impressed with my driving up to that point, having been able to drive through eight states with no real issues.

He looked at me intensely for a long moment, as though assessing whether I deserved a ticket or not. Then his eyes looked past me and softened, and he nodded toward the back seat of my vehicle, where Thembi was grinning. Without uttering a word, he slowly got back into his truck, and went off into the Texas sunshine to find some other deviant motorists. Kate simply looked at me and shook her head. Thembi was jubilant. He had never seen his father in trouble with "the Man" before.

The ornate gas station and café, located on the north side of Shamrock, now had our full attention. It had been restored and well preserved and was now the visitor information center. The original structure, completed in 1936, was built to house three distinct businesses, including the U-Drop Inn Cafe roadside diner.

As the story goes, local businessman John Nunn opened the U-Drop Inn in April 1937. The design of the café was originally drawn in the dirt at a nearby motel. Unsure of what to call his new business, Nunn decided to launch a contest to get some help. The winner would receive fifty dollars—the amount of a week's pay for a waitress and a fair sum at that time. The winner was an eight-year-old boy who suggested the name U-Drop Inn. The café and related businesses became hugely successful and a major stopover for travelers passing through Shamrock. At the time, the café was the only place to get a decent meal within a hundred miles in any direction of the little town. John Nunn died in 1957, and his wife, Bebe, sold the business to Grace Bruner, who renamed it Tower Cafe and added a Greyhound bus station to the property. The building changed hands several times over the years and eventually closed in the late 1990s and steadily fell into disrepair.

Once considered one of the most unique roadside stops along Route 66, due to its architectural design, which included a visually appealing tower, the landmark was saved when the board of directors of the First National Bank of Shamrock petitioned for it to be listed on the National Register of Historic Places. They were successful, and the iconic building was listed in September 1997. The bank then purchased the property and subsequently donated it to the city. In recent years, the Tower Conoco Station and U-Drop Inn Cafe has become famous once again, featured in the hit film *Cars* as Ramone's automotive body and paint shop.

"Can I take your picture?" a woman asked as we stood admiring the property.

"Umm, I think we're fine, but thank you," I responded.

"Well, if y'all would like to stand together, I can take your photograph. Maybe with the tower?" she suggested.

"We're good, but thank you for the kind offer," said Kate.

She paused thoughtfully. "Are you sure? When the gentleman [who had improperly and rudely blocked the front of the building with his car, ruining everyone's once-in-a-lifetime photograph] leaves, I can get a real nice family picture."

We tried to politely pass on the photo, but she simply stood by, smiling warmly until we cracked. She had worn us down with kindness. So we agreed to pose for a family portrait to commemorate our time in Shamrock.

Teresa was a volunteer at the visitors' center, who had come outside into the tremendous heat of the morning to greet us and encourage us to venture inside to learn more about the Tower Conoco Station and its noteworthy history. Stepping into the air-conditioned building and out of the sweltering ninety-degree temperature was a bit of a shock and brought on some immediate shivering. Now a gift shop and tourist center, the building was packed full of bumper stickers, T-shirts, key chains, and memorabilia from Route 66 and the film *Cars*. Inside the large space was an adjoining room—the U-Drop Inn Cafe. Set up to resemble how it looked in the 1940s, the museum-like café setting was completed by mannequins playing the roles of staff and customers. It was nicely done and offered a revealing glimpse into Shamrock's proud past.

"Can y'all sign our guest book?"

This had been a common thread in each of the state-sponsored attractions we'd visited. Signing the guest book is such an important part of Route 66 attractions, to not only record the number of visitors per day and season, but to also make the case for the government to renew the grants that help these important places survive.

Teresa was bubbly and chatty and a real fountain of knowledge about the route.

"Do you think the Mother Road has changed very much over the years, from your perspective living on it?" Kate asked. We had made it a habit to regularly ask local folks this question. We loved hearing their stories and learning more about the development or demise of the road in their communities.

"I grew up along Route 66. I saw the route every day of my life, but I didn't realize the historical importance of it until I'd grown up," Teresa responded. "When I was a small child, I remember my grandparents managed motels and gas stations along the Mother Road, but their history with Route 66 goes back much further. My grandfather was the first manager of the Tower Conoco gas station, alongside the U-Drop Inn Cafe. Slowly, those motels and gas stations closed. My father was a cotton farmer, and as he plowed his fields, he started counting the cars pulling campers and tents. He came to the conclusion that putting in a campground would be a great idea, giving his wife the perfect stay-at-home job as she raised four children. I was in second grade at the time, so around 1965. When the campground was first built, we saw a lot of hitchhikers and gypsies. You seldom see a hitchhiker these days. People aren't as trusting anymore."

"In the past, the route was pretty different, as far as who ventured down it, right?" I asked.

"My parents' campground started out with families in tents and small campers as their customers," Teresa explained. "By the time we finally closed the campground, our customers were retired people in large motor homes, and if there were any children, they were usually traveling with their grandparents. From my experience, families traveling Route 66 dwindled over the years, and now the only ones that have the time and money to travel are the retired people. This wasn't always the case."

"We've noticed that there are a lot of European visitors and older Americans on the route, at least in our experience," said Kate. "Do you think visitors are finding what they're looking for in today's world of Route 66?"

She thought for a moment before answering. "I feel like the people who travel down the route are both disappointed and excited. They're sad that there are so many old buildings in disrepair, yet they're excited to see the buildings that have been restored and brought back to life. I feel as though people are surprised more about the people they meet along the way. People love to hear the personal stories of those who lived along the Mother Road in its heyday. Many of the stories people share have been handed down through generations. And there are so many interesting characters who love the route and are actually, in some way, part of the history of it."

"You sound like you have your own stories to share," I said.

Teresa smiled. "I have a few. I was looking out the window of our house one day and seen this fellow arrive with long shaggy hair and no shirt, very short shorts, and a bandana on his head, looking a bit disheveled. I was concerned. 'Oh no, are we going to have to run this guy off the property?' But no, he turned out to be the nicest, smartest person. And that was Bob Waldmire," shared Teresa about her first meeting with the eclectic artist. From the top drawer of the counter, she pulled out some sheets of paper with Waldmire's signature artwork, some newspaper clippings, and some old black-and-white photographs. It was really vintage stuff. We hung around for some time, enjoying Waldmire's precious work, and then said our goodbyes. I was glad that we went inside and grateful for the nudge from Teresa.

The afternoon was beginning to disappear when we opted to stay in town for the night and take in the extraordinary neon that wraps around the Tower Station. Across the road was the nicest looking of the generic motels, so we decided to head over and see if they had a room. The road outside was still silent, but I spent some extra time at that traffic light, looking around very carefully to make sure that the sheriff was nowhere to be seen.

After checking in, we decided to wander around and look for dinner. Shamrock is small and unassuming, to say the least, but in the late-nineteenth century, it was the most important town in Wheeler County. Today, however, there are only a handful of food options, not counting a few standard fast-food brands, and we determined that the local pizza shop (they only did takeout) was the safest bet. But first we walked across the street to the local dollar store to replenish our supply of drinking water and snacks. Emerging back into the dimming heat, we saw two police cars parked in front of our room and four officers escorting a middle-aged lady in handcuffs toward their vehicles. She was not resisting, but she did look perplexed. Her shoulder-length, blond hair kept blowing in her face.

Intrigued, we cracked open a chocolate bar and watched from a distance. Sadly, before we managed to finish our treats, the officers turned off their flashing lights and pulled out of the parking lot. The late-afternoon entertainment was over.

As we headed out of town, pizza in hand, to a grassy RV park that some local townsfolk told us about, the road quickly became more interesting. The shell of an old school bus, abandoned long ago, sat rusting in the Texas sun. Dense foliage had grown around it, covering its roof, snaking through broken windows and a crack in the windshield. It is amazing how fast nature can reclaim the land. We had pulled off the highway to get a better look, mesmerized by the uncanny sight. We are always intrigued by the likely backstory that accompanies deserted buildings and vehicles, but a discarded school bus is somehow extra creepy, especially in the lonely Texas vegetation. At one point, the town must have been bustling enough to require the bus, but one day, someone parked it on this spot where it now rests, and simply walked away. There was something unsettling about that. A warm breeze began to blow and crickets came to life in the roadside grass. I looked down the highway toward Shamrock, and ahead toward where we were going. It was empty. We were all alone. After a few moments in contemplation, we decided that it was most respectful to simply move on.

The sun began to set lower as we traveled westward. The drive was peaceful, and we drifted off in our reveries. Up ahead stood a solitary house with a long gravel driveway. Several large dogs rested placidly, patiently waiting for nightfall. With the huge Texas sky swallowing us, we were enjoying the sweet sound of Arlo Guthrie, absorbed by our surroundings, when suddenly, out of the blue, the dogs jumped up and lunged at us in an incredibly measured attack. It scared the shit out of me. I swerved and hit the gas, the car almost veering crazily into a ditch.

"Holy cow! Did those dogs just try to attack the car, Dad?" Thembi asked, stunned.

"Those animals are a menace," I said, shaken. "One day someone is going to kill one of them! Imagine if we were on foot or a motorcycle! The owner needs to chain them up." I got the feeling that this was a regular activity for these dogs.

Kate cracked up. "Your father was almost jumping out of the car and taking cover," she squeaked out between hysterical peals of laughter.

I was still annoyed with what had just happened, but her contagious laughter made Thembi and I start giggling, and broke the tension from the near assault.

The attempted attack shocked us back to reality, but it was most likely that the dogs were simply trying to reduce the tedium of their day. From the rearview mirror, I watched as the biggest one, a brown-and-black mutt, stretched indifferently and flopped back down onto the drive, throwing dust into the still air.

The RV park appeared in the horizon and we pulled in to take in the last rays of the serene summer afternoon and enjoy our pizza on one of the available picnic tables. The sky was clear of clouds and the sunset was fantastic. Sometimes it's surreal being in the middle of "nowhere" without a care in the world, without anyone actually knowing where you are.

In the distance, a rotund middle-aged man was bent down inspecting something on the side of his RV. Kate and Thembi had cracked open a crossword puzzle, so I decided to stretch my legs and walk over to say hello.

"Good evening!" I said, approaching carefully. It is never a good idea to startle a stranger when out on the road.

He turned around quickly and looked in my direction, warily.

"To you too," he responded.

"This is quite a nice rig that you have here. Have you been on the road for long?"

He regarded me cautiously. "Oh, well, I guess for a bit of time," he said. "I've been driving across the country and stopping to see some of the things that I missed out on for most of my life. I'm fifty-eight and decided this year that it's now or never."

There was no sound coming from inside and I hadn't noticed anyone around him as we ate. So it looked like his trip was a solo one.

"Are you traveling all by yourself?"

"Well, sort of," he answered. "But I have my dog with me."

"Does it get lonely being out on the road alone so much?" I asked.

He stared at me for a moment, unblinking, lost in consideration. Then he frowned.

"It can. It's easy to get lost in your own head out on the road, but I like to keep to myself these days." He paused and looked away. "I was married for thirty-two years this past May, but I recently lost my wife . . . " He turned back around to look at the RV and the work that he had been doing before I interrupted him.

"I'm very sorry," I started to say, but his body language made it clear that our conversation was over.

I think it's time for me to leave, I thought.

"Thanks for stopping by," he said without turning back in my direction.

Darkness was almost upon us when we packed up and worked our way back to the motel.

"You have to be kidding me," Kate said as we approached the home with the crazy dogs. They were still on the tranquil road and appeared to recognize us. Quickly back on their feet, they rushed out onto the road, though without the same gusto they had demonstrated a few hours earlier. Perhaps even for them, it was time to call it a day.

Shamrock was even quieter when we pulled into the motel parking lot. The lone traffic light blinked in the night, leaving the mesmerizing lights of the Tower Station and U-Drop Inn to illuminate the emptiness of the dark night. It was wonderful to sit outside, as we had done at numerous other places along America's Main Street, and contemplate the complicated history of the country. One of the most memorable parts of traveling down Route 66 is the constant reminder of those who stood there before you, and of the sensation of being an unobtrusive observer; no one knew we were there in little Shamrock, no one cared. There is a freedom in that.

26

AMERICA IS PACKED with museums. There are transportation museums and history museums. St. James, Missouri, even had a vacuum cleaner museum until mid-2019—but now we were at the Devil's Rope Museum in McLean, Texas. But what is devil's rope, you ask? Good question. It is, simply put, barbed wire. Okay, so before you decide that this sounds like a very boring place, let me dissuade you. To our surprise, this museum was actually quite fascinating, with a wonderful Route 66 display right off the gift shop, a huge collection of different types of barbed wire, and a lot of history that was pretty darn neat.

Some important discoveries: modern-day barbed wire was first developed by Michael Kelly of New York in 1868, but the fancy, mechanically produced barbed wire was actually the brainchild of Joseph Glidden of DeKalb, Illinois, in 1874 (Glidden is often called the Father of Barbed Wire). Today, there are over 2,000 types of barbed wire and 450 unique patents held. Who knew? The Devil's Rope Museum, which is a tribute to barbed wire, had the largest and most unusual collection of barbed wire in the world, including the most complete history recorded of this wire fencing that changed the West. It was a really cool place, and we enjoyed wandering around and discovering its vital contribution to the country.

"That is a dangerous-looking piece of metal," a woman commented as she joined us in front of a very clear display on the effectiveness of the wire.

We laughed. The wire was called the devil's rope early on due to its potentially harmful effect on cattle and other livestock that were cut or hurt beyond healing by the vicious metal, and had to be put down. Its effects were so savage in the early days that ranchers referred to barbed wire as being from the devil.

"Have y'all been here before? How do you like our little town?" the woman asked.

"This is our first time to McLean, but we really like it so far," I said. "We were certainly not expecting to find out so much about barbed wire when we came into the museum!"

Thembi agreed. "I had no idea there were so many different types!"

I'm pretty sure that no one who has not visited this museum has any idea.

"We hear that a lot," she responded. "We get people coming here from all over the world, thanks to Route 66. Most of them have never heard of McLean, but we are pretty proud of our little town." And so they should be.

McLean was the last Texan town to be bypassed by the interstate, and was also the former site of a World War II German prisoner of war camp. Now almost a ghost town, McLean's quiet, vacant streets belied its once exceptional history.

She seemed happy to hear that we had been investigating McLean. "You know, until recently, we used to be a 'dry' town. Do you know what that means?" We didn't.

"Well, alcohol was not permitted to be sold within the town limits. So folks would drive twenty miles to Shamrock or ten miles up the road to Alanreed to buy beer, wine, whatever. Actually, they didn't really have that good of a selection. They have a little gas station over in Alanreed that used to sell a few different types of alcohol. It just changed last year—we are now a 'wet' town. There are lots of developments going on here in McLean." She seemed to be excited about this new one. It would have seemed silly to us only a month earlier, but while traveling through Indiana, on the way toward Illinois and Route 66, we visited a small Amish town, Shipshewana, and desperately wanted a cold drink after eight hours driving in the hot sun; they, too, were a "dry" town, and we were forced to make do with soda.

The road to Alanreed climbed and dropped quite dramatically, with the interstate cutting across the land on the left and open pasture and fields covering the right. At one point, the old road dipped lower than the interstate and the fast-flying highway disappeared, only to reappear as the road rose again and continued to run parallel. Then, unexpectedly, we were entering Alanreed, a real-life modern ghost town.

There was not much to see or do there, so we pulled over and inspected an old 66 Super Station filling station and took a gauge of the mood of the remnants of the town. The station had been lovingly maintained by someone and was adorned with neat beige bricks and a rather fresh coat of green paint on the door and around the windows. A plaque on the side of the building announced proudly that it was built by Bradley Kiser in 1930. That was a long time ago.

The once-busy settlement was silent now, populated only with memories, periodic travelers, and Route 66 road warriors.

27

THERE IS A sadness that pervades Jericho. The ghost town feels grim, haunted even. Once a rather busy area that took advantage of the Great Depression–era traffic that passed through its borders, little is left now to show that a thriving farming community once dwelled there. The original alignment of Route 66 that ran from Jericho to Groom brought trepidation to even the bravest of motorists, with treacherous mud and ruts that stopped travelers dead in the miry clay (until 1932, when a new alignment was created). Less-than-neighborly farmers were always ready to lend a hand and pull them out, for some cash of course, further victimizing those already in peril. As a matter of fact, legend has it that inhospitable farmers would pour buckets of water over the already slippery road in the evenings in order to ensure business in the morning.

It had rained earlier that day, in fact, not a big shower but a steady pour. Coming into Jericho, the road was slick, causing the vehicle to slide haphazardly and careen toward long-abandoned fields. It was a brief and scary picture of what migrants, in their heavy, overladen vehicles, would have been forced to endure as they fled drought and famine.

Wandering through tall grass toward ghostly wind turbines, I kept an eye open in the bushes for snakes who might have made the area their home. Broken-down structures—a once-happy tourist motel and a local store—now littered the otherwise pretty setting, their walls crumbling in the fierce Texas sun. An old remnant of an automobile, missing windows and headlights, seats, and an engine, sat dead in the distance, almost invisible beneath the long, scraggly grass that had grown up around it like a tomb. The Jericho cemetery, dating to 1894, rested about a mile down the muddy road. The interstate roared past with a muffled rumble in the distance, out of sight but always within faint earshot. But it did not break the eerie sense of abandonment. Rather, it added to the atmosphere, giving us the sense that humanity was so close by and yet totally unaware of Jericho. We quietly departed and left the ruins and their ghostly residents to the past.

———

DRIVING THROUGH THE Texas panhandle was like entering a different dimension. Yes, the Friendship State had a multitude of curious sites: the Giant Cross (the second largest in the Northern Hemisphere) and the Leaning Water Tower of Britten (built that way to attract attention) in Groom; the spooky backcountry town of Conway, with its VW Slug Bug Ranch full of rusting Volkswagen relics; and the reticent ghost towns. But there was something else, a hypnotic unsettling effect as we drove mile after mile through tiny towns with nobody really around. There were plenty of stops, but they did not feel touristy. They felt more like remnants of lost hopes and dreams. An abandoned past.

There was a definite different feel to Route 66 in Texas. While the Midwest portion of the trip had been fascinating and enthralling, the roadside destinations and attractions had the impression of having been taken care of, restored, and preserved for the purpose of attracting visitors. In contrast, in rural Texas, the roads were lonelier, and with the numerous cotton fields, grain elevators, and windmills that dotted the dusty landscape, there was a shadowy feeling of being removed from the rest of the world. Attractions seemed like they had been left behind and motorists would simply stumble upon them, uninvited, but welcomed nonetheless. It can create a disquieting feeling. We loved it.

Voyaging down Route 66 is very much a long excursion of contrasts.

———

WE WERE LOST in Amarillo. We had been trying to get to the Big Texan

Steak Ranch for an hour, to no avail (the *EZ66 Guide* did the job until we got into the city). We were hungry and eager to check out the famous restaurant, a colorful, flamboyant sort of place that offers a free meal if customers can finish a seventy-two-ounce steak and all of the side trimmings within an hour. Should you fail, the dinner is a whopping seventy-two dollars. The notion of consuming an inordinate amount of food in order to get a free meal was ridiculous to us. Eating is not a sport; it is meant to be enjoyable. And the gastric consequences of winning this competition seemed to outweigh the free steak. But when in Texas . . .

Navigationally challenged, we unexpectedly spotted a lively distraction: the celebrated Cadillac Ranch. We had been eager to see it but had intended to pass by the following day. However, with the landmark so near, we put food on hold and headed toward history. Assembled in 1974 by Northern California artists and architects Chip Lord, Hudson Marquez, and Doug Michels, and financially supported by local millionaire Stanley Marsh 3, the ranch consists of ten Cadillacs that have been buried nose down in the earth. Famed for its graffiti-covered remains, Cadillac Ranch attracts visitors from around the world and has become synonymous with Route 66, even though the attraction was not originally on the route. In 1997, the vehicles (and, as such, the ranch) were relocated two miles to their current site, in order to move them farther away from the encroachment of a very quickly growing Amarillo. At the original site now stands a sign adjacent to the ten empty holes that once held the bodies of the Cadillacs: "Unmarked graves for sale or rent."

In the distance, the cars rested like colorful pillars. The ground was still muddy from the earlier rain shower, churned up by those who came before us. The Cadillacs looked different than we expected. Often photographed rising from dry crumbling soil, the image of the carcasses that day set a different tone, glossy from the recent wet weather and bogged down in a pool of brown water. We treaded carefully through the slimy earth, cautious not to slip and fall. A couple was cavorting with a middle-aged, red-haired woman, who was greedily photographing the vehicles. They appeared oblivious to others around them and the redhead was hell-bent on capturing the vehicles from every angle. Bending over too ambitiously to capture a shot, she stumbled and fell sideways, facedown in a deep brown puddle. As the water rippled, she did not get up immediately, but stayed stagnant for a few uncomfortable seconds. The couple, perhaps concerned about getting their clothes soiled, stepped back quickly. Unamused by their lack of concern, the photographer struggled to her feet and marched off in a sulk to the road, the sheepish duo hot on her heels.

As they disappeared slowly back toward the road where we had all parked, the sun went behind a host of fluffy clouds, shining a heavenly light on their backs. Against the kaleidoscopic vehicles, the shapeless fields looked bleak and empty. Thembi and Kate stood together for quite some time, without words, staring at the metal corpses that have been planted into the rich Texan soil. While not a true historical setting, Cadillac Ranch creates a peculiar atmosphere as it overlooks a sea of wheat fields. As the sun dipped farther down, giving way to the fast-approaching Texan night, we were reminded of the great many people who had passed this way to pay tribute to the artistic vision of not merely the ranch but the pure essence of roadside Americana itself.

Hunger shook us from our reverie, and we decided to try again to locate the Big Texan. Back at the entrance of the ranch, a pair of young women, one quite thin and pale and the other a bit heavy and decked out in overly baggy shorts and a T-shirt that hung well past her waist, were making their way in. The heavier girl had extremely short brown hair and was wearing a wide-brimmed baseball hat that advertised the name of a popular farm equipment company across the front. Not wanting to wait for us to exit via the turnstile gate, they decided to climb through the barbed-wire fence protecting the front of the ranch. The slender girl climbed through rather effortlessly, with her friend pulling the rows of wire apart. However, when the larger girl attempted to follow suit, the barbed wire snagged the seat of her shorts and she yelped in sudden pain. She was stuck. The Devil's Rope had struck again! We watched as they tried to get her out, wanting to help, but not wanting to further embarrass them.

"Lift your leg," suggested the slender girl.

"I'm trying, damn it!" she hollered. "I told you we shouldn't go under the fence." She was attempting to remove her clothing from the teeth of the wire. "Careful! You're going to rip the ass of my shorts," she yelled.

What ensued next was truly a sight to behold. The frantic girls tried desperately to break free from the fence, with the captured girl standing (as best as she could), squatting, lifting her left leg, her right leg, lowering her weight onto the wire, pulling at the fabric—but the barbed wire simply would not let her loose. Finally, the slimmer girl stepped away from the ordeal and reexamined the situation. Her trapped friend merely slumped down, crouching just above the razor sharpness of the metal.

"Excuse me," I called over. "Can we lend a hand? You seem to have gotten caught."

They stopped. The stout girl immediately turned red in the face and then frowned. "No, we got this. You guys can go about your day." She looked irritated by our interference, so we decided to leave them in peace.

As we drove back east toward the outskirts of Amarillo and, hopefully, the Big Texan, we watched from the rearview mirror as the pair continued to struggle unsuccessfully. I am sure that theirs was a precautionary tale for all other visitors who followed that day, and I would not be surprised to find a pair of shorts still stuck to the fence when we next visit.

28

IN THE DISTANCE, we finally saw the unmistakable sign that has been luring people off the old highway for decades. A smiling cowboy decked out in full Western attire—a broad-brimmed ten-gallon hat, huge belt buckle, right hand resting on his six-shooter—stood next to the announcement that travelers had reached the Big Texan Steak Ranch.

In the parking lot, in front of the vibrant-yellow wooden structure, sat an enormous green lizard wearing equally large cowboy boots, seemingly excited and ready to pounce. Close by, a gigantic brown-and-white cow with a pair of sharp horns advertised the seventy-two-ounce steak competition, and a sign that hung from the front of the building shouted, "The public is invited. Come one. Come all." Even from the parking lot, it was impossible not to hear the unmistakable sounds of country music blaring from inside. Thembi's face clearly demonstrated his excitement as he exited the car uncharacteristically fast. We had arranged to meet the owner, Bobby Lee, for an early dinner, so we hurried in.

"Dad! Look at these pictures," called Thembi as we wandered through all the fun, kitschy attractions that were on display and hung on the walls. "See how they start out old and normal and then suddenly change? Check out this one!" The photographs on the walls represented the Victorian era, with its prim and proper restrictions, but changed dramatically to become vampires and ghouls, altering their appearance as patrons pass by. It was pretty creative. We walked back and forth, observing the changes half a dozen times before being distracted elsewhere.

A life-size dummy of an old miner sat alone on a bench adjacent to the photographs. He looked real and was a character in his own right, but as we glided past toward the dining room, he loudly passed gas before blurting out, "Excuse me!" Taken by surprise, we jumped and then burst out laughing. The Big Texan is not just a restaurant—it's a destination unto itself.

The large dining area was bustling, and bursting with energy. There were people there from all around the world and we were met, almost aggressively, with a hive of liveliness. I told a waitress (actually, I shouted over the loud music) that we had a reservation and were supposed to meet Bobby, and we were quickly shown to our table, where a tall man— six feet two—with silver hair and a charming mustache stood to greet us. Bobby had a kind face and mischievous grin, like a little boy who is up to something.

"You must be Brennen!" he said with a hard but jovial handshake. "Glad you could finally make it down to see the Big Texan. And who do we have here with you?" He shook Kate's and Thembi's hands and beckoned us toward a window booth.

"Sit down, sit down. I've booked us my favorite booth."

His eyes scanned the room, constantly aware of both his patrons and his staff.

"Why is this one so special?" Kate asked.

Bobby perked up and turned his gaze quickly in our direction. He grinned and his eyes seemed to glimmer. "I was the Friday closing manager and it was a slow night," he said. "My busboy came to tell me that Wolfman Jack was in booth 49 alone, eating a big T-bone. I approached him, introduced myself, and he invited me to sit down. We visited about old monster movies, *American Graffiti*, Alice Cooper, and Route 66. He was incredibly gracious, and curious about the Big Texan. The true highlight of the evening was when a full moon rose over the motel, while I was sitting across from him. He leaned toward me and said, 'There's my partner.'" Bobby laughed heartedly, clearly still living the moment.

Wolfman Jack, aka Robert Weston Smith, was an American disc jockey who rose to prominence in the 1970s and was famous for his raspy voice on radio and in pop-culture film and television. He was connected—likely due to his voice—with a number of horror and Halloween projects and went on to appear in numerous films and TV shows.

Wolfman Jack died in 1995 from a heart attack and is buried in North Carolina.

Time passed quickly that evening. So much was happening all at once. Waitresses whizzed around carrying huge trays of food and were sassy and smiling, obviously enjoying their job. To the left, three contestants were laboriously trying to finish their enormous meals, while a giant clock ticked away, edging them further and further away from winning the iconic competition.

The steak-eating challenge first began in 1962, when Bobby's father, R. J. Lee, took notice of how much visitors enjoyed watching local cowboys try to outdo each other as they consumed their meals. The restaurant attracted a lot of locals who relished the generous portions that were provided. One Friday night, R. J. put several tables together in the center of the dining room and, sitting all the cowboys in the middle, offered a challenge to the men: whoever could eat the most one-pound steaks in one hour would receive their dinner for free. The cowboys were game, with one individual consuming two steaks in the first ten minutes. Upon completion, he requested a salad and a shrimp cocktail with his third steak. In the end, this gastronomic marvel won by finishing off four and a half pounds of steak, a baked potato, a shrimp cocktail, a salad, and a bread roll—an insane amount of food for any human being.

Amazed by what he witnessed, R. J. announced then and there that from that day forth, anyone who could finish a seventy-two-ounce steak, with all the trimmings, would get their dinner for free. And so a tradition was born.

29

A TUMBLEWEED DANCED across the road in front of us, narrowly missing being swept under the vehicle. The late afternoon was hot and sunny, with an intensely warm wind that blew brush and debris through the air. It had been an awesome day of traveling the cowboy country of Bushland, Wildorado, and Vega, the latter a small town complete with Dot's Mini Museum, a 1920s Magnolia gas station, and the empty, spacious city-center streets that we had come to expect. It had been a good ride and it felt great to be cruising along the historic highway. We were eagerly heading to our last stop in Texas, the small, unassuming town of Adrian. Beyond that lay Glenrio, the long-abandoned ghost town that borders the Cactus State, New Mexico, and some of the most astounding scenery on Route 66.

Our destination in Adrian was the fittingly named Midpoint Cafe, a title that signifies the diner's enviable location as the geographical midpoint of the route. It is exactly halfway between Chicago and Los Angeles. But there was a catch: the owner of the café kept unpredictable hours and often closed after three o'clock.

As I drove, a large furry creature inching its way across the road narrowly missed getting squashed. I thought that I knew what it was, but I needed to make sure before making an announcement. In the backcountry of Texas, a great many beasts had become part of the tarmac as they attempted to reach the other side. As I reversed our vehicle, Thembi was concerned. "What is it, Dad? What did you see? Did we hit something?" he asked anxiously.

Kate was a bit more blasé. "Do you need to pull over and pee again?"

"Oh my gosh! Look, Mom, Dad found a huge tarantula! You've got amazing eyes, Dad," Thembi gushed. I did a little bit too. Every father can appreciate how it feels when their child thinks they are a mini-superhero.

Jumping out of the vehicle, slowly—we didn't pull off to the side, as we hadn't seen another car for more than an hour—we spent the next half hour alone with our new friend, observing as she made her way across the deserted road and back again, and again. Thembi was trans-fixed.

"Dad, look at her colors. It's definitely a female." He was online with my phone, checking out details on the species. "It's a Texas Tan Taran-tula!" he exclaimed, beaming.

"Don't get too close, buddy. No, don't try to move her with that stick. Move your foot away from her face, you're wearing flip-flops!"

Kate was excitedly filming the encounter on her camera. It was, after all, our first real run-in with a tarantula. "Good job, honey!" she said. "I would have missed it for sure." It was quite a moment of accomplish-ment for me, it seemed.

Finally, after what seemed to be a reasonable amount of time, another vehicle approached, slowing down to see if we needed assistance.

"No, we're good, no car trouble. It's just a tarantula," I said. Thembi was all smiles, certain that his adoration for nature would be infectious.

"It's over here, on the edge of the road," Thembi offered. "My dad seen her while we were driving to Adrian." He tried to indicate where the motorists should look.

The driver, a kindly, heavyset woman missing several of her front teeth, stopped and looked down at the arachnid, gasping in shock before hitting the gas and speeding off without a word of goodbye.

"I don't think she likes spiders, Dad," observed Thembi as we watched her pickup truck disappear into a cloud of dust.

It was three thirty and we were just a little behind schedule, thanks to our timeout with the spider. But we found the Midpoint Cafe and were hopeful, as it was a day of good tidings. Not that good, though, as the eatery was closed and locked tight. The staff were gone for the day. We let out a collective sign and stepped back from the entrance to look around.

Adrian was quiet, with a solemn air to it. The heat from the afternoon radiated off the asphalt and shimmered down the long, straight, silent road ahead.

"How can they close a café, on Route 66, at three in the afternoon? That is insane," Kate complained. "Let's go ask next door at the Sunflower Station. They may have some idea if it will be open later."

Adjacent to the café stood a shop with an assortment of merchandise that we had come to expect on the trip. An otherwise simple and nondescript peach-colored building, it was decorated with an old pickup truck, complete with wide eyes and a pair of worn-out buckteeth—definitely meant to be a tribute to loveable Tow Mater from *Cars*. Around the entrance of the shop were chairs and a table, welcoming visitors to take a break from the sleepy road, and a grocery store cart filled with pretty flowers.

"Excuse me?" I called, entering the doorway.

A slim older man with a friendly face emerged from the back room, drink in hand. "Can I help you with anything?" he asked.

"Do you happen to know if the Midpoint Cafe will reopen today? It seems to have closed really early," I said.

"Yeah, the owner keeps odd hours. He's gone for the day. Sorry," he answered.

"Do you guys happen to sell any soda or food here at the shop?" I asked.

"No, only water. Sorry."

Gazing around the store, I noticed that it was covered in memorabilia from *Cars*. Again, that was something we were getting used to. The gent took sight of this and asked me if I had seen the film.

"I have, actually. Several times. It is one of my son's favorites," I answered.

"Oh," he responded excitedly, "you need to talk to Fran. She's the real Flo." He called toward the back of the store, "Fran, come on out here!" At first, there was silence. I looked toward the rear to see who he was hollering to.

A voice shouted out from the shadows. "We're just back here drinkin' and smokin.' How y'all doing?"

This is how we met Fran Houser and her friend Budd.

The previous owner of the Midpoint Cafe, Fran had sold the business after twenty-four years, seeking a slightly simpler life. Originally from Massachusetts, she moved to Adrian in 1989 to try to find a more suitable place to live for her asthmatic six-year-old daughter. Initial plans were to open an antique shop, but locals wanted a restaurant. And so the Midpoint Cafe was born. Well, actually, it was originally called the Adrian Cafe, but its name was changed in 1994. First opened in the 1930s by Zella Crim and then expanded in 1947, the original café ran twenty-four hours a day during the route's heyday; it is now the oldest operating café between Amarillo and Tucumcari, New Mexico.

"We had so many amazing people come through the café, from all around the world," shared Fran. "When I first purchased it, our business came from I-40 . . . a lot of folks from California heading with their families back to Mississippi, Georgia, et cetera. But as plane travel became more affordable, business dropped off. Around that time, I became acquainted with Tom Snyder, founder of the U.S. Route 66 Association. He called and told me that the café was the midpoint and suggested that I needed a webpage, as people from all over the world had been contacting him with questions about the road. A few years later, we started hearing folks speaking in German, then French, and then it became the United Nations at the café. And they were so excited to be there. We've even had celebrities like Willie Nelson, Tanya Tucker, Ewan McGregor, Gerald McRaney, the music group Sawyer Brown . . . I remember arriving to open the café one day and a young guy was waiting outside. I told him he could take a seat inside while I got the place ready for business. 'Can I help set up?' he asked, 'I have some experience as a waiter.'

"Later on, when we were open, someone asked me, 'Do you know who that is?' I didn't. 'That's Bryan Cranston, the famous actor!' He was pretty good at helping set up too. Now I know who he is, of course, but back then I didn't have a clue. So many memories."

Fran's life and that of Adrian changed in 2005 when Pixar paid her a surprise visit while touring Route 66 with Michael Wallis. Arriving in their Cadillacs with steer horns protruding from the bonnet—think Boss Hog's car from *The Dukes of Hazard*—the visitors began to snap photographs of the café. The venue later became the inspiration for Flo's V8 Cafe, with its neon and flair, and Fran became the influence for Flo. Looking at the woman behind the character, it is immediately clear that Fran is very much the fun, friendly, easygoing lady that Pixar sought to craft into the cool, ready-to-tackle-the-world 1957 GM Motorama show car. As a matter of fact, Fran reminded me of the favorite auntie that so many families have, the one who is a world of exuberance and totally unpredictable.

Heat shimmered off the ground as we ducked out of the Sunflower and absorbed our surroundings. We had now reached exactly halfway. Our trip was half over. Thinking back to Wilmington, 1,044 miles to the east, where we were struck by the miles ahead of us, it was difficult to conceptualize that we had arrived at the exact middle of Route 66. Each day had been a dream, an attack on the senses as we attempted to wrap our minds around being in Cuba or Carthage, Missouri; Baxter Springs, Kansas; or Arcadia, Oklahoma. Places did not blend into one another. There was a very clear and vivid distinction. To be on the road and moving from town to town and state to state, making our way across America's Main Street, was a trip in more ways than one. Sometimes it did not feel real. We had so much behind us, but just as much in front of us. There was nothing left to do but drive on and take it in as it came.

30

THE DAY WAS getting late when we found ourselves in the atmospheric ghost town of Glenrio, which straddles the state line between Texas and New Mexico. It was by far the most ethereal of the abandoned towns we had encountered thus far on the trip. Other than singing birds, a bevy of overly gregarious crickets, a five-foot-long Trans-Pecos rat snake who sat completely frozen in an attempt to remain invisible in the brush beside the road, and the town's only remaining resident and her barking dogs, we were alone. A decaying 1968 Pontiac Catalina, with long-stemmed yellow wildflowers on it, rested beside an old Texaco filling station that was slowly crumbling, while a vacant eatery, the Little Juarez Cafe (originally called the Brownlee Diner) stood perhaps thirty feet away from the station. Toward the end of the remaining buildings was the largest of the lot—the once-impressive Texas Longhorn Motel and Cafe. Operated by Homer Ehresman from 1955 to 1976, the motel's sign is still one of the most photographed on the route. The sign is now largely destroyed, but once read "First Stop in Texas" on one side and "Last Stop in Texas" on the other. It still stands high in the sky and is striking in its own right.

These businesses are sad reminders of the life that was snuffed out when the bigger, busier I-40 came crashing through a mere two miles north of town. We wandered around the sprawling motel grounds, stepping over broken glass and scattered nails, careful not to cut our feet. The back of the motel, where the shells of the rooms now lay, was a panorama of wide-open doors and overgrown earth. It was a spooky surprise. Remnants of broken-down property was sprinkled everywhere. Behind the motel was a deathly silence. The natural sounds that were so boisterous on the highway had disappeared and an eerie stillness dominated the deserted motor court.

A single door was closed, and fragments of curtains partially covered the undamaged window. It was uncanny standing in front of the room, preparing to try the door handle—as though someone might actually be residing in the deteriorating venue. I thought I observed the curtains slightly open but then there was no movement. It was probably my imagination, but not wanting to antagonize anyone who may actually be calling the motel home, I briskly abandoned the idea. Truth be told, there are a lot of bizarre people who call the quieter spots in America their own.

"Thembi, stick with me, please," I said as I warily strolled around, entering rooms that looked reasonably safe. A dirty mattress lay on the floor in one bedroom, its once-white color now soiled by years of dust and neglect. A small bee entered the forlorn room, buzzed around for a moment, and then flew back outside and toward the multitude of dainty wildflowers.

"Imagine," I said to Thembi, "all of these old possessions once belonged to someone. They were important to them at one point. Now those people are long gone, and the motel is steadily disappearing too."

He rested his slight frame against mine and put his hand on my shoulder, as he liked to do. "I can't believe that the owner just got up and left," he said. He lingered a moment before carefully walking back toward the front of the building and the warmth of the sunshine, where Kate was busy taking photographs.

"I like this place," he told her. "It feels like we're all alone, but we can still see the cars on the highway in the distance flying past and they don't even know that Glenrio is here. It's weird and creepy, but in a good way."

Soon it was time to vamoose and get some more pavement under our tires, but we had one more thing to do before returning to the highway. There were almost fifteen miles of dirt road running between the picturesque but unearthly Texas ghost town and San Jon, New Mexico, and Thembi was itching to take the wheel. He has always loved driving, and used to jump in the driver's seat, or should I say, onto my lap, when we would do game drives in the parks at home in Kenya. He takes his role very seriously and has great control of the vehicle.

Rural eastern New Mexico is dry and dusty, filled with scraggly grass and short, unremarkable trees. But the vistas were undeniably magnificent and the simple wood-trestle bridges offered a reminder of the railroad's influence along Route 66. As we neared Endee, a few dilapidated structures came into view: a crumbling dirt house whose roof had crashed in, a tilting and soon-to-topple concrete restroom with the fading word "Modern" painted on its side, tiny square homes that were once proudly constructed with sturdy rock and stone, and a rusted big-body car surrounded by shrubs and long grass. All sat lifelessly in the tepid wind, their only residents now the birds and snakes. Large fallen trees lay almost on top of some of the houses, and the wide, graded dirt road, with San Jon to the west, was desolate. A barbed-wire fence to the left of the road reminded us that someone lived around there, but their influence was otherwise unseen.

The sun was getting low in the sky and we needed to motor on, but I wanted one last photograph of the broken buildings and stepped into the long, prickly grass to try and ease my way a little closer. It stuck through the slits in my sandals and clawed painfully at my legs. I slipped slightly on some loose soil. Down the highway, a truck was heading fast in our direction, coming from the path to Tucumcari. I suddenly felt vulnerable and uncertain. I didn't think I was trespassing, but it is hard to know in some remote areas. The truck, a white two-door pickup, came to a halt across the two-lane dirt road and the driver put his window down. Inside were two Latino men dressed in loose fitting T-shirts and sunglasses. Kate called to me from where she was resting on the front bumper of the car. "Do you think we should get moving? We may be on someone's property."

The men sat in their vehicle staring at me without saying a word. I decided to break their gaze and walk over to say hello. As I sauntered over, the driver unexpectedly jumped out of the truck. I stopped. He looked as uncertain as I felt. I took that to be a good sign. I continued to cross the road.

"Good afternoon!" I said. "We're not on your land, are we?"

"No, no, not at all. We were just curious about what you were doing. That grass has big snakes in it and other things. I'd be careful if I were you."

His passenger said something in Spanish and they both laughed.

Seeing the confusion in my eyes, he smiled. "He says that those buildings you were taking pictures of seem to be very important to travelers. We often see people stopping to take pictures. And of the old Glenrio motel too. To us, they're just falling-down buildings."

I was reminded that so often, the people closest to the old road are the ones who least feel a romantic connection to it. In many cases, to them, it is just a road. Fair enough.

His friend said something, and he turned back to me. "He wants to know where you are heading to?"

"We're driving across America, but using Route 66," I said.

"Is that your family?" he asked, motioning his chin toward our vehicle. Kate smiled and waved.

"It is."

"Are they enjoying it? How are you guys finding America so far?"

"It is definitely a big country, but people have been so friendly. By the way, I'm Brennen," I said, reaching out to shake his hand. "Do you guys live near here?"

"Sort of. We live down the road a ways in San Jon. It's not far from here, but we have to pick up some seed in Vega, over in Texas."

He asked a few questions about our travels and was genuinely curious about what we'd encountered.

"Have you ever driven Route 66?" I asked. "Even just the New Mexico or Texas portions?"

"Ha!" He shook his head. "I've never really driven anywhere, but my wife has. Her father used to take her and her sister on long trips. They'd go to California to visit relatives." His eyes lit up. "I keep telling her that we'll go, but you know, life just gets too busy sometimes."

His friend, still sitting in the shade of the pickup, called out something and they both started to laugh.

"He says that my junkie truck is lucky to make it to Vega."

The three of us laughed together. They were both really friendly, kind guys.

The sun began to scorch the back of my neck and we had to get to Tucumcari. It had been a long but fulfilling day. We bid farewell and watched from the rearview mirror as they disappeared into the distance, enveloped in a cloud of dust. As we drove, we realized that they were likely the first people from New Mexico that we had ever met.

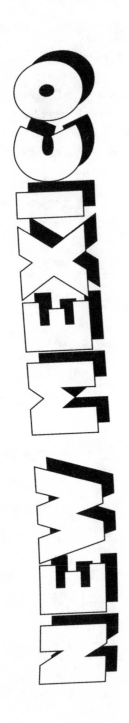

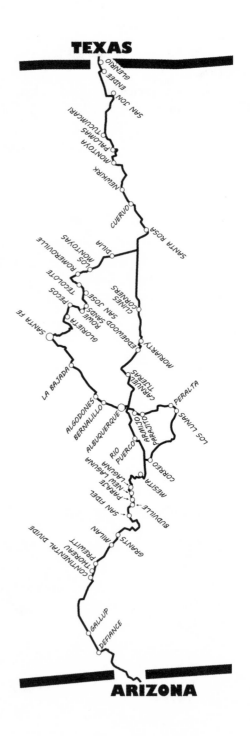

31

IT WAS LATE afternoon when we rolled into Tucumcari. It would have been later, but we were moving toward the sun, and by simply crossing into New Mexico, we had gained an hour. It was an exciting discovery. The town itself is small in size—5,300 people—but big in Route 66 history and culture, with a fair assortment of themed motels and a few good eateries, and it even boasts a state-of-the-art dinosaur museum that was on our hit list.

There is a beautiful legend surrounding the name Tucumcari. In this southwestern version of Romeo and Juliet, a maiden named Kari, the daughter of an Apache chief, Wautonomah, is deeply in love with a young man, Tocom, but is inconsolably devastated when a rival suitor kills Tocom in an act of jealousy. Kari seeks revenge and stabs the murderer to death before taking her own life with the same knife. Distraught by the death of Tocom and his young daughter, Chief Wautonomah kills himself. But at the moment of dying, the chief was heard bitterly calling out "Tocom! Kari!" And, as such, the name was born.

However, that is probably just a myth, believed to have been fabricated by a Methodist minister in 1907. According to historians, there is no evidence that the Apaches ever actually settled in the area, and Tucumcari most likely gets its name from the nearby Tucumcari Mountain. The widely agreed-upon academic explanation is that it comes from a Plains Indian term, possibly Comanche, "tukamukaru," which may have meant "lookout point." The town has been around since 1901, when it was established as a construction camp by the Chicago, Rock Island and Pacific Railroad. Originally named Ragtown, the camp quickly picked up a new and more colorful nickname—Six Shooter Siding—due to the numerous gunfights that took place within its violent borders. It then became Douglas, before receiving its final title of Tucumcari in 1908.

Tucumcari, roughly pronounced "two-come-carry," is the largest town on Route 66 between Amarillo, Texas, and Albuquerque, New Mexico. Back in Route 66's heyday, at the height of the family road trip phenomenon, the town's reputation as a bustling destination with over two thousand motel rooms was loudly broadcast on billboards along the highway and within leading travel guides and literature. It was a sought-out destination for travelers as they motored along the historic road. But then the mighty interstate swooped in around 1981, and without warning, the town's booming economy dried up to but a trickle. Today, there are only a handful of these motels left, beacons of a bygone era.

The pride of the animated town is the Blue Swallow Motel, arguably the most respected motor court on Route 66. The story of the Blue Swallow began in 1939 with carpenter turned entrepreneur W. A. Huggins. The venue was officially opened in 1940 as Blue Swallow Court, with ten rooms and a café located on-site. In 1948, the lodging was purchased by Ted Jones, a prominent local rancher, who wisely added two additional rooms, recognizing the growing demand. After Jones and his wife passed away in the 1950s, the motel was then purchased by locals Floyd and Lillian Redman and modernized by installing a new and larger sign, and changing the original "Court" to the more fashionable "Motel."

It was during the Redmans' long tenure that the Blue Swallow introduced an interesting practice that I imagine must have been rare even in their day, but totally unheard of in modern hospitality. Should a visitor not have enough money to rent a room, rather than turn the needy traveler away, the owners accepted personal belongings in trade or, for some, went as far as providing the room free of charge. But these were, of course, different times. And the slogan of the day back then was a cheery "Tucumcari Tonite."

With its pink stucco walls decorated with seashell designs, and its attractive neon sign hanging proudly in the front, the motel has been a beacon for visitors for over seventy-five years. At the time of our visit, the motel was under the proud ownership of Michigan natives Kevin and

Nancy Mueller. Recently named "the last, best and friendliest of the old-time motels" in *Smithsonian Magazine*, the venue was full for the night when we checked in. It was a good thing that we had made our reservation a month earlier. (Some venues on 66 require a bit of pre-planning to make sure that visitors are not disappointed upon arrival.)

"You guys have had a long drive," said Kevin, laughing as he searched for our room key. "When you get settled in, feel free to pop back around if you want any suggestions for dinner or what to see and do in Tucumcari. I would recommend Del's down the street for tonight, but it can get pretty busy."

The motel lobby was full of 66 paraphernalia and, of course, tributes to *Cars*. (In the animated film, the neon lighting at the Cozy Cone brightly displays what has long been a Blue Swallow slogan, "100% Refrigerated Air.") The Muellers' dog wandered about freely, to the delight of some children whose family had also just checked in. There was an energy flowing at the Blue Swallow that was contagious—a feeling of being in the right place, at the right time, where something memorable is happening.

All around the property, visitors were sitting outside their rooms on colorful metal lawn chairs, greeting each other, swapping stories of the road, and taking a deep breath of classic Americana.

"So you drove down to California, from Ottawa, alone, in order to join your family who flew down? Then you guys went to Hawaii, and now you are driving back home together via Route 66?" We were impressed by this rather complicated and ambitious travel story.

"Correct! It's been a long trip, but we thought it would be a chance of a lifetime as a family, and for the kids to experience Route 66," said David, a Canadian who was now on his way home and whose room was near ours.

"What a fabulous holiday," chimed in a British girl called Wilma, without looking up, who had been fiddling furiously with her phone. She and her companion, Betty, had been sitting on the step outside of their room trying to sort out a problem with one of their devices.

"I can't seem to get this bloody phone to work. It's so stupid," Wilma moaned.

"Look, look! You're not doing it right, eh! Give it here. Let me take a look," chided Betty, growing increasingly frustrated with her friend and the situation.

We watched and listened as they tried to sort their dilemma.

"I have an idea," said Betty, "Why don't we call Derek and ask him what to do? He's quite clever with these things, innit?"

Wilma looked up at her with distain. "Well now, I can't quite do that when the bloody thing refuses to turn on, can I?"

Betty shrugged. Wilma stood up abruptly, followed by Betty, and the pair disappeared into their room and shut the door. I turned to David and smiled. His story had been hijacked. He gave me a knowing look.

"I better get going," he said, reaching out his hand to shake farewell. "We need to get these kids fed before they have a real meltdown. If I don't see you guys before we leave tomorrow, have a great trip and be safe out there."

He turned to give chase to his two young and precocious children, who had discovered a resident cat. "No, Michael!" shouted the mom, who had emerged from their room with sunglasses in hand. "Don't pull on the cat's tail. He can bite or scratch you. Michael, stop hitting your brother!" Thembi looked on with slight interest.

Down the semicircle drive, some guests looked harried as they hung freshly laundered clothes over the backs of chairs to dry, while others took the opportunity to reorganize the trunks of their cars, prepping for the next day's departure.

The Blue Swallow is a hub for people watching, a place to absorb diverse personalities and cultures from around the globe. Sitting and taking in all the activity was mesmerizing. Everyone was there for the same purpose: to experience fabled Route 66 and the magic of the iconic motel.

The sun was hanging lower in the enormous desert sky when we decided to stroll down to Del's Restaurant to grab some Mexican food for supper. It wasn't a long walk and it felt nice to get in a touch of exercise. Most of the town's remaining neon signs were still off, as nightfall was not yet upon us. But to say that there was tremendous expectation on our part would be an understatement. I think everyone on the strip was eager to have the Muellers switch on the famous motel sign with the delightful little bird.

"There it is!" Thembi called, kicking a stone down the street as we walked. The Del's Restaurant sign was hanging in the distance, a lighthouse to all hungry voyagers looking for a safe port of call. Of course, being in the Southwest and on Route 66, there was a gigantic steer standing proudly on top of the neon sign. Approaching the parking area, we suddenly realized that patrons were arriving in droves, on foot, on motorbikes, in vehicles—we even saw a pair of cyclists show up and quickly chain their bikes to a nearby pole. It appeared that every motel operator in Tucumcari had shared the same dining recommendation. There was a commotion as the line trailed out the door and people began jostling to get in. The hostess was doing her best to have tables cleared and people seated, all under the aggressive glare of a hungry crowd.

"Matthews, table for three," announced the flustered hostess after a tense thirty minutes.

"Here!" our hands shot up into the air in response, like zealous school children pleading, "Please, allow us to take a seat and pay you for your food and service." Okay, we didn't say that, but it certainly felt like an unstated privilege to be given a table. This was not trendy Manhattan, but quiet, out-of-the-way Tucumcari. However, the rush was pretty indicative of this eatery's success.

Dinner was a relaxed, tasty event with delectable spicy chicken fajitas and an amazing salsa with fresh corn chips. Totally worth the wait. Our waiter was hilarious and witty, constantly dropping well-timed sarcasm and humor. The room buzzed with voices from across the globe. Thankfully, within all of the chaos and commotion, we were able to exhale.

The sun had surrendered the day and a full moon greeted us, high in the clear night sky as we made our way back to the motel. A light wind had began to pick up and the air got a little cool. Kate leaned in for a cuddle as we walked. Neon shone beautifully up and down the strip, from the Roadrunner Lodge Motel to Motel Safari to Tee Pee Curios up to the Blue Swallow; it was mesmerizing, and the once-hectic street was now almost empty and oddly hushed. Where there was just recently a horde of frenzied people, there was now a faint loneliness and an indescribable quietude.

At the Blue Swallow, the neon sign was brilliant, a wash of color keeping watch over America's Main Street and its long-enthralling past. A No Vacancy sign shouted from the window, and the office was dark and closed for the day. I suddenly felt a deep sense of gratitude for being able to be there, and pulled Thembi in close. A burst of wind blew through the air, tussling my short blond hair and carrying with it a sweet scent of desert flowers.

After getting Thembi ready for bed, I went back out front to the curb and stood on the highway for a long time, alone on the road that had carried so many dreams. There was a deafening silence as artificial sounds had vanished, all but the steady hum of the neon, and for the first time that day, I was fully reminded of the ninety years of hopes and aspirations that defined Route 66 and created its lore and mythology. Here we were in the heart of America, in the hauntingly beautiful desert of New Mexico, anonymous travelers permitted to claim our own little piece of Tucumcari, like so many who had traveled this land before us.

When we set out on a road trip, we don't always realize that we are unlikely to return in the same state as when we left. The road impacts us, people impact us, our hearts and minds are changed. I was really starting to understand the spiritual essence of America's two-lane highways and the small friendly towns that they run through.

32

A VAST CLEAR sky welcomed us the next day. There was not a cloud in sight, and already, at seven in the morning, there was palpable energy around the rooms as people strategically packed their vehicles and carefully arranged their belongings, ready to head off. I saw Kevin walking toward the office and rushed over to say good morning.

"How did you sleep?" he asked.

"Fantastic! It was a really peaceful night." We were given room 10, as it was one of the only rooms that had two queen beds and was perfect for a small family.

"That's good to hear. I'm just holding down the fort, as Nancy is traveling for a bit. You have time for a coffee?" he asked.

"Sure! Then you can tell me about yourself and how you ended up in New Mexico and owning a Route 66 icon!" I suggested.

"Well, it's been a journey, that's for sure," he responded as we walked into the crammed little office.

"So what brought you guys here, to Tucumcari? It doesn't seem like the obvious place for most people to wind up," I asked.

He then began narrating his own journey.

Kevin and Nancy found themselves on Route 66 the way many others have in recent years. Kevin lost his job in 2011 after twenty years with the same company, and was shell shocked by the unexpected development. He needed to clear his head and Nancy suggested that he hit the road, visit some family, and figure out what he would like to do next. He agreed. (That sounded strangely familiar.)

Initially, Kevin headed to Kentucky to visit his son, Cameron, before continuing south to find some solace with his parents. It was from there that he began to ponder a life on the old highway. Kevin and Nancy had visited Route 66 in 2007, and while the trip had faded into a pleasant memory, obviously the bug was still with him. Energized, he quickly jumped on his computer and began to search for businesses for sale along Route 66. It was not long before the sale of the Blue Swallow caught his eye. Fascinated, he called Nancy and shared his musing.

With Nancy's support, Kevin picked up the phone and contacted the owner. However, the response was not what he was expecting. A blunt voice on the other end quickly advised him that the motel was no longer for sale. It was off the market. But Kevin would not be deterred. He continued to communicate with the owner and finally managed to arrange a visit to the motel for March 2011. For the couple, it all felt like a new adventure. When they arrived at the venue, owners Bill Kinder and his wife, Terri Anderson, who had owned the classic venue since 2006, took Kevin and Nancy around the property, showing off the rooms and amenities. The Muellers were now keen to make their pondering a reality and by evening on their last day, they had hammered out a purchase agreement.

As I walked back to our room to get my troops ready, I realized that Kevin and Nancy's story had a common thread with several others that we had heard along the road. Route 66 had provided many people with an opportunity for a second or even third act. That is a unique trait to American life that most Americans don't seem to recognize: the ability to turn a potentially tragic life occurrence—loss of income and maybe career—into a second act and a chance to dream a new life into existence. Route 66 is a perfect example of the country's very real ability to allow people to reinvent themselves.

33

THE ROAD OUT of Tucumcari was dotted with remnants of what the town once was. A deserted trucker's terminal, its sign missing several letters but still calling for long-haulers from fifty feet in the sky, sat on the left-hand side of the tarmac. Once a safe port for big-rig drivers who needed to stop for the night, the rest haven now gave off only disturbing vibes. It felt downright haunted. Piles and piles of rotting onions were scattered across the sun-scorched concrete—how they got there we had no clue. Dozens of birds had made nests atop the derelict sign, the only life to still frequent the stop. Beside it was a burned-out Shell station with old oil drums and huge concrete blocks that had been put up in front to try to bar entry. This only added to the moroseness of the town's outskirts.

The safety of Tucumcari felt well behind us as we stumbled onto the remains of the Paradise Inn Motel. More than any other deserted motel so far on the trip, Paradise emanated a freaky forlorn feeling, as though we were being watched from inside the abandoned structure. If Glenrio gave off that sensation, Paradise Inn did so tenfold.

We walked around the grounds, hesitantly peeking into the long-forsaken rooms. Old photographs were strewn across the ground, flapping in the morning breeze beside castaway personal belongings and old furniture and mattresses, which I assumed came from the motel's empty rooms. And if that was not weird enough, visitors have often reported hearing a radio playing from the forgotten venue's garage area. It has been assumed that the owner was doing this in order to dissuade trespassers from taking up residence.

All around the property, long, scraggly grass grew, providing a home for plentiful grasshoppers. Otherwise, there was a deafening silence. The heat of the morning was already shimmering off the ground. I bent to pick up an old photograph of a woman, young and pretty. Her eyes looked distant, and I got a sense of dread as I held the picture in my hand, as if I was disturbing something that was perhaps best left alone. I placed the photograph gently and respectfully back on the ground and almost stepped on an unblemished egg. Like the onions at the truck stop, I had no idea how this egg had found its way to this cheerless, long-left-behind locale.

"Let's get out of here," Kate said. "This place is really ominous. I'm getting the feeling of being watched."

"Yeah, me too," said Thembi. "Dad, what did you see in the back?"

I had carefully walked through the wasteland to try to photograph the large Paradise Inn Motel sign but was so unsettled that I came back quickly after taking only a few pictures. "Nothing much, buddy, just more of the same family photos, stuffed animals, and old junk. Come on, let's get going."

In 2017, a mysterious fire razed what had been the main office of the motel and one room, further cementing its sinister reputation and bleak future.

A fair portion of New Mexico's Route 66 has disappeared in modern times, swallowed up into private Native reservations, and is no longer accessible to motorists. As such, traveling in the state is a mix of using the interstate—which has amazing scenery in its own right—and hopping onto Route 66 when the opportunity allows.

Before Clines Corners, a large travel stopover and Route 66 mainstay that has been around since 1934, but just past Santa Rosa, home of the freezing-cold but very popular Blue Hole, we took Highway 84 north. We were now driving on the original alignment of Route 66, which existed between 1926 and 1937, called the Santa Fe Loop. This was some pretty old road—the tales it must have witnessed! Wide-open spaces, deep valleys, plains, and forests painted the landscape with dramatic views through the small towns (more like villages) of Dilia, San Jose, Rowe, and Pecos, all evidence of the richness that rests underneath the soil.

The heavens suddenly darkened, and the vehicle shuddered violently as a savage wind grabbed hold of it and the clouds opened up with a fierce shower of gigantic raindrops. It startled me and I tensed up, trying to keep the car on the wet road. The storm had come out of nowhere and swallowed the SUV whole. Late-summer storms are a somewhat common occurrence in the Southwest and can be a bit jarring. They reminded us of the intensity of the rains during the monsoon season back in Africa. It was impossible to see anything in front of us, so I slowed to thirty miles per hour and hoped that no one driving behind us was foolish enough to maintain highway speed. I switched on our hazard lights, just in case. In the passing lane to our left, a BMW zoomed by at a breakneck speed, splashing us with a wall of water before disappearing almost instantly. Kate and I looked at each other and shook our heads. We listened as the rain pounded on the roof of the vehicle and enjoyed the experience, while also feeling a sense of panic at the lack of visibility. Thembi was napping, bored from too much time in the confines of the car. But then it was suddenly over, and the torrent stopped as quickly as it had started. It is amazing how a storm can come and black out a perfectly beautiful day, if only for a few moments. Loud, angry thunder clapped in the sky as lurid clouds danced above and headed toward some dusty hills in the distance.

———

FOUNDED BY SPANISH colonists somewhere between 1607 and 1610, the City Different, as Santa Fe is lovingly referred to, is New Mexico's capital and the fourth-largest city in the state. It's also the oldest state capital in the nation. Santa Fe is a place with a full and diverse history, matched only by its natural beauty. There was a unique quality about the city that really did make it feel different than many of the New Mexico sites we had encountered by that point.

Originally, Route 66 ran straight through the town, but only for a brief period. At the time, New Mexico was heavily influenced politically by a group of businessmen and officials known as the Santa Fe Ring. They were mostly Republican in their political persuasion, yet somehow, in 1924, Democrat Arthur Thomas Hannett was elected as the state's governor—but he would only serve a single term (1925–1927). He blamed the Republican establishment, largely based in Santa Fe, for his loss. Upon losing his second run for governor in 1927, in an act of what some say was revenge, Hannett forced through a sixty-nine-mile cutoff road from Santa Rosa directly to Albuquerque that effectively bypassed the scenic town of Santa Fe entirely. In some ways, that was a real shame, but it seems to have helped Santa Fe to shape its own future away from the busier road.

In its earliest alignment, however (1926–1937), Route 66 ran straight through Santa Fe and past our momentary destination, La Fonda on the Plaza hotel (situated, as the name suggests, on the historic Santa Fe Plaza).

"Now you're talking!" Thembi declared as we entered our room. He had grown weary of the road and was excited to put down some roots for a few days. And if one is to spend any extra time at a venue, La Fonda on the Plaza is, without a doubt, the hotel you want to call home.

Positively spectacular, La Fonda—"the inn" in Spanish—was totally different than anything else we had experienced on the route thus far. The architectural motif was Pueblo in nature, with rounded corners and irregular parapets, as it has always been at La Fonda on the Plaza. The venue's prestige and influence have been felt since it first opened its doors in 1922, and grew even more once it became one of the iconic Harvey Houses of the West in 1925.

Fred Harvey was born in the United Kingdom and immigrated to America in the early 1850s, at just seventeen years old. Harvey began his American journey working in restaurants in New York City and New Orleans before deciding to open his own venue in St. Louis. Luckily for Southwest travelers, Harvey's restaurant failed, and he moved into a new role, serving as a freight agent with the railroads. In this job, he traveled through the Great Plains, an experience that hugely impacted him as he witnessed the poor state of lodging and dining that rail passengers endured in the American West. He was inspired.

In 1876, Harvey entered into an agreement with the Atchison, Topeka and Santa Fe Railway (AT&SF) to open a restaurant at the company's depot in Topeka, Kansas. The British entrepreneur believed that travelers longed for a finer dining experience, and he was right. Soon, with the success of the Topeka location, Harvey opened up additional locations along the railroad's route. These eateries became part of the Harvey House restaurant chain and evolved to also include comfortable, clean accommodations for rail travelers. This would develop into a chain of luxury hotels that included La Fonda—in 1925, AT&SF purchased the property and leased it to the Fred Harvey Company—and became known as Harvey Houses. Most are now gone, but a few remain, heralding the dreams and vision of a man who is said to have "civilized the West."

With over 180 rooms and a very popular restaurant (where reservations are recommended), La Fonda on the Plaza is, in every sense, the pure essence of southwestern hospitality. The hotel had been recently renovated, and just walking down the halls, we were very aware that we were walking through history, a compliment to the management's attention to detail in maintaining the hotel's authentic spirit. Our room was tastefully decorated and had many distinct design features, such as a hand-painted headboard and original art dressing the walls that celebrated the uniqueness of Santa Fe charm. The history of the hotel and the ambience created the perfect place to unwind during a Route 66 journey.

34

WE WANTED TO take advantage of the sunny afternoon, so we headed out to explore the town on foot. Down the road from La Fonda, the historic Santa Fe Plaza was bursting with people from across the globe, each enjoying the day in their own unique way. The focal point of the plaza is a serene, tree-lined green space peppered with benches for people to sit on, and a gazebo at its center. It is surrounded by boutiques, art galleries, and overflowing eateries. Old Latino men sat, sipping coffee and debating politics, while tourists stared, perplexed, at complicated maps of the city. We wandered around casually, soaking in the diversity of culture. On the edge of the plaza waited several pedicabs, pedal taxis that reminded me of tuk tuks from back in Kenya, but that rely on leg power and not noisy, gutless motors.

Colorful Mexican blankets hung from storefront windows, and huge strands of red chiles, neatly threaded together, decorated open market stands. Two men, one with a saxophone and the other with an acoustic guitar, entertained an appreciative audience in the center of the square, while both locals and visitors to Santa Fe sat and chatted, laughing together and whiling away the tranquility of the day. It was an interesting amalgam of old and new.

However, in the midst of all this animated and colorful vibrancy, we also noticed that a fair number of young transient people had made the shops' doorways and the city's public spaces their home, at least during the summer months, creating an uncomfortable clash with the ultra-upmarket Santa Fe vibe. The disheveled, boisterous youth didn't seem to be dangerous, but they were loud and unkempt and brushed past others on the sidewalks in a belligerent, pushy manner that enormously contrasted with the otherwise serene nature of Santa Fe, especially on the plaza.

We strolled along the narrow streets that were once a part of Route 66 and admired the wide variety of art and distinctive Pueblo architecture, enjoying the warm colors of Santa Fe that were visible at every turn. With us in tow, Thembi had spent our first morning in Santa Fe visiting nearby rock and mineral shops, admiring the wealth of natural bounty available and discovering a notable number of really cool dinosaur fossils. This town was perfect for our budding amateur naturalist.

After exploring the plaza area, we contemplated walking down to a shopping mall some miles away. Malls are not the norm for us on a beautiful summer day, especially while on holiday, but we were excited to check out a unique insect and reptile museum that a member of La Fonda's restaurant team co-owned. The opportunity to explore the bug museum had Thembi over the moon with excitement. He has been an insect enthusiast since his toddler years. The plethora of creepy-crawlies and the abundance of open space really does make growing up in Africa a golden experience for kids. There is an indisputable sense of freedom to move around and digest life. Since relocating to Toronto, we had struggled with the indoor culture of television and video games that pervades Western life. In Kenya, children still go outdoors at every opportunity to play sports, explore, or just enjoy the gift of space.

"Let's take one of the pedicabs," suggested Kate. "It looks like a pretty long walk and you know Thembi will get tired." In Kenya, I don't think that we have ever taken a tuk tuk, because of the potential dangers on the roads. But Santa Fe's streets have a totally different, calmer sense—they looked safe enough. A number of men were standing on the other side of the park waiting for clients.

"Hello," I called to one of them as we walked over. "How much to get to the DeVargas Center?"

After some relaxed negotiation—I have always hated bargaining, though it is part of daily life in Africa—we were on our way, wind in our faces and Santa Fe revealing itself before us, all from the comfort of a padded bicycle bench. Our driver, Juan, transported us not merely down mysterious side streets and through quaint neighborhoods, but back in time to a Santa Fe of long ago. As he peddled, Juan shared tales and history, pointing out fascinating antiquity as we passed. His world and realities were a far cry from those of the average plaza hotel guests. Born and raised in the city, Juan was one of twelve children, each steeped in the Catholic faith. He took pride in showing off his hometown, a city marinated in a mélange of Native American, Hispanic, and Anglo culture and history.

"I come from a big family, but I have no kids of my own. Not even a wife. But that's okay, it gives me more time on the bicycle and to do my job." People waved from the roadside, calling out greetings and warm wishes to Juan. He was undoubtedly a man of the people.

"Have you seen much change in Santa Fe over the years?" I asked.

"Yeah, for sure, but you know, legally, construction cannot be modernized. The general look and feel of the area, especially on the plaza, has stayed the same for decades." Juan hit an incline and started breathing with a little more difficulty. As a man in his midforties, he was working hard to keep the momentum of the ride going.

"Do you want us to jump off until you get the bike up the hill?" I offered.

"No, no," he said, laughing. "This is good exercise and I'm used to it. But I appreciate the offer. And your patience!"

Cars drove slowly behind us, unmoved by the slow pace at which they were forced to proceed behind a fatigued pedicab driver. To our surprise, no one was beeping or shouting. Back in Kenya, drivers would have been aggressive, perhaps even causing an accident as they sought to push past, but not in Santa Fe. There was a deep sense of community in the historic city that seemed to bond residents together.

It was a perfect ride down to the mall. I was incredibly happy that we decided not to walk—on foot it would have been a bloody-far journey! Inside the sprawling DeVargas Center, the scenic face of Santa Fe disappeared, quickly taking on the generic visage of shopping centers the world over. But that was okay, as we were there to enjoy some nature. The Harrell House Bug Museum (since relocated to the Santa Fe Place Mall) was quiet as we entered, devoid of the large and manic crowds that often disrupt and distract from a museum experience. As we handed over our tickets, the owner promised us that we would be able to touch some of the bug life on display once we had finished the tour. That made Thembi happy.

With 2,400 mounted exhibits and over 150 live ones, there was a ton to see. Alone in the museum, we had all the time in the world to slowly enjoy our discoveries, as we wandered from tank to tank, taking in the beetles and snakes, scorpions and fish. Harrell House even had a large monitor lizard; a beautiful Jackson's chameleon that reminded us of our garden in Kenya, where they were wild, plentiful, and roamed free; and some of the most striking butterflies we had ever seen. It was a fun, unusual experience and a great addition to our cultural stay in Santa Fe. The museum was certainly not what we would have expected to discover in a shopping mall.

Outside, Juan was nowhere to be found. His cab was chained to a nearby pole, but he had ventured off.

"I'm hungry," Thembi said. "Can we get something simple tonight? Maybe pizza?"

"You don't want to eat in the restaurant at the hotel? It's getting a bit chilly to stay out," I answered. The cold air had picked up as the day wore on, and the recently sunny afternoon had all but vanished. Santa Fe's weather can change quickly.

"No, we can eat there tomorrow, but I want something that I know tonight. Please!" Thembi pleaded.

"Okay, if you—"

"I'm here, I'm here!," Juan called out. "Sorry about that, guys. I needed to go and buy a new hat, and I figured that since I was already down here, and you would take some time . . . how do I look?" he asked, trying it on.

Clouds filled the sky as we followed the evening traffic, which moved placidly through chaotic main streets and down quiet, narrow residential ones. We were concerned that the rain might arrive before we did, but Juan deposited us safely back at the hotel, just as a crash of loud thunder shattered the tranquility of the night. The monsoon season poured down, squashing our plans for pizza.

35

THE RAIN FROM the previous night had pushed out the high-pressure system and summer was back. It was a perfect day and locals were out in droves. There was bliss and excitement in the air. People were enjoying their outdoor freedom once again.

"The museum is just over there," said Kate, pointing across the road. "Why don't we check it out?"

The Palace of the Governors was constructed in the seventeenth century and served as the place from which Spain ruled the American Southwest. It's now a protected site, chronicling the history of Santa Fe, New Mexico, and the region. A well-respected state museum, the building was registered as a National Historic Landmark in 1960 and a National Treasure in 2015.

The portico of the Palace of the Governors was occupied with people sampling the arts and crafts sold by local Native American artists seated on the floor atop colorful woven blankets—a long-standing tradition to help preserve New Mexico's Pueblo and tribal cultures. We went around the busy market scene and headed straight to the New Mexico History Museum, which is connected to the Palace of the Governors. One ticket gives visitors access to both venues. We strolled leisurely through the three floors of the impressive history museum, soaking up the exhibits on display. We took in the story of New Mexico, then and now, the car culture of northern New Mexico (I now have an appreciation for lowriders that I never had before), a photographic exhibit on the artist Agnes Martin, and more. At the Palace of the Governors, Thembi absorbed himself in a scavenger hunt for religious iconography, an activity provided by the museum. As he went around ticking off items he had located from his list, I wandered behind him, reading and looking at the numerous cultural artifacts and historical biographies that were on display. Santa Fe is steeped in an enormous amount of history, and it can be overwhelming to take in all at once. We were beat by the time we were through, and we headed out for some fresh air in the courtyard area that connects the Palace of the Governors to the main museum.

A gentleman ambled over after seeing Thembi trying to throw a pebble into a large hole in one of the two trees in the courtyard. "Hello there, young man," he called. "Can I show you a very special tree?" Thembi nodded in agreement and walked over to the stranger. We kept a close eye on him.

"This tree here, this one, was planted by His Majesty, King Juan Carlos I of Spain in 1987 when he visited Santa Fe!" he said.

Thembi's eyes grew big in amazement and I felt a sense of pride at his young thirst for knowledge and new discoveries. "What type of tree is it?" he asked.

The gentleman stopped for a moment, charmed with Thembi's interest. Perhaps he was not expecting that. "Well, that's a very good question. It's a cottonwood tree." He patted the tall, leafy tree's strong bark admiringly, and then bade us farewell, hurrying ahead to rejoin a friend who had caught up after lingering at the museum. Thembi went back to tossing stones.

"Where to next?" I asked Kate.

"Let's check out the Loretto Chapel!" Kate is a history buff at heart and could have spent an entire day in the streets and historic buildings of Santa Fe, if Thembi and I had agreed.

The chapel is located right on the Old Santa Fe Trail, aka Route 66, and is famed for its mysterious floating staircase. Kate was particularly interested in going inside, even though neither Thembi nor I had much interest.

"Why do we need to go in there?" Thembi complained. "Look, there is a long line and it is probably pretty boring." He wanted to go to lunch. I did too. We had been investigating the town's romantic past for hours.

But Kate was keen on seeing the old church and insisted that it was time well invested. As a child, she attended a primary school in Mombasa that was started by the Sisters of Loretto, and she was enamored by the supposed connection.

"Let's go inside and check out the building. It's very old and will be interesting. Who knows what we might discover inside? And besides, Mom wants to go in," I said to Thembi.

"Okay, but then we can go and get pizza?" he bargained.

The main seating area of the old church was swarming with visitors, many of them believers who were engaged in prayer. We spent a good amount of time sitting in silence on the smooth, handcrafted wooden pews of the small center of worship, marveling at the intricate architecture, beautiful stained glass, and the uniqueness of the famed staircase, which is miraculously unsupported and was once used by the nuns to ascend to the choir loft.

We wrapped up our day by grabbing pizza at a popular joint around the corner and then heading to a grassy park to sit on a bench and watch Thembi run around and play. As an only child, he often gets treated much more like an adult—but even though he is mature and responsible for his age, he is still a little boy. As he practiced somersaults and methodically collected sticks and stones to build a home for the local squirrels at the base of a wizened old tree, Kate and I observed and soaked in the lull of the day.

"I am really glad we included Santa Fe into our schedule," I noted casually.

Kate stared at me for a moment, before adding, "I am really glad that we decided to come on this trip, period. We needed it. Do you think it is giving you any clarity on what you'd like to see come about in our next chapter?"

This was something that I had been thinking about a lot as we crossed America, but at that point, I still had no idea what was next for us. I felt responsible for pulling my little family into the unknown. If I had only hung on to my cushy job with *Destination Magazine*, we would not have been in this soul-searching mode. But Kate has always been a supportive, wise wife, and she knew from experience that things always work out.

"I'm not sure. I know that I am discovering that I want bigger changes in life than I thought—maybe we could do something along Route 66?

Wouldn't it be amazing to meet people from all over the world who are excited about small-town America?" Then I heard the words of Kevin Mueller of the Blue Swallow Motel in my ears. "It is not a life for everyone."

"Would you mind not going back to Africa right away? I mean, if we did stick it out here for a few years, maybe on 66?" I asked.

Kate smiled, her imagination spinning wildly.

"You know me, I'm fine to be here, or anywhere really. I just want to be where we can find some good opportunities that allow us to live an interesting life."

An older couple walking in our direction nuzzled against each other as they stared at Thembi, who was still in the grips of construction. "What a beautiful little boy," the woman said to her partner, adjusting a strand of pearls that decorated her long neckline.

"He certainly is a busy little guy," added the gent. "It brings back memories!"

She threw her head back and laughed. "It certainly does." He leaned in and gently kissed her thin lips as they continued past, and the pair gave off an aura of ease, of gratitude. I wanted what they seemed to have. Contentment. It is not always easy to come by.

Later in the evening, I found myself standing on East San Francisco Street, just adjacent to La Fonda, a spot in the city that is blanketed in memories. As I absorbed the peace of dusk, the bell at the Cathedral Basilica of St. Francis of Assisi chimed out, as it has numerous times a day throughout the decades. There was a chill in the air again, and I shivered. The traffic had slowed to a handful of vehicles, and the picture-happy tourists had largely fled to the comfort of their cozy hotels. An enormous full moon rose high in the desert sky above me, bouncing its bright light off the sandy walls of La Fonda and onto the sidewalk in front of me. Nearby, an artisan was humming softly as she finished packing up for the day, carefully arranging her wares. I was lost in my thoughts and deep in contemplation when, unexpectedly, I felt a small hand in mine. I pulled back, startled, but quickly realized that Thembi had ventured out from the hotel to join me. Kate stood back at the hotel entrance watching to make sure he was safe. We stood hand in hand for some time, just he and I, breathing in our last night in Santa Fe.

36

WE WERE RELUCTANT to leave Santa Fe's charm, but we needed to be in Arizona in four days and had a few stops to make first. With a late start to the day, we were grateful that I-25, which was to take us toward Albuquerque, was somewhat empty. The scenery was made up of quaint adobe houses and beautiful mountainous vistas. We spotted a herd of seemingly wild horses out on the open landscape, a real taste of the Wild West. New Mexico has a fierce rawness to its beauty.

On the outskirts of Albuquerque, the highway became faster paced, choked by the movement of hundreds of hurtling vehicles. The Western highway system is always impressive to us, as its design allows a crazy number of speeding vehicles to all intricately weave their way this way and that way, methodically keeping in step with one another as if performing a curious tribal dance.

Albuquerque is a big city. It has a population of around 560,000 people but feels larger and much more crowded, despite being very spread out geographically. More than Santa Fe, Albuquerque has a cool mix of the old and the new, the traditional and the ultramodern. It has a big-city mentality, mixed with a laid-back southwestern attitude. Neighborhoods like Nob Hill and the Brick Light District along Central Avenue (as Route 66 is known as it runs through the center of the city) celebrate some of the best cuisine and shopping in the region. Trying to make sure to follow some advice we'd gotten, we avoided turning north or south off Central between San Mateo and Wyoming—an area officially known as the International District but scarily referred to as the War Zone due to its problem of gang violence. Homeless people were standing at every set of lights along this stretch of Central—and there are many—with placards in their hands pleading, "Please Help Me, I Need Food and Any Little Bit Will Help." A Native woman knocked on the window of the car in front of us, begging for money. This was not really what we were expecting when we descended into the tranquility of the Southwest. But it is a big city, so we likely should have been more prepared.

We decided to put up at Hotel Andaluz (opened in 1939 as a Hilton)— one of the nicest boutique hotels in the city. The venue is located downtown on Second Street and is within easy access of Route 66 and all of the street's picturesque neon and historic locations. Once we were settled in, we ventured out to explore the nearby area.

The afternoon was hazy but bright, and the desert's heat was offset by a gentle breeze that made it pleasant to stroll. The area had a lot of shops and office buildings, with wide streets and a fair share of foot traffic. We turned the corner and walked over to Copper Street and across to First Street. A young man with tanned skin and short twisted cornrows flashed past on his skateboard, pushing us from the sidewalk and up against a building. He didn't look back. Across the road, another guy was staring blankly into the distance, resembling a zombie. It was obvious that he was high on some sort of drug. He did not stagger. He didn't blink. He simply stood, motionless, and lost in his empty gaze. What was he possibly thinking about, if anything? Behind him, his compadre was shaking his head violently while jabbing himself in the face and mumbling incomprehensibly.

"This place looks dangerous, Dad," Thembi commented. "Are those guys over there drunk?"

"No, they are probably high on drugs," I explained.

"Wow, drugs can make you behave like that? They look crazy!"

"Drugs can cause good people to do all sorts of bad things," I said. "That is one big reason for you to never even consider trying them."

"Let's just go back to the hotel and get a drink on the rooftop bar," Kate suggested. So we quickly retreated to the safety and comfort of the Andaluz, where we enjoyed a cool beverage and watched people several stories below as they walked the pavement or rushed to catch a bus across the street. It was time for people to call it a day and head home, and it was enjoyable gazing from the safety of the terrace and watching as life played out.

———

OUR INITIAL INTRODUCTION to Albuquerque was not what we had expected. The city was bigger and busier and somehow more cosmopolitan than we expected. But we wanted to give it another chance to charm us, so we set out for dinner in the famed Old Town neighborhood. A destination unto itself, the beautiful Old Town has been a central part of life in New Mexico's largest city since Albuquerque was founded in 1706 by Governor Francisco Cuervo y Valdés. Alive with people, commerce, and music— gifted street musicians strummed away on their instruments in quiet narrow corners, tucked in between shops—Old Town is jam-packed with old-world allure and appeal. The construction reflects the Pueblo Revival style of much of New Mexico's architecture, with flat roofs and gentle adobe contours. It fits perfectly into the southwestern landscape. There are over a hundred shops and galleries tucked away down curious little pathways, waiting to be discovered. Wandering through the neighborhood felt more like an adventure than a shopping trip, as we found ourselves running into dead ends and bumping into impossibly beautiful pottery, clothing, and jewelry. Pale-red bunches of chiles hung from doorways, and quaint wooden and ceramic signs welcomed customers to mysterious storefronts. The entire area is designed around a central plaza and only made up of about ten blocks, but it felt larger. It was like we were trodding on historic but incredibly fashionable ground.

We popped into a dozen shops on our way to Seasons Rotisserie & Grill for dinner, amazed by the bright, intricate designs of pottery, blankets, carvings, and ceramics. There was a welcoming air in Old Town and less of a push to purchase than in Santa Fe. The area is a refuge for curious visitors looking to discover the secrets of an iconic southwestern city.

A young girl was sitting behind the counter of a small, out-of-the-way shop in the corner of one of the many open courtyards. Making eye contact, we decided to say hello and investigate what she was selling. Kate wanted to buy some ceramic flowerpots to take home.

"Hello!" we said with a smile, entering the shop.

She nodded but did not respond. She was busy typing on her cell phone.

"You have some really nice items, is this your shop?" Kate asked.

"It's my parents' place, yes," she said, tearing her eyes away from her phone. "Are you visiting New Mexico?"

We explained about driving Route 66 and shared about our time in Albuquerque thus far. She was not very familiar with Route 66—she had never left New Mexico. As we spoke, she frowned slightly, her body language becoming more rigid.

"That must be very exciting," she responded, "getting to travel across the country. You must be seeing so much. I would love to travel."

"Why don't you?" Kate asked.

The young girl shrugged and looked back down at her phone. "My padres would never agree. They need me here to help out. But maybe in the future."

"Do you enjoy working in this shop?" Kate continued.

"Yeah, I do. I guess. But I would love to get to experience more outside of New Mexico. I have a cousin who moved to Phoenix to go to school. He likes it a lot and said I can come to visit anytime." She sighed and asked more about our trip.

We said our goodbyes and promised to try to return. It is sad to see young people trapped in other people's dreams, even their parents'. But it also reminded us of the differences that culture often brings. We have a lot of European friends, for example, who would never dream of putting their lives on hold to work in their parents' business.

We invested three days in Albuquerque, exploring some of its amazing museums, restaurants, hiking, and shopping opportunities. Albuquerque had redeemed itself and reminded us that first impressions are often misleading. This large but dreamy desert town may have its faults, but it is a gem in the Southwest—a jewel in the crown of Route 66.

37

KATE SPOTTED THE sign that read "66 Pit Stop: Home of the Laguna Burger" and remembered Kevin back in Tucumcari recommending it as a great stop for lunch. "There's also an old 1933 Rio Puerco Bridge nearby that we can check out," Kate added, in an attempt to sell her burger craving.

Laguna Burger is located at a gas station in Rio Puerco, with one end of the building housing a convenience store and the other the diner. The place was very busy at midafternoon, which is when the local lunch crowd arrived. We headed to the counter to place our order and were advised that it would be a twenty-five-minute wait. We looked around and were deflated to realize that most of the patrons in the restaurant were also waiting for their orders. My first inclination was to abort the mission and just keep driving. No burger could be worth this wait, I thought, especially since I'm not the one eating it. But Kate and Thembi really wanted a burger and Laguna is famous for their food, so I just needed to exercise a little patience.

As Kate and Thembi browsed the shelves of the convenience store, I placed our order. After a couple of minutes perusing, they announced that they were going outside to explore a little and try to locate the old bridge. The heat of the afternoon was intense, and seating was hard to come by, so I stayed put.

At the table beside me, two guys wearing Pepsi uniforms were also waiting for their order.

"I loved *The Godfather: Part II*," said the older-looking one, as he casually flipped through a book from the store that reflected on life in 1974, the year I was born. The book was from a series devoted to reminding readers of what major events took place, what was on the music charts, big on television, new to the movie theater, and advertising and products unique to the year. It was a creative idea.

"I don't know. I think I saw it, but it was a bit slow, if I remember right," responded the younger one. "That was a long time ago, 1974. I find those older movies a bit slow."

The guys had been bantering back and forth about 1974 and debating cinema when Roy, the older one of the pair, leaned over in my direction.

"What do you think? You look a bit too young to remember the *Godfather* movies," he said.

I had been eavesdropping, but when he turned to include me in the conversation, he took me by surprise.

"I like all of the *Godfather* movies," I replied. "But I think the second one was the best. It seemed a bit faster paced—although it's been some time since I've seen any of them."

He looked across the table at his colleague. "See?" Looking back at me, he asked, "So what are you doing in New Mexico? You guys heading down Route 66?"

"Yep, we are heading west. We were just in Santa Fe recently but are on our way to Arizona."

They both nodded; they liked Santa Fe.

"I'm Roy and this is Carlos. You've come during a busy time, lots of people waiting for food, but boy, Laguna makes the best burgers. Do you like ketchup? I always order mine with extra ketchup," he said. "You need to get it from the counter."

Roy was Caucasian, perhaps in his fifties, with graying hair and brown, thick-rimmed spectacles. Carlos was Latino, in his late twenties maybe, and heavyset with pitch-black, wavy hair. They both had friendly faces. Roy was a chatterbox.

"I actually don't eat beef, so I ordered a chicken burger," I said.

They looked at each other for an instant. "Ah, well, yeah, I hear that the chicken burgers are good here too," Roy offered.

"Oh yeah, for sure," Carlos added. "There is really nothing not good here. It's a very popular place."

"So you guys work for Pepsi?" I guessed.

"Guilty as charged," Roy said, laughing. "We work up the road at the bottling plant."

"Pepsi has a plant in this area?"

"Oh yeah, Pepsi's all over the place. It's big business," Roy explained.

"Are you both from New Mexico?"

"I grew up around Albuquerque. Been in New Mexico almost all my life. Carlos here is from Roswell," said Roy.

"The UFO place?" I asked.

"That's right," he responded. "I don't believe in aliens or anything. But you never know, right?"

"Where is Area 51?" I asked. I know very little about alien lore, but in this part of the country, some people have turned it into big business.

"That's in Nevada," said Roy. "It's about nine hours from here."

"I've been there too," Carlos added. "It's a pretty cool place. In the middle of the desert. Nobody really knows what they got out there." He paused. "Maybe they did find a crashed spaceship or something."

"Do you believe all of the stories about people seeing UFOs in those areas?" I asked.

Carlos suddenly became very serious and the tone of his voice felt a little defensive. "Why, what do you mean?"

"I . . . I'm not sure . . . I mean, nothing . . . I'm just curious," I responded, slightly alarmed.

The eatery pulsated with energy as people continuously came and went. Roy wasn't lying—Laguna was definitely a favorite with the locals.

A young Latino guy behind the counter called out their order and Roy rushed up to grab it. I changed the conversation. "How important is Route 66 to New Mexico these days?"

Carlos looked to Roy, who was back in a flash and busy squirting a generous amount of ketchup over his meal.

"I would think it's pretty important," Roy answered, wiping red goop from the corner of his mouth. "It's definitely key for smaller places like Tucumcari and Gallup. They depend on it. But larger places like Santa Fe or Albuquerque, maybe not as much—but parts of Central Avenue in Albuquerque are still pretty 66 focused, I think."

"Will you guys drive to California?" Carlos interjected.

"Oh yeah, right to Santa Monica. My wife and son have never seen the Pacific Ocean, so it's one of the highlights."

"You plan on doing the whole trip again on the way back east?" he asked. "Driving Route 66 is a once in a lifetime for a lot of people. Doing it twice is huge."

"I'd like to do Route 66 one day," Roy interrupted. "Just not sure when I can make the time. Honestly, I don't really get what draws so many people over to do it, but there must be something rewarding about driving across the country on a historic highway. That's a long time in a car, though."

"I don't know," said Carlos. "I get it. I think people are looking for their ideal version of America. I'm not so sure we New Mexicans have a vision that looks much past our state."

"Matthews, one chicken and two burgers . . . " shouted the guy behind the counter.

Kate and Thembi returned just in time, sweaty but invigorated. "Dad, we didn't really find anything super interesting. The bridge was pretty cool," Thembi said. "Mom took a million pictures."

Roy and Carlos said a friendly hello and our conversation seemed to break. They focused on their food and personal jawing and we on ours. It felt odd and I had to restrain myself from interrupting their lunch.

After finishing their burgers and fries, the pair wished us a safe and "uneventful" trip through New Mexico. They needed to get back to work and to the rhythm of their lives. As they left, I found myself hoping that one day they will find themselves able to explore America on the country's blue highways. There really is a great deal for all Americans to discover and digest.

38

GRANTS WAS NOW in sight, and Thembi was eager to head underground at the New Mexico Mining Museum to get a taste of what uranium miners experienced in the 1900s. Up to the 1980s, when this mining industry went somewhat bust, Grants had styled itself as the "Uranium Capital of the World."

Many of the museums and historical sites along Route 66 survive due to the dedication and effort of their noble volunteers, most of whom are retirees who are passionate about the route and about meeting tourists. The mining museum in Grants was no different. As a matter of fact, the older gent who greeted us as we walked through the door was a retired miner. He was enormously chuffed when Thembi, discovering a treasure of unknown proportion, rushed over to inspect minerals and stones of all types that were on display.

"Do you know what this is, young man?" He winked at us. He was about to give Thembi a lesson.

"Yes, it is Blanchard fluorite," replied Thembi, who had this subject down pat.

Obviously taken aback, the miner looked over to us, more shocked than impressed.

"Well, yes. Yes, it is. But how about this one?" The challenge was on.

"Oh, that is one of my favorites. It's turquoise. Did you know that . . . ?"

Arms crossed and fully engaged, the old miner was amazed by the discussion he was having with an eight-year-old about geology.

"This little boy is a fount of knowledge. I have never met a child who knew as much as he does about rocks and minerals," the man observed.

Thembi moved on and was examining what looked like a piece of an asteroid.

"Thank you," I responded. "He reads a lot and has always been very passionate about everything connected to nature, including minerals. We appreciate you spending some time with him."

"Oh no, it is my pleasure, truly! I wish more kids were as interested as him. So few care about such things these days. They're all too busy with video games."

We headed toward an elevator, almost invisible in the colorful room, that would take us down to the lower level, where the museum really comes alive. "Watch your step now," the miner told us. "When you get to the bottom, when the elevator stops, just follow the numbers, starting with one. If you press the buttons, you'll hear a recorded description by real miners, explaining the work that they used to do underground. Have fun." With that, the elevator door closed and down we went.

I have never really been claustrophobic, but the realization that we were beneath the ground, in a relatively snug space, made my stomach tighten. I knew that we were safe, but the museum had done such a realistic job creating the "mine" that I needed to keep reminding myself that we were not really far inside the Earth. I can only imagine what real miners go through, especially the old-timers, tunneling deep into the belly of the earth. Man is not meant to go so far down into the dark realms.

As we moved through, each stage of the exhibit looked superbly accurate, complete with genuine tools and instruments to represent men hard at work. Listening to the voices of the men who worked the earth for much of their lives brought on a wave of empathy. It was obvious that many of them loved their job, but the mere thought of people being forced to venture underground in order to make an income to support their families was slightly disturbing.

"This place is so cool!" Thembi called, rushing ahead.

Kate was busy taking pictures with the exhibit. My favorite was one next to an impossibly long drill. She looked right at home there, posing as an underground worker.

Back on the main level, another family was checking out the wide assortment of stones. The same gent who had engaged with Thembi earlier was now trying to excite another boy who looked to be around Thembi's age.

"And do you know what stone this is young man?" he asked with a kindness in his voice.

The boy's dad watched, hopeful that his son would embrace the opportunity to learn. His face dropped and distorted when the boy held the stone for a moment before tossing it back into the bin. "I don't know," he responded nonchalantly. "Dad, this museum sucks."

———

THE ROAD WAS empty again as Grants disappeared behind us. We could see the interstate in the distance, hectic and cold with streams of fast-moving vehicles. On America's Main Street, tiny, peaceful towns like Milan and Prewitt, on the way toward Thoreau, welcomed us as we moved west. Thoreau is a nondescript town, except that it is the location of the Roy T. Herman's Garage and Service Station, one of the oldest remaining gas stations along Route 66 in New Mexico. A series of mountain ridges rose up on the right, with colorful swirling patterns of pink and red. The New Mexican landscape was simply spectacular.

We stopped on the side of the road to stretch our legs and inhale the history of the land. The mountain ridges in the distance marked the Continental Divide on Route 66. Also known as the Great Divide, it determines which way rainfall flows into the seas—on the west side, it drains into the Pacific Ocean and on the east, into the Atlantic Ocean. A freight train lumbered past, endless with cargo cars, and Thembi started to jump up and down, waving his arms in an attempt to get the conductor's attention. I wasn't sure that he did, but then suddenly the train let off a loud whistle. Thembi was elated.

We'd just left Thoreau in our wake and a stream of billboards began to paint the roadside. There were three in a row for the iconic El Rancho Hotel, and several for Indian Village. This was a good place to go, apparently, to buy an authentic tomahawk, or if that is too extreme, a tomahawk-shaped baby rattle. Another Indian Village sign proclaimed that the store boasted "50 State Souvenir Spoons." That is an impressive collection. Then came a fun one for Smokey's restaurant. All of these billboards were announcing businesses and attractions located twelve miles away in Gallup.

The road into town widened, and a feeling that we were moving away from the emptiness and toward something took over. Soon enough, Gallup appeared as a myriad of roadside motels and jewelry stores and pawnshops on the left-hand side of the road, and railroad tracks on the right. Pale-green shrubs and dry desert grass accentuated the horizon as our eyes gazed off toward spectacular red sandstone hills in the distance. A train heading east clanged as it traveled by, and the Hacienda Motel called from the roadside on the left. Gallup traffic lights on Route 66, and there are many, began to bring vehicles to a halt, reminding us that we were, in fact, back in urbanity. The town is a decent size—close to 22,000 people—and packed with restaurants, fuel stations, motels, and shops. The tracks suddenly disappeared as the right-hand side of the road took on a new life and historic motels began popping up: the Arrowhead Lodge; the 1949 Blue Spruce Lodge, whose awesome sign was in the shape of a spruce tree; and the Lariat Lodge, with its cool Googie-style letters. But the town's most iconic hotel is undoubtedly El Rancho.

Gallup had been a choice location for many of the old Western motion pictures, and El Rancho, an imposing and impressive venue that was built in 1936 by R. E. Griffith, the brother of film director D. W. Griffith, became a magnet for Hollywood actors like John Wayne, Ronald Reagan, and Alan Ladd, who used it as a base while filming. The hotel's employees were trained by the esteemed Fred Harvey Company, so El Rancho provided the comfort and class desired by its movie-star patrons. When Gallup was bypassed by the interstate in 1980, the venue sadly went through a series of owners and fell into a state of disrepair, finally filing for bankruptcy in 1987. It was then purchased at an auction by Armand Ortega, a well-known Indian trader, and brought back to much of its original glory.

Gallup is a town chock-full of Native American culture. Anasazi archaeological sites from around AD 300 can be found within the sandstone cliffs, and a large part of Gallup's population is Native American, including some Hopi and Zuni residents and a large number of Navajos.

Visitors are also able to witness Indian dances with traditional drums, rattles, and flute instruments, and listen as locals explain the cultural traditions that surround these dances. Along Gallup's long stretch of the Mother Road, historic trading posts dot the landscape, with family-owned businesses like Richardson's still luring motorists off the highway after 109 years.

Just over a mile west of El Rancho, we spotted the homestead for a lesser-known Gallup resident, a Muffler Man named the Dude Man. The giant was only barely visible from Gallup's Route 66 stretch, but caught our eye as we drove slowly through town. We took a quick left down Fifth Street and another left onto West Coal, making our way to John's Used Cars lot to pay our respects to this towering figure. His stoic face, cowboy hat, gun belt, and slightly tight outfit made him the perfect giant cowboy. But his location was in a crowded area and the numerous low-hanging wires and telephone lines made taking a good picture of him challenging. Nonetheless, we were glad to have found him, adding him to our collection of favorite giants.

Back on Route 66, we continued west and out of Gallup's business-district limits. The road became less busy and less populated until we were back on two lanes. The railroad tracks came back into sight. Gallup was behind us and the Arizona state line was on the horizon. Even though a fair amount of New Mexico's stretch of Route 66 had been swallowed up by the interstate or was on private property, what we had seen and experienced in the Land of Enchantment was a truly amazing part of our American odyssey.

Tower Conoco Station and U-Drop Inn Cafe, Shamrock, TX.
Photo By David J. Schwartz.

Big Texan Steak Ranch, Amarillo, TX. Photo By David J. Schwartz.

Old café sign, Adrian, TX. Photo By David J. Schwartz.

Ghost town of Glenrio at the Texas–New Mexico border. Photo By David J. Schwartz.

Blue Swallow Motel, Tucumcari, NM. Photo By David J. Schwartz.

Rio Pecos Ranch Truck Terminal, Santa Rosa, NM. Photo By David J. Schwartz.

Jack Rabbit Trading Post sign, Joseph City, AZ. Photo By David J. Schwartz.

Remnants of Twin Arrows Trading Post, Winslow, AZ.
Photo By David J. Schwartz.

Grand Canyon Caverns, Peach Springs, AZ. Photo By David J. Schwartz.

Historic Seligman Sundries, Seligman, AZ. Photo By David J. Schwartz.

Oatman Highway, west of Oatman, AZ. Photo By David J. Schwartz.

Route 66 in the Mojave Desert, CA. Photo By David J. Schwartz.

Roy's Motel and Cafe, Amboy, CA. Photo By David J. Schwartz.

Wigwam Motel, Rialto, CA. Photo By David J. Schwartz.

Part 3

Into the Desert

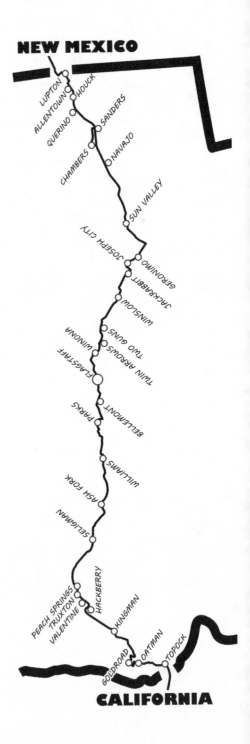

39

WITHOUT A DOUBT, when pondering our American odyssey and planning the itinerary, we were hugely excited to get into Arizona, and experience the state's famed natural beauty and Wild West pioneer heritage. There is something magical about the American Southwest. Not only has it historically been a place of pilgrimage for adventure seekers, but it is also a land steeped in legend and lore. It is home to people who have built their lives and futures in these remote spaces, under the glaring sun—and for some, far off the conventional gridiron.

Crossing into Arizona, we were greeted by the high sandstone bluffs that keep watch over Lupton and the start of the celebrated Arizona Indian trading posts that stand out firmly at the base of the hills. We cruised past unassuming little towns like Allentown, Houck, Sanders, and Chambers. Time was not on our side, so we decided not to detour into the Painted Desert National Park, but from the roadside, we could still appreciate the incredible scenic beauty that defines the area: hues that ranged from earthy red to more vivid shades of lavender. Colorful rocks were sprawled across the spectacular land, painted an orangish gold. It was astounding.

We kept a watchful eye for a marker pointing us toward the Jack Rabbit Trading Post in Joseph City, a location that has kept a respected star on the Route 66 map since 1949. The building, rumored to have been built by the Atlantic and Pacific Railroad (which later became part of the AT&SF), once housed a snake farm and gift shop, and then was used as a restaurant and dance hall, before Joseph City resident James Taylor leased the property in 1949 and turned it into the Jack Rabbit Trading

Post. During the glory days of 66, numerous giant billboards urging motorists to visit the trading post lined the highway, each depicting a giant jackrabbit silhouette on a bright-yellow background and a mileage countdown to its location. The advertising campaign, stretching from Illinois to California, became an emblem of the road itself. These were the days when road travel was fun and offered an adventure. In modern days, the iconic road signs no longer exist, save for one that is located at the site of the Trading Post.

We took the exit into Joseph City, known as the oldest Mormon settlement on Route 66 in Arizona, dating back to 1876, in search of the store. As we drove down the quiet main street, there was that great apocalyptic vibe typical of so many small southwestern towns. There was a pulpable emptiness as we passed abandoned crumbling structures that decorated the thorny landscape, a testimony to dreams that failed to stand the test of time. We ended up at a dead-end section of the road and had to double back, slowly tracking our way across I-40 and down a slightly rutted frontage road toward the outpost. And then we saw it, the emblematic billboard depicting a large rabbit followed by a bunch of bunnies running along the top with big bold letters: "HERE IT IS." We had found it.

"Welcome to the Jack Rabbit Trading Post. Can I help you find anything?" a man asked when we entered. This was Tony, we learned, who owns the shop with his wife, Cindy. Tony was stocky in build, with a friendly face, short brown hair, and warm eyes. His ample mustache ran down the sides of his mouth, meeting again at his chin to form a goatee. He was dressed in a simple white T-shirt that had "Route 66" emblazoned on the front pocket and a pair of faded jeans. He appeared totally relaxed in his surroundings.

Kate and Thembi moseyed over to some hand-carved wooden guns that had caught Thembi's attention, while I entered into a serious conversation with Tony over the best hot sauces to select from their decent assortment.

"I don't want something too sweet, or so spicy that I can't taste the food," I explained.

"I totally get ya. Well now, let's look. We do sell a number of good brands. It comes down to individual taste, of course, right? But I would try this one—at least it's the most popular one here. I've not heard any complaints," Tony suggested.

I was reading the ingredients on the back of a second option when a younger man with short brown hair, wearing a dark-gray hoodie with "I Dig California Girls" across the front in big white letters, looked up from the shelves. "You don't want to get that stuff," he said. "It's shit, man. Totally glorified ketchup."

"Yeah, it's a bit bland. I think they use weak chiles or water it down or something," added his female companion, flipping through a book. "He's right, I would get the Arizona Cowboy stuff."

An old man inserted himself into the discussion, emerging from behind the back shelf as though from thin air and startling the California-girl lover. "Damn, man! You made me jump. Damn!" the young man shouted, bending over with his hands on his knees and shaking his head.

The old man ignored him and continued his interjection. "You know, a good hot sauce is hard to find, hard to find, indeed. Say, where y'all from anyhow?"

Tony hollered to his wife to come over. "Cindy knows more about these hot sauces than me." Down there in Arizona, it seemed that hot sauce was an emotive topic.

After much discussion and debate from seemingly everyone in the shop, I settled on both a red and a green Arizona Cowboy Hot Sauce, as Tony had suggested. A lot seemed to be riding on my choices.

"I'll take this one," Thembi announced, grinning proudly. In his hands was the largest of the guns, a double-barreled toy shotgun, equipped with a zillion elastic bands in place of bullets.

"No, get a smaller one, maybe a handgun, please," I suggested. Guns are not very common in Africa, believe it or not, unless you are a criminal or a member of a militia group, so he was thrilled to be able to choose from such a wide selection.

"Aw, Dad. Okay, let me look." After another twenty minutes of debating the qualities of a dozen pistols, he finally chose. The wooden gun was used a dozen times after the trip but was quickly broken within a week of getting home. He didn't seem to even notice.

Outside, when we had finished our shopping for the day, the desert sun had become blinding, causing us to take a step back. An impressively heavyset man with a bushy beard and a minute, two-door silver car, covered in stickers from every place he had visited on the road—and there had been many—relaxed beside the large fiberglass hare that guarded over the shop. We noticed that his plates were from Nova Scotia. We have family on the East Coast and I went to university in Halifax for my master's degree. What a small world.

"Have you driven all the way from Halifax?" I asked. (That was around 3,100 miles!)

"Yep," he said, passively. "Just me and Sammy, my Boston terrier."

The small dog was jumping around from seat to seat in the car, excited to see some new faces.

"He's likely the best travel companion I've ever had. He just sleeps most of the time, but when he's awake, he likes to sit on the passenger seat and keep me company," he said. "Are you guys doing Route 66? All the way? Where did you get on? I was just over in Vegas and decided to check out some of the road. I met some folks in Vegas who were from France and they said that Arizona was a great place to jump on, so Sammy and I decided to do so. I told my sister I'll try to be home for my birthday, though."

"Oh, when is that?" Kate asked.

"The end of October." He had a few months.

"How long have you been on the road?" I asked. His car looked rather weathered. I was surprised that it had carried him that far, and he still had a lot of tarmac to put under his balding tires.

"About two months now. But I think I'm ready to head back east again. I've seen pretty much everything that I care to now."

Thembi was playing with Sammy through the half-opened driver's window. He was tickling the top of the dog's head and laughing. The back seat of the small vehicle was a disordered mess of clothes, blankets, food wrappers, and everyday items. The car looked lived in.

"So where have you been sleeping?" I asked.

"We try to camp whenever possible. Often we just crash in the car. It's good enough for us. Sammy doesn't seem to mind."

It was difficult to imagine how such a large man could bed down in the back seat of the overcrowded, miniscule vehicle, but he seemed to be making do. Traveling America's two-lane highways is an adventure unto itself. You meet a lot of unusual characters, each with their own peculiarities and stories.

40

IT WAS EARLY morning and the street was empty when we approached the corner of Kinsley Avenue and East Second Street in Winslow, Arizona. This was the corner that became internationally famous after the release of the hit single "Take It Easy," penned by Jackson Browne and the late Glenn Frey, and recorded by the hugely successful band the Eagles. Many people may not know that the track was actually the band's first single, released in May 1972, and partially the result of an eventful road trip that Jackson Browne had taken through Arizona in 1971.

What great lyrics. So simple and honest. And now, standing on that corner in Winslow, Arizona, the town that inspired the musician to write the song, there was a true sense of being somewhere that had helped form a significant piece of pop culture. With no one around, it was easy to tune out the insanity of the modern world and ponder Browne's personal experience, right there on that corner in the middle of America— that is, until a horde of manic tourists descended on the landmark, eager and impatient to get their picture taken next to the statue of an unnamed musician that decorated the spot. We sat on a nearby bench, watching the chaotic scene play out, in the hope that they would soon depart. I was amazed at how many pictures of the exact same snap they took. How many variations does one's vacation photo album require? Apparently a lot. After about a half hour, we finally gave up and decided to check out some of the souvenir shops that lined East Second Street, pay a visit to the Tiny Church of the Mother Road—which was just big enough to fit our family of three—and explore Winslow's Old Trails Museum.

We had been told about a pretty outdoor water recreation area just outside of town called McHood Park Lake, also known as Clear Creek Reservoir. Later that day, we went over to have a look. The lake came into sight after driving southeast on Highway 99 for a little over six miles, but it felt much longer as we made our way through barren earth and empty roadway. It is funny how getting somewhere always seems to take much longer than going back. It must be the anticipation of searching for something new.

The road toward the recreation area followed the creek to its left, tracing its path along the shore, while the water wound its path close to the one-hundred-foot-high Coconino Sandstone cliffs on its right. The water can reach depths of up to twenty-five feet, so it remains cool, but not too cold, all year round. It was a tranquil place, dotted with other vehicles, each parked at a sufficient distance from one another so as not to disturb other enthusiasts. It is definitely a hidden haunt, largely kept secret by the locals. In the distance was a cute little bridge that we would have crossed over to get to the other side of the creek if we had continued down the road.

"Let's park on this hill," suggested Kate. "We can walk down to the edge of the water and still keep an eye on the vehicle."

"Can I get in?" asked Thembi. "I feel like a swim."

"No," Kate and I answered at the same time. We didn't know this place or what lived in its depths.

"Look," pointed Thembi, "There is someone down in the water."

An older woman was busy playing with her dog on the shore, throwing a ball into the brown lake, to the dog's delight. Sensing us coming, the canine froze and began to growl. He was not a large dog, but he was effectively menacing.

"Oh, stop it," she told him. "Leave these people alone."

Smiling, she waved to us as we walked carefully down a steep incline toward the water. "He's all bark and no bite. Don't worry about him." Bending down to pat his wet fur and rigid, alert frame, she soothed him. "Isn't that true, Angus? You're a good dog, aren't you?" She spoke to him in that irritating way that people do to small children and animals. The dog just looked up at her.

We began to speak softly to Angus, and he relaxed. Behind him, a huge splash upset the water as a man emerged out of nowhere, startling us. We had no idea that someone was beneath the surface.

"Oh, don't worry about Tom," she said, noticing us jump. "He was down under looking for shells and treasure, I guess. Tom, come on out and meet . . . sorry, dears, what are your names? I'm Margie."

We introduced ourselves and Thembi reached down to pat Angus, who was now calmer but not overly interested in us. Garbage was strewn in the long grass just on the edge of the water, with plastic cups and empty beer bottles scattered along the ground.

"Isn't it just terrible?" Margie quipped. "I went around and collected a bunch of trash the last time that we were here, but people, I think they're teenagers, like to come here and have bonfires and party, and they just leave their trash everywhere. They have no respect for keeping nature as they find it."

Mosquitoes were starting to bite as they emerged from the long grass with the cooling of the afternoon. Kate swatted at one that was flying around her face, which caused Angus to start barking excitedly again.

"Angus, settle down now," said Tom, shooing the dog away. "That's the bad part of being down by the water at this time of day. The mosquitoes will eat you alive!" He laughed while drying off and threw on a T-shirt that he grabbed from the open back of their pickup truck.

"Do you guys live near here?" Kate asked.

"Oh yes, we live not too far from here, just about ten miles away. Tom used to come here to swim all the time when he was young. I'm originally from Scottsdale myself, but we've been in Winslow for . . . well, a long time now. We raised our two daughters and son here actually," said Margie. "They're all grown and have moved on to start their own families. Now we have grandchildren. But we don't get to see them as much as we would like to. They're all very busy with their work and lives."

Tom wrapped his arm around her and acknowledged her sentiments.

"Our son works for the railway, just like his father used to," added Margie.

"I'm retired now, but I spent my career with the railway, mostly in management," Tom explained. "I think he got the bug from me. It was a good life. A man could make a decent living on the trains and there were always opportunities for advancement. But now even that has changed . . ." Tom's last words trailed off in a sad reverie of times past.

"So what do you guys like to do with your time now? Winslow is a bit of a sleepy town," I asked.

"We travel a lot. We also volunteer at the retirement home in Winslow," Margie said. "A lot of the senior citizens can't get out and get around like we can. Many of them are people we've known for a long time. We enjoy visiting with them and helping out as we can."

"Might be us in there soon enough," Tom joked.

"True, very, very true," she said, laughing.

As darkness approached and the Arizona sky turned from blue to vibrant shades of orange, pink, and red, we bade the pair goodbye and thanked them for their time and conversation. It had been a full day in Winslow.

41

"I JUST HAD my picture taken with Ziggy Marley and my dog, Goya," said Tina Mion, co-owner and resident artist at La Posada. "She also has dreadlocks. It's so cute."

"Ziggy is around?" I asked, surprised but excited at the possibility of seeing him again. I worked with Ziggy in 2014 when we did a big cover story for *Destination Magazine* in promotion of his *Fly Rasta* album. It was fascinating listening to him discuss his reggae-legend father, Bob Marley, and hear him talk about trips they took and the icon's philosophies on life and happiness.

"He's really a nice person," Tina said. "He was here en route for a concert he's performing in Tucson. But he checked out this morning."

I was disappointed.

That is the world of La Posada in Winslow. It attracts holidayers, history buffs, celebrities, artists, and philosophers from around the world, each of them looking to experience the magic of the gem of the Fred Harvey railway hotels.

La Posada, our home for the next few days, opened its doors in the 1930s, during the Great Depression, but was never very profitable during that period. The brainchild of Fred Harvey—who developed and ran all of the hotels connected to the Santa Fe railways—La Posada (which means "the resting place") was intended to be the finest hotel in the Southwest, complete with the best linens, china, silverware, and service. And it was, for twenty-seven years, until it was closed to the public in 1957. By 1993, the railway announced plans to do away with the hotel and bulldoze it to the ground. However, as with so many wonderful places on Route 66, the National Trust for Historic Preservation found out about La Posada's peril and added it to their endangered list, where it caught the attention of Tina Mion and her husband, Allan Affeldt.

Affeldt and partners tirelessly negotiated with the transportation giant for three years before finally resolving a myriad of legal, environmental, and financial obstacles. Finally, with a truckload of patience and commitment, the trio of Allan, Tina, and their university friend and fellow artist, Daniel Lutzick, took ownership of the property in 1997. They have been injecting their love, artistic talents, and energy into the property ever since. In modern times, La Posada stands as a testament not only to their efforts and forethought but to the vision of Fred Harvey and the creativity of the building's designer, Mary Colter, arguably the most influential female architect of her time.

Sitting outside with Tina, I listened to the trains rattle as they passed and admired the beautiful landscape that makes up the hotel's lush garden. Amtrak stops right in front of the hotel, just as the other passenger trains did in olden days.

"When we first took over La Posada, the building was in a terrible state of disrepair," Tina said. "We used to have to chase squatters away. There was a great deal to be done. But we heard about this amazing hotel that was about to be destroyed and just had to do something to save it. And, little by little, we've managed to restore La Posada to its former glory. It's such a wonderful place."

Tina beamed as she spoke about the hotel, carefully watching the groundskeeper as he mowed the expansive lawn. Route 66 is packed with wonderful vintage motels and properties, but upmarket, classy hotels like La Posada are no less important to the experience and speak to the eclectic style of the Mother Road in the Southwest.

———

I WAS MEANDERING La Posada's spacious lawn, looking for Thembi and Kate, when I heard giggling coming from a miniature haybale maze that decorated the property. Thembi was hiding from his mom and refusing to be found. Kate was no longer having fun—I could hear it in her tone—but Thembi loved a good game of hide-and-go-seek.

"Oh, Dad's here," Kate called, with gratitude in her voice. "Let's go, *now*." She stressed the final word.

He remained hidden. She called again, but still no movement. He was committed.

"It's time to go for lunch, Thembi," I finally chided with a slightly sterner voice. "And we have a surprise for you. We're going to visit a famous rock and mineral shop in Holbrook."

That was all it took to displace him from his well-chosen corner in the maze. He was a rock-and-mineral fanatic. Bursting upright, he blew past us toward the hotel parking lot.

Backtracking thirty-three miles east, an easy jaunt from Winslow, we found Holbrook to be a cozy little town, famous for its midcentury Wigwam Village Motel, where guests get to sleep in an "actual" wigwam. Well, maybe not a real one, but it certainly offers the aura of a traditional structure. In fact, the design is not that of a wigwam at all, but rather a tepee. A wigwam is traditionally a semipermanent, dome-shaped structure that was prominent with the Indigenous people of the Northeast, while tepees were temporary, cone-shaped dwellings that were popular with the people of the Great Plains. However, when entrepreneur Frank A. Redford was first inspired to dive into the motel business in 1935, he supposedly did not understand the difference and inaccurately named his motel Wigwam Village.

Redford was a man with a vision. But what most people do not realize is that he himself was on a road trip when he conceived of the idea for his motel chain. While visiting Long Beach, California, Redford spotted a lunch stand that was shaped and painted in the fashion of a tepee. He loved the concept. Once back home in Horse Cave, Kentucky, he set to work to build his own lunch counter and fueling station. And yes, he built them in the shape of what he thought was a traditional wigwam. He finished in 1933, and customers soon began encouraging him to add rooms to the eatery—and, again, his dreaming took off. The original, which he called Village #1, was completed in 1935 and constructed around a large shop that housed his impressive collection of Native American artifacts. He applied for a patent on the ornamental design of the structures, which he received in 1936.

Village #2 in Cave City, Kentucky, close to Mammoth Cave National Park, was born in 1937. Three more were to come by 1940. In 1950, Chester E. Lewis purchased the design rights from Redford and constructed the Holbrook property—Village #6—selecting a key location right on Route 66 and an easy drive to the Grand Canyon, Petrified Forest National Park, and Meteor Crater. Like #1, Holbrook's village also originally had a gas station. The motel closed its doors in 1974, when Holbrook was bypassed by the faster-moving interstate. Two years after his death in 1986, Lewis's children renovated and reopened the motel.

In a nod to Village #6's role in classic Americana, it was listed on the National Register of Historic Places on May 2, 2002.

Today there are only three motels of this unique style left in the country, with another Route 66 one in Rialto, California, and the third in Kentucky. At one point, the nation was graced with seven Wigwam Village Motels, but true roadside kitsch and hardcore Americana has been steadily fading over the decades and we have sadly lost the others. But the story of the classic Wigwam Village Motel remains a good one.

We hadn't planned to spend a night there, but wandering the quiet compound, alone with the wigwams and old, rusting vehicles, we could appreciate the role that these villages played in inspiring roadside Americana.

———

Holbrook has long been a favorite among Route 66 travelers. It is a destination that is, according to its own website, "steeped in Native American culture, Hispanic roots, and pioneers from all walks of life." The town has some very picturesque architecture and faded but expressive murals on a number of its downtown walls. After a quick visit to the supposedly haunted Navajo Courthouse (we didn't see any ghosts) and a stroll through its lively older section of town, we decided it was time to grab some food.

One café called out to us in particular, as it was noted in many of the guidebooks, but after a disappointing lunch, where we barely touched the food—and questionable hygiene practices, we discreetly paid the bill and made our exit. Our experience echoed a complaint that we had had since we started the trip: Guidebooks seem to wax lyrical about many of the same vintage Route 66 diners, praising their service, cuisine, and atmosphere. However, we'd had a number of misses on this journey and no longer trusted recommendations that romanticized a venue simply based on its history and location on the Mother Road.

Traffic began to build up along West Hopi Drive and we were forced to wait for a few minutes to cross the road. Two policemen passed us on foot as they headed to their patrol car, nodding hello to us and chatting in Spanish as they went. Traversing the crosswalk, we saw two giant, green, cartoony-looking brontosauruses on the right, standing guard over a wide variety of colorful geodes and rocks. We had discovered one of Holbrook's famed rock shops. To me, the offerings were little more than bright earthy stones, no big deal. But Thembi felt like he had hit the mother lode, and began roving neck deep through a veritable treasure trove. Rushing from table to table, he was enamored with everything on display, busily explaining to us what each rock or mineral was. The proprietor, a slightly heavyset older man arrived and opened the front door. "Welcome inside," he beckoned.

Under the shop's roof rested shelves and shelves—and even more shelves—of minerals, rocks and gems, petrified wood, dinosaur bones and claws, and pretty much anything and everything that a geologist could ever hope to discover. As Thembi and Kate spied out the place, I walked over to the checkout counter to strike up a conversation. At first, the owner seemed standoffish, but soon, he relaxed and began to share his story. "I moved to Arizona from Mexico when I was six," he began. "You know, I learned hard work early. By eight years old, I was picking fruit in the field. It taught me responsibility. Kids these days do not know responsibility. At the age of fifteen, I learned to weld and then got a job with Toyota, as a welder. I taught myself. Did you see the dinosaurs out front? I built those myself. No one showed me how. I taught myself. You do not know me, but I know myself," he said.

Okay, that was deeper than I intended to go when I went over to talk with him, but I listened intently. His story was interesting, but probably not unique to the region.

"You know, Anglos—do you know what an Anglo is? You are an Anglo, a white man. Here in America, Anglos speak better English than some of us, and so they feel superior and other people consider them superior. They don't know me, but I know me. I built those dinosaurs and did not go to college. Anglos go to college, but they cannot build those dinosaurs. You cannot build those dinosaurs. You don't know me, but I know who I am. Do you understand?" he continued.

I think I did. In a clearly earnest manner, he was expressing an inner understanding of his own perceived abilities and potential. In a world where people are easily cast off and disregarded due to their appearance or education, accent or skin tone, he had a solid self-awareness and was proud to proclaim his accomplishments. If more of us possessed his quiet confidence and had more respect for each other, the world would likely be a much better place.

Amazingly, it took him around twenty years to build the seven dinosaurs situated out front, using cement and reinforcing rods. That was serious commitment.

It had been about forty-five minutes since we entered his shop and it was now time to go.

"Thank you for sharing your life experiences with me," I said. "You have an amazing shop."

He nodded. "Sometimes I talk too much. I'm sorry if I've kept you."

"Not at all, you've given me something to think about," I reassured him.

Outside, the bright sun shone down in our eyes, blinding us after being in the dimness of the shop for so long. "Wait!" he called, rushing around the counter and to the door. "This is for the young man." There was a gentleness as he handed Thembi a small plastic triceratops.

"Thank you very much. It is my favorite species of dinosaur."

The old man grinned, making his way over to a new group of customers who had arrived.

———

THAT EVENING, AFTER a fantastic dinner at La Posada's famed Turquoise Room restaurant, we decided to grab a bottle of wine and head over to the Little Painted Desert County Park to enjoy its spectacular scenic views and take in a desert sunset. The park is only eighteen miles from La Posada, and as we made our way up a long lonely paved road, we were uncertain of what we would discover.

"Are you sure we are going the right way?" I asked Kate. The drive down County Road 282 felt like it was getting a little long.

Gazing down at the information she had recorded from an online map, she was confident that our turnoff was just up ahead. So we continued.

The light from the day was already beginning to slant, and a slight breeze began to build. We drove with the windows down, our arms outstretched, soaking in the air. Then on our left, we spotted it, the turnoff to the park. The short drive in took us to a small picnic area with sheltered tables that provided an exquisite view of the red and orange hills as they rose and undulated in breathtaking folds. God sure does know how to weave a beautiful tapestry.

We walked along the rim for some time, tossing stones down into the creases of the dry earth. There in that lonesome spot, the three of us had only each other. We laughed and joked, pretending to stumble over the edge, competing to see who could throw pebbles the farthest. It was a wonderful night, until a van made its way toward the picnic area and a half dozen teenagers exploded from inside the white vehicle. It was a youth group doing a short excursion to supposedly watch a sunset for themselves. Their noisy chatter and shouting disrupted our tranquility and we began to pack up, disappointed and irritated—but, hey, they had a right to be there too.

Then, to our horror, they excitedly removed a large car tire from somewhere inside the van and worked furiously to thrust the rubber over the edge and down into the canyon. We watched in disbelief as the leader of the group, an older man in wiry glasses and a beige T-shirt, encouraged them on. We wanted to say something, to scold them or warn them, but we didn't. I'm not sure why. When they had successfully done their part to damage the environment, they crowded back into their van and headed off. Thembi and I walked over to the rim and looked down—perhaps we could climb down and retrieve the tire? But it had disappeared and was nowhere to be found. What was the point of jetting an old tire into a park?

As we turned around to head out, we noticed a locked-up restroom that had itself become a tapestry for local graffiti. Why can people not simply appreciate history and natural beauty without feeling the need to leave their mark or destroy it? The sun set peacefully as we turned onto the county road and made our way back to the hotel in silence.

42

THE GRAND CANYON State had thus far proven to be all that we had hoped and more, with its endless diversity and laid-back but boundless energy. There is an ethereal beauty to the state. In many ways, Arizona reminded me of northern Kenya. Only 280 miles outside the capital city of Nairobi, the gateway to the north, Samburu, could not be more different than the city center if it tried. The topography and culture change dramatically once one passes Mount Kenya, giving way to arid and semiarid land and groups of people who resist "modern enlightenment." Arizona, outside of the bigger cities, is very similar. The desert attracts freethinkers who are looking for space and liberty—to be who they want to be and embrace life in a manner that best suits them, often far outside of the accepted norm. The air, both literally and symbolically, just seems clearer and easier to breathe in the lonely desert of Arizona.

We were pushing on west of Winslow and decided to spend some time alone with the wind and the birdsong, some five hundred feet into the heavens, staring down at a gigantic hole left by a giant meteorite crashing to earth. Known as Meteor Crater or Barringer Crater, after Daniel M. Barringer, one of the first people to propose that the crevice was the result of a meteorite impacting the earth approximately fifty thousand years ago, it is an amazing natural phenomenon. We stood alone at one of the lookout points, high above the crater, quiet and in awe of the fantastic views of the surrounding landscape. We were by ourselves; the multitudes that we found upon our arrival had come, seen, and left. It was a peaceful moment on the top of the world. Far down below, miniature dust devils blew across the barren earth.

"*Scusa*," someone said, tapping me on the shoulder. "Is it you?"

It took me a second, but I recognized them. It was the honeymooning Italian couple from Galena.

"Oh, hi! How are you guys doing?" I asked. It was so crazy to bump into them again, especially so far down the road from southeastern Kansas.

They were the first people we had stumbled upon a second time during the trip.

"You here long?" asked the gent, his brown eyes open wide.

"Not really, just about an hour. You guys?"

He stared at me, and then turned to his wife, who seemed to translate my question. "Ah, no, we just arrive. It is, how you say . . . amazing, no?"

"Yes, it is. By the way, we don't know your names," I responded. "I'm Brennen," I said, touching my chest. "And this is Kate, and Thembi."

"Marco, *e mia moglie*, Sophia." She smiled, embraced him, and then walked to the edge of the wooden platform to admire the view. It was getting warmer as the morning rolled on.

It was quiet for a few more minutes as we admired the natural wonder together, until a large crowd made their way excitedly to the platform to encounter the unearthly phenomenon for themselves. Bidding farewell to the couple again, we dashed to the vehicle and made for the hills. Literally.

As we headed back down the dusty road, we took a quick detour and found a peaceful place to hide out of sight. Kate threw down a picnic blanket and we relaxed in the shade of the vehicle while we consumed our first meal of the day and listened as cars passed us in the distance, heading toward and away from the crater. The hard ground was covered in small anthills and the voracious insects marched to and fro across the desert, scurrying in all directions. A bevy of flies soon discovered us and, more importantly, our food. They proved to be relentless. After forty-five minutes of waving our arms in the air to brush them away, we decided to push on.

On the interstate again, lots of vehicles were cruising by, with odd breaks in traffic, leaving us alone for a few moments on the roadway before another surge of semi-trucks and cars from across the country approached mysteriously from behind before whizzing past. I've always wondered where these bursts of traffic come from. One minute the road is dead quiet and the next you are inundated with a hoard of flying vehicles that appear as if from nowhere before vanishing into the distance. It is bizarre. The desert stretched out beside the highway, its emptiness hiding all of the diverse wildlife that call the wasteland home, only emerging in the cooler, safer hours of the night.

We made a quick but memorable stop at the Meteor City Trading Post—opened by Joseph Sharber in 1938 as a Texaco service station. Sharber then sold it to Jack Newsum in 1941, who renamed it Meteor City, after the nearby crater. Visitors could purchase gas, food, and assorted curios. A roadside sign at the time advertised the location as having a population of one. (When Newsum married in 1946, he updated the population to two.) Defunct at the time of our visit, the attraction once seduced motorists off the speeding roadway and was the location for a scene from the 1984 classic movie *Starman*, starring Jeff Bridges. Once a creatively crafted shop, now the post's adjacent tepees and giant dream catcher simply sat idle, shaking in the wind and baking in the desert sun. It is a moody place that holds a forlorn atmosphere. A long, lonely dirt road runs past it, traversing the land in a mysterious, eerie manner as it rolls past dilapidated billboards that ceased to pull traffic long ago. Pieces of the rotting wood rested on the ground at the feet of the structures, making the trading post look all the more abandoned. We loved it.

After the trading post, we made another short stop at Two Guns, a totally abandoned tourist destination whose resort was now covered in graffiti. Vandals had not been kind to the lonely relic. It was another sad reminder of lost dreams from a bygone time, another in a long line of discarded places that had been ruined by local graffiti artists who seemed unable to appreciate the value of simply enjoying the deserted without any form of molestation.

"This feels a bit creepy," Kate said, carefully observing the thick brush and mounds of broken concrete. "Why would anyone want to destroy such a place?"

"I'm not sure. But it makes me angry," I responded. "These places are such an important part of history on Route 66. And if they close, at least visitors should be allowed to experience the ghosts of the route. This just ruins the moment."

A large black lizard with vertical white stripes jumped up on a rock beside me, waving his long tail to the side. Another quickly joined him, and then another. The area was packed with them.

The picturesque but now-deteriorating Canyon Diablo Bridge rests behind the broken-down structures, providing a window into the canyon and the surrounding areas. Even in its wildness, it remains a serene, lovely scene. Hidden from plain view, a path leads down to a spot overlooking the cliff where the famed Apache Death Cave is located. This mysterious place attracts curious travelers searching for a ghostly experience, but the steep hills and shifting gravel deterred us from venturing too far down. That said, the tale is a tragic but fascinating one.

As the story goes, in 1878, forty-two Apache warriors raided two Navajo camps located along the Little Colorado River and killed everyone except for three girls, whom they took captive. Discovering what had happened, twenty-five Navajo warriors pursued them, tracking them to a cave where they could hear voices. Soon the warriors located the mouth of the cave in a ravine and, after killing the two guards who were placed to keep watch, dropped large amounts of wood into the entrance of the cave and started a huge fire. The Apaches tried to negotiate their way out but that did not work. Then they tried to use whatever water they had to douse the fire, and when that did not work, killed their horses and tried to use their blood to put the flames out. Finally, in desperation, they stacked the dead horses near the entrance to try to keep the flames away.

In the end, they all perished, including the captive girls, and the Navajos departed. Legend has it that from that day, local tribes avoided the cave due to a deeply held belief that the area was cursed. It is a story that fits perfectly into the rocky desert landscape and the mystery of Arizona's Route 66.

And if that was not enough, there is more death and sadness connected to the location.

In 1922, Earle Cundiff, a World War I army veteran from Arkansas, and his wife, Louise, decided to construct a trading post at what seemed to be an ideal spot, right where the Little Colorado River crossed the National Old Trails Road. The business had big plans and included a restaurant, a fuel station, and some cottages for road travelers. Route 66 would be born four years later, so their timing was terrific.

In 1925, the couple, needing a bit of cash infusion, decided to lease out a portion of their land to a dubious character named Harry "Indian" Miller. The conman successfully convinced the couple and anyone who would listen that he was in fact an Apache chief who went by the name of Chief Crazy Thunder. The pair entered into a ten-year agreement with the crook, and excitedly planned for the future.

At this time, Miller, or Chief Crazy Thunder, employed Hopi tribesmen to construct phony stone ruins just above the Apache Death Cave, calling the attraction Mystery Cave. He even sold skulls and bones of supposed dead Apache warriors as tokens and souvenirs. It was an idea for its time, and business boomed.

In addition, Miller constructed a stone structure that he called Fort Two Guns. The establishment included a gift shop and a zoo with mountain lions, bobcats, and snakes, among other things.

On March 3, 1926, Miller and Cundiff got into a dispute over the terms of their agreement and Chief Crazy Thunder shot and killed an unarmed Cundiff. The act was committed in cold blood but after a trial, Miller was surprisingly acquitted and returned to Two Guns.

Louise remarried in 1934. When she and her husband sold Two Guns in 1950, the once-bustling tourist trap entered into a decade of decline.

The cursed nature of the otherwise picturesque stopover was undeniable, but then again, so was the surreal, magnetic pull of the place's history and story. Alone in the desert, it is slowly wasting away.

"Let's get out of here," Kate suggested.

The walk back to the vehicle revealed a minefield of sharp nails that had been scattered over the dry earth, each waiting to puncture unsuspecting tires. We were in the literal middle of nowhere and multiple punctures would have been a disaster to both our tires and our plans for the day.

"Thembi and I will pick up as many of these nails as we can," I said to Kate. "We'll make a path and you can drive slowly behind us and get the car out of the parking lot." She nodded and jumped behind the wheel.

Rumor has it that the current owner of the defunct property put the nails on the ground himself in order to discourage visitors from frequenting the attraction. If true, it is a really nasty way to get a message across. But after twenty minutes—there were a lot of potential pokers—we had managed to clear the assault and get safely back on the tarmac. As we did, an SUV pulled in and a large family excitedly jumped out.

"Give me a second," I said. "I want to go and warn these guys to be careful where they park."

Grateful, the heavyset, gray-haired father of four from New York offered a heartfelt thank-you. "Okay, everyone, back in the truck," he insisted. "We're going to give this one a miss." He nodded to me as he pulled out.

It was ninety-five degrees in the sun and back in the vehicle we had the AC on full blast, but it was only denting the onslaught of the Arizona heat. The sun was intense. Back in Winslow, we had been told about an older couple who were hiking out in the California desert of Route 66 at the wrong time of day. Ill prepared, lost, and somehow separated from each other, the woman had managed to call 911, but when help arrived, her body was found lifeless. Her companion was never located.

Apparently, this is not a lone incident. Hikers and road travelers fall victim to the elements and oppressive heat more often than people realize. Desert travel needs to be given its due respect.

43

ONLY AN HOUR and a half west of Winslow, Williams is a tourist town through and through. It's a fun place full of activities and entertainment, geared toward the large numbers of visitors who are heading out to the Grand Canyon or to discover the quirky joys of Route 66. Williams boasts the Bearizona Wildlife Park, many museums, including the Planes of Fame Air Museum, innumerable restaurants and 66-era cafés and bars, and even a classic train ride to the Grand Canyon. There is also the Route 66 Zipline, which Kate was determined to try.

"Come on," she pleaded. "Let's just do it once. It'll be fun."

"No way! Look at that thing," I said as I watched a couple screaming as they flew through the air. "Not a freakin' chance."

"Thembi, you'll come up with me, right?" she asked.

Thembi was not quite certain himself. His eyes demonstrated clear distrust for the contraption hurtling across the still Arizona sky.

"Oh, come on. You guys are so boring. This is why we are traveling, to make memories. We'll never forget riding the Route 66 Zipline." That was my fear.

"Fine, but only once," Thembi said, breaking under the pressure. But I think he was actually excited to go for the ride.

They made their way up a set of stairs toward the contraption of death, and climbed in. From the safety of the ground, I watched as the zipline chairlift slowly went in reverse, the vintage red vehicle at the top of the carriage appearing to back up as my family's legs dangled precariously over the edge of the seat. Then I heard a click. They had reached the end and were ready to motor into oblivion. Suddenly, Kate started to scream and there was a rush in the sky. It was over before I knew it, but the zipline vehicle flew past in the air above Williams and deposited my family safely onto the platform at the bottom.

Back down on the reliable concrete, the pair had different responses.

"Let's do that again, Thembi!" Kate said excitedly.

"No, no way!" said Thembi, putting his arm around my shoulder and coming in for a cuddle. "Once is enough." I laughed and shot Kate a knowing glance.

Above our heads a new couple shrieked madly as their vintage vehicle flew by. They were obviously having the time of their lives.

Williams has an interesting, even unique, fact going for it: it was the last town on Route 66, between Chicago and Santa Monica, to be bypassed by the interstate. President Eisenhower's Advisory Committee for a National Highway Program sought to modernize America's highways. The plan that was eventually put in place was meant to make road travel safer and faster. And from 1970 to 1985, the Mother Road slowly disappeared from popular use. The new interstate highways were now in vogue. In October 1984, I-40 replaced the town's enviable stretch of old Route 66. On June 27, 1985, Route 66 was officially fully decommissioned.

When an Elvis impersonator approached us with a curled-up lip to ask if we would like a photo op, we knew it was time to leave.

———

WE WERE LOOKING for exit 146 off I-40, for Ash Fork, when we saw a purple cross adorned with a picture on the side of the road. There were bunches of flowers surrounding it, and the photo was of a pretty Latina, maybe eighteen. We saw a lot of these crosses on the roadside once we entered the Southwest, reminders of the loss that families had experienced on the road. It was sad.

The ponderosa pines were behind us by that point and the cooler weather had given way to intense heat once again. Ash Fork was empty as we rolled through, save for a lone hitchhiker who waited patiently on the side of the highway. There must have been little traffic passing that day, as he seemed to have given up on finding a lift. He was sitting down next to his pack, his head buried in his lap. He struck a lonely figure all by himself in the midst of such a barren desert landscape. I couldn't decide whether I thought him brave or stupid, hitchhiking in today's unpredictable world. Then again, even back in the glory days of road travel, picking up a hitchhiker or looking for a lift with a stranger was not safe. You never knew who you were getting into a vehicle with.

The romantic notion of making your way across the country without money or a car, with only your wits and a warm smile, seemed a little dangerous and haphazard as we watched the young man sitting alone on the side of the highway. I was forced to reflect back to my own senseless wanderings as a once-intrepid traveler. The things I once did without hesitation now often look irresponsible and risky.

Once we got into the center of the small town, we headed to the Historical Society's Museum/Tourist Center, which was sadly closed, so we made a right to see what else might be cool to see. Suddenly, without warning, the sky erupted in a violent storm of hail, blinding us to the road ahead. We slowed to a crawl, hoping that any other motorist would do the same, should anyone else fantastically appear on the deserted route. Alas, there was nothing to see in Ash Fork that day.

Back on the interstate for a spell, we kept our eyes open for exit 139, which would take us to Crookton Road, seventeen miles of some of the prettiest Route 66 still drivable. The interstate was peppered with speeding semi-trucks and the odd lumbering vehicle, but otherwise it was relatively calm. Kate kept looking down at the guidebook and back up again.

"Make sure you don't miss the turnoff," she cautioned. Then suddenly, there it was.

We took the off-ramp and ran into grassy plains and a slew of Burma-Shave signs—humorous, lyrical road advertisements that once lined American highways of yesteryear. Each sign, one after the other, contained a sentence from a larger slogan, with the last sign delivering the final punchline: "IT WOULD HAVE BEEN MORE FUN / TO GO BY AIR / IF

WE COULD HAVE PUT / THESE SIGNS UP THERE / BURMA-SHAVE." They were a throwback to a simpler way of life, now long gone.

True to the spirit of the signs, this is a portion of the road that requires time. As we drove, the road curved to the right and then to the left, and then back to the right. Nineteen light-brown horses were grazing in the open field. It was a beautiful scene. We climbed a hill, and just over the top, thirteen cows, with five calves among them, were standing in a group watching the road. We continued to climb, and then the train came into sight, passing slowly, its whistle ringing out in the afternoon air. Westwood Ranch was on the right and then some more Burma-Shave signs: "THE ONE WHO / DRIVES WHEN / HE'S BEEN DRINKING / DEPENDS ON YOU / TO DO HIS THINKING / BURMA-SHAVE."

I was lost in my thoughts as we rolled along. This was country where I could live. I love the hot dry climate of the desert, the immense openness and unpredictability. There is a wild, untamed beauty to this part of the Southwest. I found myself wondering what properties might be available. The more I contemplated it, the more the appeal grew, the more viable the idea became. But, once again, I remembered Kevin Mueller's words back at the Blue Swallow, "It is not a life for everyone," and I began to doubt. How did one go from being in a place of transition and driving down Route 66 to investing one's life into the route, or any new town for that matter? I was wrestling with my fears and dreams when a lone motorcycle roared past, his noisy bike shattering my daydreaming.

"Look at this guy," I complained as he weaved from lane to lane, passing no one. I hate such antics, for especially personal reasons. My father was killed in a motorcycle accident when I was seventeen years old, and while I am not against motorcycle enthusiasm, I am very well aware of the dangers they pose and the need to exercise caution when on the road. Suddenly, in my rear, a dozen others approached, each pushing forward, maneuvering haphazardly in unison. Thembi looked up from his book, curious about the racket that interrupted the rhythm of the uneventful afternoon.

Harley-Davidson motorcycles surrounded us on three sides—at the rear, the front, and the left—their riders determining our speed.

Maintaining their posture, they traveled beside the vehicle for what felt like forever before thrusting forward, the last one of the group slowing down to nod as he passed.

"Just let them go," suggested Kate. "They're going to cause an accident if they keep driving like that. Luckily the road is so quiet."

Just as quickly as they appeared, they were gone, vanishing down the desert highway. We settled back into the gentle ease of the drive, once again alone with our dreams.

44

MUCH HAS BEEN written about Seligman, so we had enormous anticipation as we neared the town. Not only is it significant to Route 66—as
the destination played an integral role in the highway's development and
very survival—but it maintains a reputation for being a quintessentially
kitschy Route 66 town. For us, the stranger the better. As we entered,
we started to see small homes surrounded by scrub grass and "Route 66
Cavern or Bust" signs. On the left-hand side of the road, there was an old
pickup truck rusting in the breeze and a bunch of old worn-out tires left
in a discarded pile. Already, the town was living up to its reputation.

Starting out as a railroad camp back in 1895 before developing into an
important railroad stop along the AT&SF line, Seligman wholeheartedly
embraced the hype, popularity, and economic success that the early
Route 66 brought with it. But when the interstate circumvented Seligman in the late 1970s, it had a deep impact on through traffic. However,
unlike many of the other towns that literally died, Seligman stood its
ground and fought back.

Funky to its core, Seligman is a little different than most other Mother
Road towns. Delgadillo's Snow Cap Drive-In, the Historic Route 66
Motel, the Roadkill Cafe, and other old-time stores and shops all bring
life to this one stretch of preserved history. Seligman is, in its own right,
one of the oddest places on America's highway. As we drove into town,
several mannequins, decked out in 1920s garb, were posed in various
positions on a storefront balcony. Farther down the road, the tail end of
an airplane that had "crashed" into the side of the shop building (for
show), hung precariously from the upper level, with a tag at the end of its

tail advertising airplane rides for five dollars. The spirit of the shop was cheeky. The front entrance was cluttered with precious classic Americana items like an old gasoline pump, a vintage Ford with eyes in the windshield that made it look worried, a barrage of vintage signs, and even some type of life-size tin man. The store was the Historic Seligman Sundries, built in 1904 and still standing today. We ventured inside, where we met the new owner, Uschi, an American of Swiss origin, and a longtime Route 66 motorbike tour guide. She sold us on Seligman Sundries' "best coffee on the route" fame and reminisced about the time she spent in Kenya when she was younger. It's crazy how small the world can seem at times.

"But how did you end up here in Seligman? I mean, it's a cool town, but not necessarily the place most people end up," Kate inquired.

Uschi paused, collecting her thoughts. "My partner, Thomas, and I were both in the tourism industry and had been conducting motorcycle and bus tours across the US for many years. Our tours often brought us to Seligman, on our way to the Grand Canyon. We liked this little town for its appearance that makes people feel like they've gone back in time, and for the great job the local business community had done preserving this precious pearl on Route 66, against all odds. We had always stopped at Seligman Sundries for the European-style coffee, which was much appreciated by our international clientele. Over the years, we noticed that the motivation and efforts of the old owner had declined. The store looked neglected, to put it politely. We knew about the potential of this place and told the owners we would be interested in purchasing it. We were actually living in Flagstaff at the time and saw the chance to have something ourselves and be at home [on Route 66] and not traveling all the time."

"This town seems really popular with Europeans. Actually, the whole route has a lot of European traffic," I said. "We've met a lot of people from Italy, France, Spain, the UK, and elsewhere since the first moment we set foot on 66 tarmac."

"The myth around Route 66 and what you can see here in Seligman reminds people from these countries of a time when they looked at America with envy," she explained. "Right after World War II was a very difficult time in Europe. In the US was a wealthy middle class that was able to afford big, shiny cars, holiday travel, and comfortable accommodation along the way. For the Americans, this was just an episode in time, but for Europeans it symbolizes a period when they dreamed of a better life, and that life was believed to be found in America."

While it is safe to say that Africans do not know much about Route 66, we share a strong commonality with Europeans on how America is perceived. Back home, few people comprehend the difficulties of real life in the States. It is widely believed that the United States is the land of milk and honey and that by simply setting foot on its soil, one's life will be transformed for the better. Forever. Those who have settled in the United States and try to explain the realities to people in Africa are often viewed with suspicion, as though they do not want to share in the wealth and privilege found in the "land of the free."

Driving down Route 66 is an eye-opener for anyone interested enough to pay attention. Contrary to the sales pitch, life in the United States is not always grand and is most certainly not always easy. But many Americans do work hard and there is a definite belief that a little bit of luck and a lot of determination make a difference. Americans seem to have a huge respect for the idea of being "self-made."

Our quick stop in the store had taken on a life of its own, as we swapped stories and shared laughter with the owners, but that is the thing with Route 66: you never know what you will see, who you will meet, and what you will experience, and you can't rush it. But I could sense that my family was getting tired, and we still needed to grab a bite to eat before we checked into our motel. When the next customers walked in, we excused ourselves with a quick but heartfelt goodbye and a promise to be back to taste some of their famous coffee.

———

The streets were mute as we walked toward Delgadillo's Snow Cap, and it was easy to feel the specters of Seligman's past. A giant ice-cream cone flashed in front of us, drawing our attention to the lively diner. The exterior was a hodgepodge of vintage cars (including the "Christmas car" with an intoxicated-looking Santa Claus), jocular "outhouses," and a no-frills seating area on a covered patio. The outside of the joint was colorful and creative—almost an assault on the senses. But it was the inside, in the narrow hallway covered top to bottom with notes, IDs, and business cards from thousands of visitors from around the world, that really stood out. Thembi ordered a small root beer, and when the cheerful lady behind the counter handed him a miniscule cup of shredded ice and pop, the size of a paper ketchup holder, his eyes went big in shock. "Oh! Is that it?"

"Well," she said in a defensive tone, "you did order a small soda!" She really did look annoyed! What an actress.

Then, breaking into a huge grin, the successful gag revealed itself as she placed a real root beer on the counter. She then turned to me: "Would you like mustard on your chicken burger?"

"Yes, please."

Suddenly, without warning, she reached forward and squirted mustard all over my shirt—but thankfully, it was not real, just a yellow string that popped out of the plastic mustard bottle. Delgadillo's Snow Cap has been playing practical jokes on unsuspecting customers for over fifty years now.

Started in 1953 by the late Juan Delgadillo, who passed away in 2004, this small, peculiar eatery has become world famous for its uniqueness, tasty food, and the comedic essence of its late owner, who cultivated the restaurant's prankster culture.

We planted ourselves on the outside patio and watched the world of Seligman go by as we ate. A British couple headed for the entrance but were quickly stopped in their tracks. A look of surprise washed over their faces. The woman vigorously yanked on the doorknob, getting increasingly frustrated as the door refused to budge.

"I can't get the damn door to open," she complained, exasperated.

"Maybe they make their doors different over here?" Her partner simply shrugged.

"Why won't this bloody door open?" she lamented.

We watched in amusement, entertained by the ensuing debate over the unbudging door.

Trying again and again, she finally stopped and examined the door more closely. With a sheepish, embarrassed grin, she turned another doorknob on her right, the real doorknob (there are two). She, too, had been fooled by the antics of the Snow Cap, but visitors seemed to be taking the experience all in good stride.

My chicken burger was delicious, and I devoured it in a few quick bites. Which was a good thing, because, without warning, three full-size tour buses pulled up outside the diner, spilling forth a group of tourists. I had read about this in our *EZ66 Guide*: "Seligman is best in the early morning before the flocks of tour buses block the view." But it was surreal to see firsthand, in such an out-of-the-way place.

Seligman has been dubbed the Birthplace of Historic Route 66, not in the same official way as Springfield, Missouri, but because it is the source of the rejuvenation of the Mother Road as a historic highway. And this is credited to Seligman's most famous resident and brother to Juan, Angel Delgadillo. In 1987, residents of Seligman, led by Angel and other Route 66 lovers in Kingman, formed the Historic Route 66 Association of Arizona, and it is through their vision, diligence, and advocacy efforts that the State of Arizona dedicated US 66 from Seligman to Kingman as Historic Route 66. This was the spark that the Mother Road needed, and other states soon followed with their own associations.

Angel Delgadillo has told a story in numerous published interviews about how he and his brother would go to the road and watch the convoys of destitute Okies go by down Route 66, on their march to the promised land of California during the Dust Bowl era of the 1930s. They would make fun of them, young and unaware of the seriousness of their plight. Then one day their father cautioned them that they too were Okies—the only difference was that they were too poor to move west. It was a lesson that Angel Delgadillo would take to heart and never forget.

45

THE ROAD FROM Seligman is mostly flat, with wide-open landscapes of high-desert terrain, shielded by steep-sided mountain ranges. Running through the Hualapai Reservation, it is covered in juniper and mesquite trees and accented with lovely cactus growing in the dry, brittle soil. We had now begun the longest stretch of intact old Route 66, 158 miles of it, from Seligman all the way to Topock. Barbed-wire fences periodically decorated the highway, with huge black crows sitting atop in sinister rows, staring blankly at us as we passed.

As the only car on the road, we relished the solitary experience, surrounded by America's epic western scenery. We had entered Mohave County and soon drove through the modest town of Peach Springs, the tribal headquarters of the Hualapai Reservation, which is surrounded by breathtaking mountainous backdrops on both sides. There was a sign advising motorists to watch for wildlife for the next twenty miles. Sure enough, tucking gently around a corner, we suddenly saw a herd of grazing deer, placid and unperturbed by our intrusion. They were safe on the reservation. Hualapai houses came into view—they were square and varied in color. Some were beige, some were brown, and some were even pink. We cruised through the small town of Truxton, with its superwide roads and a vintage, hand-painted mural on the side of the once-popular Frontier Motel and Cafe. Next was the lonesome ghost town of Valentine, home to Keepers of the Wild Nature Park, and then, without warning, we drove right into the past and arrived at the Hackberry General Store.

As with many unique Route 66 locations, you can easily drive right past this relic of a store that has been in operation for eighty years.

Looking around at the decaying shells of old cars and long-empty gas pumps, old-fashioned soda dispensers, vintage signs, and an assortment of discarded junk spread around the front of the store, it was easy to step back in time and visualize the general store as it was at its high point.

First opened in 1934 as the Northside Grocery & Conoco Station, the store served the small mining town of Hackberry, situated across the railroad tracks, as well as travelers using Route 66 between Seligman and Kingman. But the shop sadly faced the same fate as many of the towns on Route 66 when the interstate bypassed it, and Route 66 and the store were shut down in 1978, leading Hackberry to eventually became a ghost town. Then in 1992, legendary Route 66 artist, the late Bob Waldmire, bought the discarded property, reopening it as the Hackberry General Store & Visitor Center. The store changed hands again in 1998 when Waldmire sold it to John and Kerry Pritchard, with Waldmire stating in an interview with *Route 66 Magazine* that with the increasing flood of traffic on Route 66 and visitors to the store, he had lost his "ability to achieve any peace and tranquility," which he had sought when he moved to Hackberry.

I can totally appreciate the lone-outpost lure of this place. A large historic Route 66 sign hanging between the old gas pumps creaked hauntingly, its whine a perfect fit with the spartan desert existence of this once-popular settlement. We were truly in the middle of *absolutely* nowhere. Thembi was busily engaged with his digital camera, trying to capture in totality the Burma-Shave signs that lined one side of a fence: "BIG MISTAKE / MANY MAKE / RELY ON HORN / INSTEAD OF BREAK." Funny. On the opposite side was what looked like a service garage displaying a Model T flatbed truck, with cast-aside mannequins dressed as mechanics relaxing next to it, giving the scene a sinister spin. More cacti, more nostalgic signs, a water tower, and a rustic sheriff's car all seemed to keep a mute lookout for incoming visitors.

"Dad, come and look!"

Thembi had discovered a huge green caterpillar struggling to make its way across the sandy compound. Next to it was a large brown beetle, scurrying in the opposite direction. Which one of the two would become lunch for one of the many birds nesting from the nearby treetops?

Locating a small stick, Thembi gently scooped up the caterpillar and placed him safely underneath one of the old cars. "Hopefully that will keep him safe for now," Thembi said as we watched the insect wiggle his way back toward the open air.

Our peaceful, isolated wandering among all the reminders of a bygone era and Arizona insect life was suddenly cut short with the arrival of the entourage of motorcycle riders we encountered a few miles outside Ash Fork; the Mother Road was calling. This is a piece of Route 66 best experienced alone.

46

NOT MUCH WAS happening when we rolled into Kingman, a Route 66 town that takes its Mother Road heritage seriously. As a matter of fact, the town proclaims itself as the Heart of Historic Route 66. It is also a gateway to Las Vegas, which is less than two hours away. The city is divided into two unique agglomerations: the north side is largely home to the majority of Kingman's businesses and is where most of the population resides, and the older south side is home to most government buildings. The two halves are separated by a ridge of the Cerbat Mountains.

After a drive down historic Beale Street, we stopped into Mr. D'z Route 66 Diner, a kitschy, popular restaurant right across the street from the Powerhouse Visitor Center on West Andy Devine Avenue. The bright-pink-and-turquoise 1950s-style diner hit the national spotlight when Oprah Winfrey praised its homemade root beer in 2006, after she stumbled upon the eatery during her own cross-country journey. Inside the diner, pink vinyl booths, shiny chrome counter stools, and gorgeous classic jukebox all resonated with the international visitors as they settled into the cool midcentury vibe. The restaurant was packed with a constant stream of would-be diners entering and exiting, and the overflow was being asked to wait outside until space became available. It was a fun scene but far too much energy for us at that moment. Finishing our burgers (mine chicken, of course) and fries quickly, we headed into the Powerhouse to take a look.

There was a lot going on. The building itself is historic, built in 1907, and was once the home of all electrical power generated for Kingman. Its beautiful stone exterior reminded us of Kenyan architecture. By now, we'd been on Route 66 for a month and had seen more than our fair share of museums—mostly small and highly specific to a town or region—but the Arizona Route 66 Museum inside the Powerhouse was one of the best. Through colorful murals, life-size diagrams, and stunning photography and storytelling, the museum did a spectacular job showcasing the creation and life of Route 66. As a bonus, it also highlighted the Dust Bowl era of the 1930s and fascinating culture changes throughout the decades. It's definitely a must-visit.

"We should get moving," said Kate. "I'm eager to get to Chloride."

We had debated spending the night in Kingman and the afternoon in Chloride, a onetime silver mining community in Mohave County that was only twenty-three miles to the north, but decided that the opportunity to overnight in an actual ghost town was just too good to pass up. Almost no one online seemed to know much about the town, other than its basic history, and we were keen to explore it for ourselves; there was a mystery surrounding Chloride. We were excited to make our final push for the day and check into our lodging, the romantic-sounding Shep's Miners Inn.

After a forty-five-minute-long drive along US 93—the traffic was crazy, and everyone was speeding to Las Vegas, hence that highway's ranking as one of the most dangerous in the nation—we found the turnoff and escaped the insanity of the frighteningly fast artery. A sign rested to the right on the long straight gravel road leading into town, announcing—via a thin, rusting arrow—that Chloride's downtown was a short four miles away. We loved it. Its old-fashioned font and simple wording that promoted the town's rock murals, petroglyphs, and mining heritage was way cool. We were on the right track and, already, Chloride did not disappoint. But that last four miles up Tennessee Avenue—named after the town's largest (now closed) mine—felt like an eternity. It is funny how the closing miles of a drive seem to take forever when we are overly tired or eager.

But arrive we did, after driving past a turnoff to the cemetery (the oldest in the state) and some curious homes and businesses. Digger Dave's called out from the right-hand side of the avenue, slightly overwhelming with its wooden cutout of a sexy cowgirl and signs advertising the sale of lotto tickets, tourist maps, ice cream, coffee, and more. A white wooden sign announced that the establishment had "Good Food" and, around a fancily written "BAR," hundreds of people had signed their names on the front of the building. It was gaudy and tacky and fantastic. We turned right onto Second Street and stopped abruptly in front of Shep's.

The three of us stood and stretched, taking in our surroundings.

"It has character, that's for sure," I said, pulling a backpack out of the trunk. "Let's ask about checking in and then we can go for a walk around town before it gets too late."

"Sounds good to me," Kate said, helping Thembi gather his back-seat belongings.

I walked toward the simple motel, looking for an entrance. The reception was not very obvious, but a small office presented itself under a big leafy treetop. Its metal door was locked, and peering inside, I could see that no one was home.

"It's all locked up," I said.

"Why don't we go into Yesterday's and ask someone?" Kate suggested.

The old-fashioned restaurant had a shirtless wooden Indian in the front, whose paint was desperately faded, his body cracked and broken. He wore a fancy, cream-colored headdress and looked noble and proud, a relic from a long-lost past. Beside the entrance, two towering vintage gas pumps—one cream and one red—stood atop the creaky wooden platform that patrons stepped up on to enter. An ancient, rusted two-seater car (from the 1930s, maybe) sat decaying on the rocky ground in front, the words "Soul Winner" written into the driver's side. The building itself was a peach-like color, with dark-green doors that had ten windowpanes each and an old buggy wheel attached to the side of the wall. Under a window, a hand-painted note read "Miners Inn 1860."

The door squeaked when we opened it, and I was careful to ensure that it didn't bang as it closed. Inside were a handful of patrons, each with a beer in hand, whiling away the lazy afternoon.

"You go and ask about checking in," Kate said. "We'll walk around a bit."

The room was large and felt rather empty, save for maybe ten tables and a large stuffed brown-and-black dog in a box near the entrance. His frozen eyes seemed to constantly scan the area.

Our entrance immediately elicited a response from a waitress who, eyeing us, made her way slowly over. "How y'all doin' today? Can I get you anything?"

"We're supposed to be checking in at Shep's for the night," I said, "but no one seems to be in the office."

"Oh yeah! Sorry about that, they must be out, but you've come to the right spot. If you want, you can take a seat, and someone will be back soon, real soon, and they can get you settled."

I thanked her and ventured over to take a look around. Hanging on the wall were odd black-and-white portraits of a frowning couple, the eerie sort that date back to the Victorian era. The pair appeared gloomy and morose. I felt a hand on my shoulder and Kate was at my side.

We looked at each other but said nothing. Kate followed my eyes and we sat down at a nearby table. When our waitress returned to take our order, she seemed disappointed that we would not be partaking in their stock of alcohol—only some soda—and encouraged us to order dinner before five o'clock, as they closed soon after. Chloride was not the type of town where you wanted to miss the last dinner order. There were no other options.

The men next to the bar chatted among themselves, glancing over at us from time to time with grimaces, or perhaps curiosity. Our waitress strolled back to see how we were doing with our Cokes, and caught us checking out the dog in the box.

"He's kind of creepy, isn't he?" she said.

We smiled.

"The owners had him stuffed when he died and transported him all the way to Chloride from the East Coast. His name is Pepper." The way she pronounced "Pepper" held a hint of disdain.

She stood at our table for a moment, staring intently and suspiciously at the unfortunate canine.

Kate broke the dreamlike moment. "And what about those old portraits on the wall over there?"

She abruptly spun around and looked to the rear of the room.

"The owners found those in the ceiling. We don't know who they are or when the pictures were taken. But they decided to put them up. They creep me out too. They remind me of those old pictures of dead people, you know the ones where they put coins over people's eyes?"

We did, and they did, and it was all a little much for us.

Sugar water consumed, quickly, we ventured back out into the placid late afternoon.

The sky was pure blue and empty of clouds as a gigantic southwestern sun dropped rapidly in the horizon. Across from Yesterday's Restaurant, towhees with distinctive orange-and-white breasts called from an empty school yard, where unused, outdated playground equipment sat baking in the late-day heat.

Tennessee appeared to be the town's main street and was home to a pretty 1873 post office that looked like it was quiet most days. A dilapidated antiques shop wore a red exterior, faded and badly washed out in the desert sun, and a second antiques store, Cactus Cowboy, sported a humble peach exterior and dark-brown doors that were quite characteristic of the shops in southern Arizona. It had big windows with fancy writing across them, and the silhouette of a relaxing cowboy perched above the door. The entire town appeared shut down, increasing our sense foreboding. As we strolled Chloride's dirt roads and quiet streets, we felt completely alone, at least out in the open. There were signs of residents everywhere, but few were clearly visible.

The sun sets fast in the Southwest. Shadows danced across the unused tarmac as we wandered the lonely streets, gazing with interest at yard after yard filled with junk and castoffs. Old barrels and used glass bottles, rusty wagons, broken clocks, discarded basins, and long-broken lights decorated residents' property. Each was defined by the owner as an art installation. Chloride took special pride in presenting itself as a bohemian sort of escape for art lovers. To us, it simply seemed like a hideaway for those not willing to conform to polite society. As we explored the town, it felt as though we were being watched from inside of the houses. We could see people peeking from narrow windows and watching as thin curtains quickly closed.

A small boy rode his bike up the otherwise empty street, ignoring us when we said hello as he passed. He didn't appear wary of us, just completely disinterested. His clothes were covered in red dust and his long, matted brown hair looked untouched by a comb in goodness knows how long. His wheels squeaked with each turn of his pedals. He turned down the next side street and disappeared from sight.

"Where did he go?" Thembi asked, a note of alarm in his voice.

Kate and I looked at each other but said nothing. The town gave us the heebie-jeebies, but oddly enough, we liked it. Chloride is not a traditional tourism town but rather a destination for those wanting a real small-desert-town experience. Only eighty miles from bustling Las Vegas, and twenty-three miles from the wonderful Route 66 town of Kingman, Chloride felt like a million miles from anywhere and a world unto itself. It is, in fact, a ghost town that never truly died. During its heyday, Chloride was booming: eight saloons, six churches, five hotels and restaurants, four red-light dens, a bank, a livery, an opry house, a billiard hall, and a hospital served over two thousand residents for years.

Today, however, that is not the case. Over the course of several decades, Chloride's once-thriving community almost disappeared. In the late 1920s, a fire nearly burned the entire town down to the ground. In 1935, Butterfield stagecoaches and the AT&SF stopped providing cargo and passenger services to the area. Finally, in the 1940s, the area's mining industry began to decline. Many miners went off to serve in World War II and, as the mines produced less and less, they became too costly to operate, forcing families to pack up and leave, rendering the formerly prosperous camp practically a ghost town.

Nevertheless, Chloride survived. About three hundred people currently call this place home—an odd assortment of writers, history buffs, artists, and hippies.

As we continued to stroll, white-crowned sparrows chirped from thorny tree branches, and buildings like the wooden Mineshaft Market and Chloride General stood closed and mute.

"Dad, look," said Thembi, pointing. An old-time wooden casket rested against the store's creaky veranda. "Do you think it's a real coffin?"

"I don't know, Dadu. Maybe. It's kind of cool, isn't it?" We love the Old West theme that is so prevalent in Arizona.

"Yeah! But a little spooky too," he said. "I can't make up my mind if I like Chloride or not."

We understood.

With the blackness of night now almost upon us, we decided to turn back toward the motel, but stopped to stand still and take in the nocturnal smells and sounds. There was a smoky scent to the air, perhaps the smell of the dust and thorny foliage. A man in a cluttered yard stood in front of a feeble-looking house on our right. Had he been there the whole time, watching us? He was dressed in scrubby, faded jeans and a plaid blue button-down hanging open over a stained T-shirt. Long, unbrushed salt-and-pepper hair framed a face with hardened features. He had a small yappy dog of no apparent particular breed at his feet. There was something in the way that he just stood in the yard staring that unnerved us. I abruptly raised my hand in a friendly hello. "Good evening!"

The man said nothing but continued to gawk at us.

"Let's head back," Kate said.

Once safely past the property, we turned back to see the man down on one knee fussing over his tiny dog.

When we got back to Shep's, the owner was in his office, smoking and reading a newspaper. The noise of a whiny fan irritatingly filled the small room. I knocked on the door, introduced myself, and received our key, and before I departed, he was back to his paper. *What a peculiar town*, I thought.

After a simple dinner at Yesterday's, we retired to our room and crashed down onto our beds. Sleep came quickly but my slumber was disturbed by vivid, uneasy dreams that caused me to wake up frequently, startled and in a sweat. When the birds began to sing from the trees with the first sign of light, I was grateful for a new day and ready to get a start to the morning.

"I slept horribly," said Kate from the tiny bathroom while washing her face. "I had the strangest dream. I was being chased by that dog, Pepper."

47

THE SUN WAS shining high in the early-morning sky when we checked out and decided to give the town a fresh look. Chloride's dirt streets were still mostly empty, but the mood is always more positive, in the brightness of daylight, and we found the place less spooky and more serene as we took in what the day offered. We wanted to like Chloride and were keen to find beauty in the questionable artistic endeavors of its hermitic residents. Even with a generous spirit, this was a little difficult to do, but we did see an odd metal robot and several giant, long-legged metal birds that were creative enough to merit a short stop to admire the curiosity of the structures. On the other hand, the town's antiquity and historical edifices more than made up for its less-than-enviable yards. A sweet little Baptist church called out to us from behind a chain-link fence, its humble doors open to worshippers since 1891, and the Chloride Volunteer Fire Department owns an operational 1939 Ford fire engine that was built especially for the town by the Ford Motor Company. Apparently, it is still used when needed.

The Chloride Historical Society maintains an old jail and the local playhouse, and on every second and fourth Saturday of each month, the society has mock gunfights in town. A daytime walk through the town gave us a slightly better understanding of the efforts that Chloride was making to attract tourism to their nearly forgotten town. It struck us as odd, though, seeing that local residents were not terribly encouraging of outside visitors.

Lost in reverie, we walked in silence, startled back from our thoughts when a pair of dogs lunged toward us viciously, crashing into a fence that shielded their abode.

"Holy cow!" Thembi yelled, surprised by the sudden barking and growling.

"Come over here," I said to him, pulling him in closer. I made sure that he and Kate were on my opposite side, away from the house and its aggressive animals.

"What the hell are you barking at?" hollered a voice from inside.

We kept walking but sounds traveled in the quiet street.

"Leave those people alone. Get the hell back inside!"

Thembi started laughing. "That really scared me. Whoa!" He held his hand to his chest and chuckled.

"Me too!" Kate and I said in unison, both laughing and a bit embarrassed at how much we had jumped.

"Dad, check that out up in the hills," Thembi pointed.

Chloride had a giant "C" painted into its hills, a marker for aircrafts flying over the Cerbat Mountains.

"Can we go and take a look at the murals and rock paintings before we leave?" he asked.

"Yeah, that would be fun," Kate responded. "I think we'll need to drive up, though. They are supposed to be a little far from town."

And with that we headed back to the motel, avoiding the house with the dogs, jumped into the car, and said goodbye to Shep's.

Up Tennessee, past the motel's turnoff, the road beings to narrow. A branch-off to the right and a bumpy road leads a mile and a half past ancient Native petroglyphs and toward the Purcell murals, a set of bizarre rock paintings that artist Roy Purcell created in 1966. Purcell's work is actually celebrated in the Southwest and can be found in the collections of major corporations like Standard Oil, the Royal Bank of Canada, and Dow Chemical Company. Even Clint Eastwood owns some of Purcell's work. A short-term resident and prospector in Chloride, Purcell found some extra time on his hands when he took a break from a master of fine arts degree at Utah State University.

"I think we need to walk from here," I said as I pulled the car off the road as best as I could. I hoped that I had left enough room for other vehicles, if any should arrive, to safely pass. The road had become incredibly rocky with deep dips and jagged pieces of boulder. I was afraid of damaging the undercarriage of the vehicle and decided that with only perhaps four or five hundred feet to go, we could finish the journey on foot.

"I'll carry the picnic blanket and, Thembi, please take this backpack with some snacks," Kate instructed.

Thembi was off to a quick start, his little legs running ahead, chasing enormous grasshoppers and eagerly spying for rattlesnakes. He was a smart, spunky little boy who loved life, and having grown up on the road, shuttling from one magical destination or another, he always enjoyed the journey.

"It's already getting hot," Kate said, wiping her brow. "We better put more sunscreen on Thembi."

It was true, it was midmorning and the southwestern desert sun already brought fire to the brown earth, radiating back onto us as we hiked. Sweat poured from my forehead and ran down into my eyes. Kate's face glistened in the shadows under her wide-brimmed hat.

As we walked, the boulder paintings seemed to be as elusive as the town folk. But we trod on. Honestly, I would have gladly given up and returned to the comfort of the truck, but Kate was committed. Finally, after what was likely twenty minutes but felt like an hour, we rounded a bend and there they were, bright and bold against the plain desert greens and browns. The artist had titled his curious gallery *The Journey: Images from an Inward Search for Self.* Purcell's search most certainly brought out some bizarre questions if his paintings are anything to go by. One image showed a western town that was home to over a dozen wooden structures that rested at the foot of a great mountain. This was presumably Chloride. Another showed a gigantic snakelike creature with talons swallowing something that resembled fire, and onward, a fertility goddess. There were nineteen restored murals in all. His work was odd and represented something that may be better understood by those who appreciate abstract art. As for us, we were just amazed that he managed to climb so high on the rocks and never fall and break his neck.

"Hey, Dad, can you hear rattling in the grass up the road?" Thembi asked.

"I think I can, let's go take a look," I answered.

The two of us walked up the incline together, leaving Kate behind, sitting on a large rock and enjoying a cold drink. A big bird flew high in the sky above us, its wings creating a break in the never-ending, impossibly blue sky. It called out loudly from the heavens. Thembi and I looked at each other, his huge brown eyes alive with curiosity. From the time of his birth, Thembi's eyes have always communicated so much.

"Let's look in here, Dad," he said, rushing toward some stones and long, scrubby grass.

"No, wait!" I yelled. "Thembi, we need to be careful in the hills. There are snakes and spiders and other things that can hurt you. Stay with me."

Up ahead, a movement in the vegetation. We walked closer. A rattle began, getting louder as we approached. We stopped.

"What do you guys see up there?" hollered Kate. "Is it a snake?" There was excitement in her voice, and she was on her way to us.

"I don't know, but why pester the local wildlife?" I responded, backing away. I've spent thousands of hours on safari with elephants and lions, zebras and giraffes, but I have always hated snakes. It was getting hot and it was time to go!

Suddenly, there was a stillness in the air, and a sense of being overly exposed crept in. The murals were isolated and secluded, just far away enough from the town that if we needed aid, there would be no one to call for help. A swift sense of vulnerability came over us and all at once we got creeped out again. With a memorable night and morning in Chloride under our belt, we decided to walk back to the truck and leave nature to its own devices.

48

THE ROAD TO Oatman, west of Kingman, is famous for its spectacular scenery and long, steep curves. Snaking through the dry, barren countryside and descending into Perfume Canyon, the road has been carved out of sheer determination, offering drivers an impossibly picturesque, albeit hazardous, trip. Rustic remnants of vehicles strewn over the edge of the narrow road attest to the dangerous character of this portion of the Mother Road, whose breathtaking vistas are deceiving. The route—forty-nine miles from Kingman—is made up of extremely tight switchbacks and many steep drop-offs that, while tremendous in their beauty, deserve to be respected.

The day was peaceful and serene when we spotted an odd vision for the desert: a ghostly yellow houseboat rested in the distance, marooned in the cradle of the barren land. Why and how did it get here? But like so many strange sightings in the Southwest, the forsaken boat somehow seemed right at home.

"Is that Oatman?" asked Thembi, peering up from his book.

"I'm not sure. It has a ton of flags, though, and I don't see a town."

Pulling into the parking lot, we realized that we had reached Cool Springs, a souvenir shop located some twenty-eight miles from Kingman, the last stop before entering the Black Mountains and the final push toward the famed ghost town of Oatman. Built in the 1920s, the venue was originally a petrol station, café, bar, and small motel before the creation of the interstate and the resulting decline of Route 66. Closed due to lack of business in 1964, the humble venue was left to slowly decay in the scorching Arizona sun, a sad reminder of a happier time from a different era.

However, as so often happens in the United States, even the worst situations can yield to hope. Cool Springs was revived in 2001 when Ned Leuchtner, a real estate agent from Chicago, purchased the station and set about restoring it, with the aid of old photographs. The restoration was completed in 2004 and now Cool Springs sits quietly at the top of the world, welcoming passersby as they make their way through the Arizona desert. An interesting piece of information on the location is that it was used in the 1991 Dolph Lundgren and Jean-Claude Van Damme film *Universal Soldier*, where it was actually blown up, but reassembled after filming.

Standing at the edge of a cliff, I looked out at the vast wilderness, awestruck by the natural beauty and expansive earth below. There was a raw, aggressive magnificence that refused to be ignored. Thembi and Kate were investigating some tables outside the station, rummaging through bins of minerals and stones. It was a weird scene. Like other moments along Route 66, especially from Texas westward, the moment didn't feel quite real. It was like standing in a dream, asleep but vividly aware of the experience.

"Dad, look at these! They have pyrite and fluoride. There is even obsidian—these are amazing."

A young couple had come to join us, equally excited by the find. In proper Route 66 fashion, the owner had simply set out the objects and, in full faith, left a jar for consumers to put their money in should they decide to make a purchase. It was almost unbelievable, but the trusting nature of the Southwest, and Route 66 in general, was one of the things that made the trip so special, so memorable. In Kenya, someone would make off with the money and, most likely, all of the stones and minerals as well. Here in the outback of Arizona, there is a tacit assumption that people will simply do the right thing.

In the end, we purchased five dollars' worth of earthy items and jumped back into the vehicle to weave our way up the mountain, past Sitgreaves Pass—whose summit sits at over 3,556 feet! From the summit, visitors can actually see across Arizona and into California and Nevada. It was an inspiring place to stop and stretch, reflecting on the wonders of the natural scenery that roll on as far as the eye can see. It was so hot that the ground had a haze and shimmered in the blazing sun.

A SCRAGGLY DONKEY slowly made his way past the vehicle as we entered town, followed by another, and another. Excited tourists buzzed around, pursuing the beasts of burden as they wandered casually around, disinterested in the fanfare. It was just after lunch and the town was filling up, dotted with motorcycles, cars, large and cumbersome RVs, and even some young guys on skateboards who were doing Route 66 in style. The energy in the air was slightly overwhelming. A popular gold mining town until the 1930s, Oatman was named after Olive Oatman, who, along with her sister, was kidnapped by Tolkepaya Indians (a group of the Yavapai tribe) as her family trekked across Arizona to the promised land of California in 1851. She was later traded to the Mohave and forced into assimilation. Mary Ann Oatman (age seven) would die from starvation while in captivity, but, following negotiations with authorities at Fort Yuma in 1856, Olive (age fourteen) would be rescued, albeit not before being branded with tattoos on her chin and arms, marking her for the rest of her life. Now, many years later, Oatman is home to approximately 150 people who make their livelihood from the multitude of tourists who visit annually. That day we joined the number.

The town was built around one main street—actually named Main Street—that maintains an Old West theme, similar to Tombstone in southern Arizona. Oatman's collection of ramshackle frame buildings offers visitors a vintage feel for how things used to be. Complete with fun shops like Fast Fanny's Place, Jackass Junction, Saving Your Ass, the Classy Ass Gift Shop, the Bucktooth Burro, and of course, the Oatman Hotel (which is no longer actually a hotel but is an active restaurant and bar), Oatman allows visitors to step back in time—at least when the number of tourists is kept to a minimum. And in case you missed it, there is a definite theme to the titles of the shops: the sleepy locale has built its claim to fame around the wild burros that frequent the town, themselves descendants of the donkeys once used by miners panning for gold in the hills.

"Do you want to use our remaining Burro chow?" offered a French tourist, holding out a hand that was clutching a large bag of specially made pellets that Oatman shops sell to visitors who want to feed the burros.

I was frozen for a moment, uncertain how to respond. "I am not really sure that we can use it, but thank you for asking. We really appreciate it."

"But you must feed the burros. It is a very giving gesture."

Maybe she saw the blank look on my face, or maybe she was feeling bad for wasting her loot on donkey food that she no longer wanted to invest her time in doling out to the spoiled beasts, but she was not giving up.

"So would you like the food?"

"No, thank you, but again, thank you for offering."

"But the donkeys . . . they, too, need to feel loved."

Okay, lady. She had that desperate look in her eyes of someone slightly unhinged.

At that moment, as though on cue, an overweight male burro sauntered up, looked us both deep in the eyes, and began to urinate violently all over the wooden boardwalk, his pee forming a small lake near the Francophone's sandaled feet. I was appalled and disgusted by the pungent aroma that filled the air.

"Aw, you naughty donkey," she chided the mule in a baby voice. "You are so cute. Yes, you are. Yes, you are. So cute!" she gushed as urine ran past her toes.

49

OATMAN HAS BECOME one of those places on Route 66 that everyone raves about. It was, in fact, one of the towns we were most excited about seeing as we planned our trip. However, as we stood there among the many other visitors, the scraggly burros, and the overpriced shops, we just weren't feeling the magic. But there was hope, as we were going to head down the road toward Nevada to get some lunch (there were only two restaurants in Oatman) and some fuel for the vehicle (there were no gas stations nearby) and then come back later, when the myriad of camera-happy people and their vehicles would be gone.

At five in the evening, we were back in Oatman, and the town was beginning to clear. A wind had picked up and clouds had started to fill the sky, dark and heavy in their mood. A lone burro remained on Main Street, slowly making his way into the hills to join his gang for the night. Perhaps he had had a busy day. He would be back in the morning, when the tourists once again arrived.

The vibe was different now than it was earlier. The boardwalk seemed much ricketier now and the Oatman Hotel sign was rocking gently in the breeze, creating that spooky creaking sound essential to all desert-based horror films. Taking a seat across the street from the sign on a bench next to the Olive Oatman Restaurant & Saloon, Thembi spied a fortune-teller booth. For only a dollar, the mechanical figure inside would give you all of the secrets that you need to know.

"Can we see what he says, Dad? Can we?"

"Sure, why not? It will certainly add to the Oatman experience."

Inserting a dollar, the mystic came to life and began to speak. We were ready, waiting on bated breath to discover what fun, but surely spiritual, guidance he would provide during our Route 66 trip. A loud ding sounded, and a small ticket-like card sprang forth. "You will find prosperity when you work hard."

What? That was what my dollar got me? A fortune-cookie statement. Sitting back down on the bench, dejected and a little poorer, we waited in silence for darkness.

An SUV sped up the empty street with an urgency that screamed "European tourist." A woman jumped from the vehicle, ready for action, her camera in hand. She looked perplexed. "I don't know where they've gone. They should be here, that is what we read." Her husband and teenage children emerged from the vehicle and split up, each searching in their own direction. They were a team, a well-honed unit in action, and emerging from their SUV they looked like they were coming out of a group huddle.

"What do you think they want?" asked Thembi, entertained by their antics.

"I am not sure, maybe to find a restaurant," I said. "They could be hungry."

The husband was banging on the door of the Oatman Hotel, but to no avail—it closed at six. They called to each other from opposite sides of the street, but the wind choked out their words and the setting sun was closing their apparent short window. After fifteen minutes of activity, they retreated back to the safety of their vehicle, disappointed and defeated. As the driver shut her door, we heard some final words. "Where the hell did those burros go?"

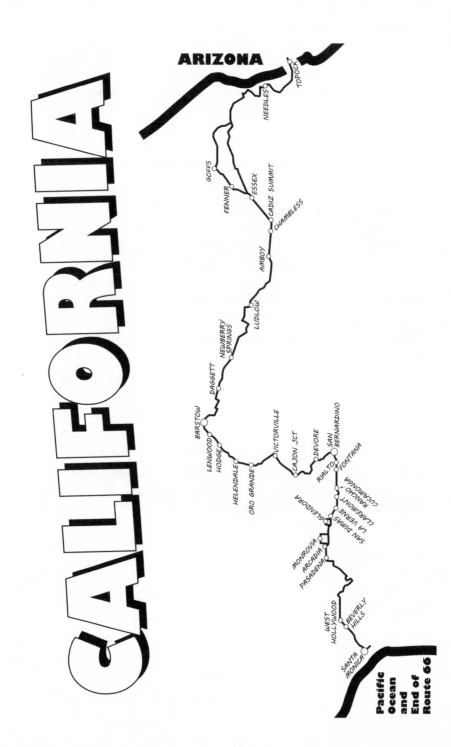

50

IT WAS BLISTERING hot as we drove through Topock, on the edge of the Colorado River, and crossed out of Arizona, saying goodbye—for a while, anyhow—to the enormous, spiky saguaros that we had enjoyed west of Kingman. The California welcome sign greeted us as we cruised into Needles—the gateway to California—and we were stoked about the final leg of our 66 journey. I had lived in Los Angeles for a bit in the early '90s and have always held a strong affinity for the El Dorado State. What I remembered most was the pulsating energy and a palpable sense of unbridled optimism that could not be quenched. It felt good to be back.

Needles is a former railroad town named after the jagged, needlelike peaks of the mountain range on the Arizona side of the border. The town had once thrived as a haven for weary travelers heading west, but as we drove through the community, Needles had a desolate look of a town dogged by misfortune. As were we. We were lost again.

Thanks to a road closure, we were forced to wander the tiny oasis for forty-five minutes looking for a way out. I became increasingly irritated as we meandered endlessly—in circles—through the modest, slightly run-down neighborhoods of Needles. Even Kate, who has the ability to remember her way to and from places like no one else I've met, was stumped. Maybe it was the heat. In 2004, we relocated to Mali, in West Africa, for a job. In preparation for the role, we drove south to Burkina Faso for six months to attend a French-language school. After the season in Burkina, we drove north again, back to Mali and in search of the sub-urb where we would set up shop while we looked for our own house. Arriving after dark, and after ten hours in the truck, Kate managed to lead us not only to the suburb, but the exact house that we had visited six months before, without the aid of a GPS or even a map. If I were in charge of navigation, we may well have become citizens of Burkina Faso.

Eventually, we managed to backtrack and got ourselves onto Route 95, then back onto 66, and mercifully began to make our way toward Barstow.

———

THE STRAIGHT, OPEN road was infinite, the immense desert, with its intense heat, stretched out for untold miles. We had been driving for an hour now and had not seen another vehicle. The route was empty of human settlement or traffic. We were heading toward the ends of the earth. Then I finally spotted another vehicle up ahead—a beat-up, tan-colored station wagon—and visions of the 1982 horror film *Death Valley* flashed through my mind. I remembered the little boy, Peter Billingsley (who would later go on to play Ralphie in the 1983 cult classic *A Christmas Story*) peering out the back of the station wagon window at a scary old relic of a vehicle as it steadily approached them from behind and then drove swiftly past. The audience could not see a driver, but the vehicle's license plate came into view: HEX 576. The Mojave Desert is indeed what nightmares are made of, but more than that, it is the most welcoming, scenic escape from the crowds and mayhem of the modern era that one could ever ask for.

Heat shimmered off the asphalt and a hawk soared high above in the cloudless sky, searching for a meal. Up ahead, I noticed something in the middle of the road. It was barely distinguishable from the asphalt surface, but in the hazy sky I could make out slight movement. Then, without warning, we were on top of it. Swerving, I hit the brakes and brought the vehicle to a stop.

"What is it, Dad?" Thembi asked, curious.

Reversing, I pulled up parallel to a large and rather irate rattlesnake that had curled up into a tight ball. Poised next to a rather attractive 66 shield on the pavement, the snake was alert and ready to strike, its signature tail rattling angrily. None of us had ever seen a rattlesnake in the wild before. We had heard the distinctive warning signs a few times throughout our time in New Mexico and Arizona when walking in the bush, but this was the first visual confirmation. How exciting!

We stayed with the snake for some time but remained in the safety of the vehicle. Thembi had wisely decided not to try to touch it with his bare foot, as he had attempted with the tarantula in Texas. A good move. He's a fast learner.

Perhaps because of the hungry bird above or maybe because it was bored with our company, the rattler suddenly uncoiled and slithered off the scalding road and back into the thorny bushes, where it was soon hidden and safe from becoming something's lunch. It was scary to realize just how close people come to such potentially deadly creatures when walking in the desert.

Songs like "Ramblin' Man" by the Allmann Brothers, "Going Up the Country" by Canned Heat, and "Carefree Highway" by Gordon Lightfoot blared from the speakers as we traced our way through the nearly abandoned towns of Goffs (population of twenty-three) and Fenner (population of zero). Soon we began to notice an interesting phenomenon: people passing this way had formed a habit of stopping and using local stones, some painted and some not, to spell out their names on the side of a slight incline on the edge of the baked highway. Perhaps it was a testimony to passersbys that they were here at one point in time and had left their mark in the barren landscape.

"Can we do that?" asked Kate. "It looks like a really cool thing to do."

"Really? You want to stop in the middle of the highway, in the searing heat, so we can spend an hour picking up burning rocks so we can write our names on the side of the road for almost no one to see?"

"Yes! Let's do it!" she exclaimed.

Thembi smiled at me and rolled his eyes. He knew his mother had a big appetite for the unusual.

Still debating the virtues of the activity, we took note of a tiny, broken-down concrete structure on the side of the road a hundred feet ahead. It was Cadiz Summit. Once a place of respite from the journey but now a graffiti-covered relic, its remains were left alone to fade and slowly crumble away in the intense Mojave heat. We pulled over and stepped out of the vehicle and into the sweltering temperature, and walked toward it.

We took a moment to acclimatize. The sun was brilliant, blinding, and its reflection off the ground startling. We looked around at the apocalyptic scene, lost in contemplation and subdued by the silence of the desolation. So much of this section of Route 66 has become a memory of the past, a harbinger of lost dreams and tangible defeat.

There was a fierce barrenness to the environment that was further accentuated by the vast emptiness on the road. If we were to run into trouble out here, things could go seriously wrong rather quickly—our cell phone signal ended back in Needles. But this didn't frighten us; rather, it added to the feeling of traveling down the same treacherous road that early travelers had endured (and not in the comfort of an air-conditioned vehicle, well stocked with snacks and water). It was genuinely a do-or-die trip for motorists when Route 66 first opened. By the 1950s, motor travel had become slightly easier, but the inherent risks of the route were always present.

In his 1939 classic novel, *The Grapes of Wrath*, John Steinbeck describes the sentiment of people reaching the end of this arduous portion of the Mother Road—"And, oh, my God, it's over"—reflecting how truly terrifying the journey was for all those vulnerable souls who found themselves with no other choice. They died in the Dust Bowl and they died en route to the promised land of orange blossoms and cascading beaches, where work was guaranteed on farms or in factories. But as they emerged from the impossible heat of the Mojave, they would have realized it was over. *My God, it's over.*

In the distance, we saw a vehicle approaching fast. It was only the second proof of human life we'd seen since leaving Needles some hours ago. It was a large 18-wheeler barreling down the road, a phantom in a ghostly terrain. Roaring past, it was an eerie, ominous vision as it faded out of sight, as though it were not real at all.

With the warmth of the day closing the discussion on writing our names on the side of the deserted road, we bid the abandoned relic farewell and took to the highway again. Ghost towns abound in California along 66, a testimony to the state's mining past and a life that so many people once pursued. Passing through Amboy, with its famous Roy's Motel and Cafe sign, and a population of four, I concluded that the Mojave Desert was, without a doubt, my favorite part of the journey.

51

THE ICONIC NATURE of this final stretch of 66 was not lost on us. The endless miles of the yawning Mojave Desert marked the last rough terrain of our Route 66 journey. Past Ludlow, where the loud chatter of a group of animated French tourists drowned out the peacefulness of our quiet lunch at the Ludlow Cafe, Route 66 gets a bit rugged, and I had to slow down to a crawl. I had pulled over to the grassy edge; Thembi and I needed a quick bathroom break. A lone car, like a mirage, appeared over the horizon, heading east. As the car got closer, the driver flashed his lights and slowed to a stop.

"How y'all doin'? Sorry to disturb ya there, but um . . . can I ask, is Route 66 bumpy all the way?" He was showing signs of serious exasperation. His small car literally may not have made it back to the interstate. Much of the Mother Road is perfectly enjoyable tarmac, but this part was somewhat rough.

"No, it's just this section. But the rest is actually not bad at all," I said, trying to button up my shorts. Thembi was already standing next to our car.

"Oh, good! I thought I would give 66 a shot, but this is getting ridiculous. I was thinking it would be nice to experience the quieter road but now I think I'll just join the interstate."

A quick "thank you" and he was gone, his car banging and complaining as he disappeared into the distance. His was actually the first small vehicle we had seen on the road that day.

THE I-40 FREEWAY was clearly visible on the right, separated by an incline and a wire fence. And even though the road runs parallel to the interstate, like on stretches of Illinois and Missouri, in no way did it take away from the enjoyment of the long, lonely stretch of desert.

Just ahead, the road edged its way slightly downhill into the miniscule town of Newberry Springs, a rather desolate place with perhaps only two redeeming factors: the Newberry Mountains, which make up its backdrop, and the Bagdad Cafe, the site where the 1987 film of the same name, about a German couple stranded in the American Southwest, was filmed. Sliding into town, we spotted the large, overhanging "Route 66 Roadside Attraction" sign outside the café, describing its claim to fame.

The site of the original Bagdad Cafe, which is in what was then the actual town of Bagdad, is some fifty miles back to the east. The town was a bustling place in its day and served Route 66 travelers when they stopped in for food, gas, or a cold drink. But both the town and the original café have succumbed to progress, with the café closing down in 1968. Nothing, literally nothing, remains of the town, or the original café, save for a "lone scraggly tree," as noted in the *EZ66 Guide*.

"Bonjour!" greeted a slight, pale-skinned, blond-haired lady behind the counter.

"Bonjour," I responded hesitantly, a bit taken aback by the French greeting. They must get a lot of French tourists, or perhaps there was something about us that looked French? I needed to give this a bit of thought.

Taking a seat at an empty table, we absorbed our surroundings. The walls of the café were covered top to bottom with customers' mementos—stickers, postcards, signed photos, folded T-shirts, and business cards. Many of the mementos were in French or from France. Obviously, there was a connection. The ceiling was completely covered with flags from different countries, and I scanned the colorful array to see if I could spot a Kenyan flag.

The woman behind the counter strode over, menus in hand. "So where are y'all headed?"

Andrea Pruett has owned the Bagdad Cafe for more than twenty years now. She and her late husband, Harold, moved to the Mojave Desert from Los Angeles back in the '90s to try their hand at something unique. "We came out here to start an ostrich farm. Harold would focus on the farm, while I would write." They bought what was then the Sidewinder Cafe in 1995 and, knowing of its link as the site for filming the movie *Bagdad Cafe*, changed the name.

"Do you always greet your customers in French?" I asked.

"Oh, many of my customers are French speaking. The French have been so good to me. And they come from all over: from France, Belgium, Haiti, even the Congo!"

The movie apparently had a deep impact on Europeans, even grabbing a nomination for a César Award in France in 1989 (as well as an Academy Award nomination for the featured song, "Calling You"). Whatever the connection Europeans have with the movie, they seem to have a special affinity not only for the Bagdad Cafe but for all things Route 66.

"I almost went under I don't even know how many times," Andrea continued. "But somehow, I've managed to stay open. It's kept me going after I lost my husband and son. It's the European visitors who keep us alive."

A shadow of sadness momentarily flickered across her face as she recounted memories of her son. "He was an actor in Los Angeles," she said, her eyes softening as she spoke about him. "Do you remember the TV show *Party of Five*? He was in it. Or the television version of *The Outsiders*? He was in that too." She beamed as she spoke of her son's achievements, her pride evident as she remembered her child. "There is a poster of him over here, come take a look."

A handsome, pensive face stared back at us from a black-and-white poster—a promising young life lost too soon. Harold Pruett (Jr.) died of an accidental drug overdose in 2002.

As we prepared to leave, vowing to keep in touch with Andrea, I was reminded of the vital enthusiasm that European tourists have for keeping the spirit of Route 66 and small-town America alive. They also play a huge role in keeping historic attractions like the Bagdad Cafe up and running.

52

BARSTOW BEGAN AS a small settlement in the 1830s, a natural place for people and their herds moving from the New Mexico Territory to Los Angeles to stop and rest, due to the abundance of vegetation and water replenished annually by the fall and winter rains. The AT&SF railroad arrived in the 1880s, and the town replaced its former monikers of Fishpond and Waterman Junction with the permanent name of Barstow, in honor of the railroad's president, William Barstow Strong. Today, Barstow is home to about twenty-five thousand people and retains its proud position on Route 66. The town is spread out, with a fair variety of cafés and restaurants, sites and attractions, and a share of modest motels. Our stop tonight was the less-than-creatively-titled, but nonetheless quite fetching, Route 66 Motel. It was the best vintage Route 66 venue in Barstow.

As we pulled in, we were taken back in time by the parking lot, a cozy piece of desert that was ornamented with a number of rusting 1950s vehicles, once-handsome machines that dominated the highway with their sleek bodies and powerful engines. Now they were a reminder of a vibrant past. Opened in 1922, the Route 66 Motel has been welcoming travelers on the Mother Road for nearly a hundred years. That is pretty impressive.

"Good afternoon, sir, how do you do? Would you like a room?" asked a slight Indian woman from behind the office counter. Her graying hair denoted her age, but there was a spring to her voice and an exuberance that showed off the fact that she had been doing this for a long time.

"Yes, please. Do you have a double with firm beds?"

"Who can know? Everyone is different, no? What is firm for one person may not be very good for another. It is hard to say. But I think you will be happy. I have been in Barstow for many years now and have not heard too many complaints. But who can know?"

We filled out the registration form, paid our fifty dollars, and grabbed our key.

Inside, the room was a fair size, with decent beds and a cozy chair for us to take turns sitting in. Thembi was delighted to be out of the vehicle and I was keen to walk around and take some pictures. In the middle of the parking lot stood a lovely creation that included a water mill wheel, an old Model T Ford, a desert display of stones and sand, and a mailbox that had been waiting a long, long time for the *Desert Dispatch* newspaper. There was even a towering palm tree. The sun was too bright for photographs, though. I would need to wait until later.

———

"THESE ARE A lot of bottles!" Kate exclaimed, taking in the refreshingly unusual creation that is Elmer Long's Bottle Tree Ranch in Oro Grande, forty minutes west of Barstow. Opened in 2000, the forest of glass was constructed out of more than two hundred handmade treelike metal pipes, with bottles of every shape, size, and color hanging carefully from them. They were accompanied by a variety of other assorted art installations; glass-bottle trees are crowned with even odder objects than the trees themselves, like rifles, animal skulls, bells, windmills, and lamps.

Elmer's held just the right amount of weird and lonesome, mixed with nostalgia and creativity, to make it perfect for the Mother Road. The story goes that, as a young boy, Elmer began to collect and salvage items out in the desert with his father, a hobby that they both enjoyed and that resulted in a massive collection of bottles. When his father died, Elmer "inherited" the entire collection and the idea of a bottle tree forest was born as a creative and unique way to celebrate his father.

Walking through the ranch, we were alone—at least, we thought we were. It was the perfect setting for a family of three to mysteriously disappear forever. The hour was late in the day and the sun was low in the sky, with a soothing breeze blowing over the "trees." Squeaking signs and singing chimes created a disquieting but ethereal tone. Meandering about, I kept a close eye on Thembi.

"Look at that, Dad!" He pointed, intrigued by the shell of an old Jeep. Nearby sat a bathroom sink and a huge assortment of other treasures that, to someone else, might be defined as junk. But on America's Main Street, people see things differently. And thank goodness that they do. It is exactly these types of places that make traveling Route 66 so special and so memorable.

The day was growing late now, and we were hungry. Intent on enjoying what we were told was the best Mexican food in Barstow, we headed back to seek out Casa Jimenez, with its famous salsa and eclectic decor. (Thembi was not overly excited about the choice; he was sick of Mexican food and wanted a burger and fries.) Off I-40 and back in familiar territory, we weaved down the main street in town, up and down steep hills, and then stumbled upon the restaurant by pure luck.

Outside, two vagrants, a man and a woman, had set up shop, hassling customers as they entered. It was odd to see in a small desert town, and we tried to follow suit as we approached the building; others had kept their eyes to the ground and ignored the pair.

"Spare a dollar, man?" the man asked, stepping in front of me as I reached for the door. His look of dishevelment was impressive. Homelessness is not surprising, but many folks are able to take care of themselves a little. This guy was grungy on a whole different level.

"Sorry, we don't carry cash," I said, which was true.

"It's okay, no worries, amigo, we can take credit." He grinned widely. He was missing several top teeth and his gums were brown. His companion, a tall lady with long legs and a pointy nose, pulled a winter hat down over her forehead and leaned against the building, picking her nose and then examining her finds.

"I am really sorry, but we can't help today. Maybe another time." Kate and Thembi were almost attached to me, pushing me forward toward the door.

"Why did you encourage them?" Kate asked, annoyed. In Kenya, we are constantly approached by beggars, and I have never been able to simply ignore them. I feel a little sorry for them, but she was right. If you give any indication that you may be susceptible to their pleas, they often will not leave you alone.

Dashing into the safety of Casa Jimenez, we came face-to-face with a large caribou, its antlers thrusting out in all directions. Animal heads—zebra, buffalo, and antelope—hung from the walls and over the tables, and a wide assortment of taxidermy creatures stood as if in motion, ready to take flight, but of course frozen for all time. It was bizarre to see. The animals were out of place, belonging on the great plains of Africa.

Many people judge a restaurant by how frequented it is by the locals. If that is a reliable indicator, Casa Jimenez was going to be a hit. All of the other clientele were large Hispanic families. Children rushed around the restaurant, gaily checking out the wildlife, their parents calling after them passively in Spanish. The place had a nice, homey feeling.

Anticipating an evening of authentic cuisine, I had again filled up on nachos and salsa and was full before the very large real meal arrived. (I seem to do that every single time.) But I love fresh salsa and warm chips. Nonetheless, we sampled shrimp ceviche tostadas, chicken tacos, and beef chimichanga. The food was fantastic and our waitress, while not overly chatty or friendly, was attentive and took great care of us.

It was dark when we rolled ourselves out of Casa Jimenez and back into the balmy air. The beggars had vanished into the desert night and the front of the restaurant was now empty. On the way back to the motel, the main 66 stretch was alight with luminous neon and the air was humid with the tease of a warm breeze. Back in the safety of our motel room, Thembi and Kate got ready for bed, knackered after a long day on the road. I was wide awake and ready to escape the stuffy room (thankfully, we had a portable fan with us). We had turned off the air conditioner due to a pungent aroma it was blowing out, making us all queasy. It didn't do much to cool the room anyhow.

Outside, I saw an Indian gentleman, perhaps the owner of the motel, sitting in the office. He was not around when we checked in earlier. I popped into the well-lit sanctuary to say hello.

As we got to talking, I observed, "You don't have any benches near the center attraction in the parking lot. It would be nice for guests to have a place to sit and enjoy the night."

"No, no way!" he responded matter-of-factly.

"Is there any reason?" I was a bit shocked by his immediate dismissal of my idea.

"If I put benches outside, we will have homeless people coming to sleep on them. No, no way," he reiterated, shaking his head vigorously.

Our conversation really didn't pick up after that, so I made my way back outside toward the main road to watch the world go by.

It was a bit disappointing that the motel had decided to make this call, but it was more frustrating that homelessness in a hugely developed country like America is such an enormous and growing problem.

Like in Tucumcari, the once-hectic road out front was now quiet; I was alone with my thoughts. So few people pass through Barstow these days, though it used to be a critical part of an even more vital route. I had experienced many changes in my own life over the year before the trip, and the very thought that this motel had weathered the storms to stay open for so many years was unbelievable. I was astounded by the sheer tenacity of the human spirit to simply hang on.

The motel's Open sign flashed, for an instant drawing my attention back to the assortment of vehicles and 66 bling. And again, like in Tucumcari, I felt a sense of peace and freedom being in a strange place all by myself in the quiet hours. I had a sudden urge to share this experience with Thembi; it would be moments like these that he would carry with him long after the journey.

"Hey, Dad," he said happily as I opened the door. He has such a sweet, gentle spirit.

"You're not asleep, Dadu?"

"Oh no! It's too hot and I'm not tired. What are you doing?" There was anticipation in his voice.

"You should be asleep! It's after midnight. But do you want to come outside with me for a few minutes and enjoy the night?"

"Really? Sure!" He was so excited that he nearly tripped getting out of bed. Kate was sound asleep.

Walking the grounds, his little hand firmly in mine, we breathed in the night. The road was quiet, other than periodic pedestrians shuffling by on foot, some in a hushed rush, others shouting at something invisible in the dark that only they could see. Thembi and I walked cautiously toward the road to take a better look at the neon sign, retreating back to the protection of the roundabout and the shadows of the vintage cars when a raucous nocturnal stroller approached the motel entrance. He slowed down near the motel but then continued on. Hearing him safely in the distance, we ventured back out. The desert town once again took on a muted tone of solitude and tranquility.

We had sojourned far, seen much, and walked in the footsteps of so many. Many who are now long gone. We had seen tremendous changes and celebrated the restoration of dreams and legacies. But that, too, reflects the realities of Route 66 and its tumultuous past; even the Mother Road does not protect you from the realities of life, but somehow makes them easier to bear.

My son and I looked up at the large orange neon Route 66 Motel sign and then down the lonely street. It dawned on me that this was almost our last night on the Mother Road. It was nearly the final time that we would get to enjoy the "discovery." By the day after tomorrow, our Great American Road Trip would be over. Then what? I wasn't sure that I was ready for it to end.

"Are you glad that we decided to do this road trip?" I asked him.

He thought for a moment and then smiled. "Oh yeah! This has been an awesome trip. I think we should do it again next year."

53

AT SEVEN THE next morning, the sky was an unsurprising deep blue and the sun washed unforgivingly over the bronzed earth.

The air was fresh in the Southwest and, walking out to take a look at Route 66 as it lazily stretched beside the motel, I felt a ray of hope and positivity. I was ready to tackle a new day and explore some of the lesser-traveled corners of California. Even at that early hour, the other guests, mostly thirty-something women from France, had already departed. We were alone. As usual, we were the last guests to depart a venue.

Our plan for the day was to head sixty-three miles northeast along the insanely fast-moving I-15 to the pretty-sounding town of Baker. The arid town was home to some old-time Americana and, best of all, the world's tallest thermometer. How cool was that? I wanted to get moving before the day got too warm. It was only ninety-eight degrees at that moment, but the day was looking like it would be a scorcher.

"Have you put on sunscreen?" Kate asked Thembi, throwing a bag into the trunk.

"Mom, I don't need it. I'm fine with my hat and sunglasses."

"Those won't protect your skin. You need to put on some cream. Brennen, talk to your son. By the way, have you applied it?"

I knew I was going to get in trouble. There was no way to avoid it. "Not yet, but I will."

"You guys, when you get badly burnt, it will be your own fault," she complained, heading back into the motel room, still muttering to herself as she disappeared into the dark.

Thembi put his hand on my shoulder and shrugged.

"We better put it on," I said. "Mom's right and, besides, I don't want her to get angry with *me*."

Safe from the sun, flimsy motel door locked, windows down and vehicle airing out, we were ready to venture off.

The ride to Baker from Barstow was pleasant but long. The highway is beautifully tarmacked, but the desert hues and long, flat road can grow monotonous. It was a nice drive but the kind that feels like it takes a lifetime to go an hour and makes you look forward to the next billboard. I-15 is mostly used as the road to Las Vegas, frequented by people from Southern California looking for an escape. We let them roar by as we piloted our way farther into the desert expanse. The land that the highway cut through rose and fell, stony hill after hill flowing its way toward Baker. Dry, empty land is all we saw for miles and miles and miles, and we had a definite sensation of wandering in a wasteland. It is hard to see anything actually growing there, and I find it astounding that people still make their homes and build up their towns in such beautiful but hostile environments.

"I am really starting to get hot," Thembi said, fanning himself in the back seat. "Can you turn the AC up?"

It was now 105 degrees and the vehicle's air conditioning was working hard to respond, but to little avail.

"We'll be there soon," I said. "Tell me what your favorite parts of the trip have been," I suggested, hoping to distract him from the heat and boredom.

He mused silently for a moment and went on to list some of his favorite stops. He was enamored with the Blue Whale in Catoosa, Oklahoma, and thought that the Big Texan in Amarillo was a lot of fun. He remembered coming face-to-face with a hairy tarantula, and my luck in spotting a rattlesnake on the lonely highway. The giant Muffler Men were memorable, and he was especially moved by the Gemini Giant way back in sleepy Wilmington, Illinois. I started to realize just how much we had seen and experienced on our journey. America really is a country for those with wanderlust. And now there we were in the California desert, traversing the country as a three-person travel bubble, sharing each and every happenstance as they came.

The highway shimmered in the distance, the desert mirage creating a scene out of a film, as though glittering water had covered the tarmac in our path. Warm air was now blowing from the vents as the vehicle could offer no resistance against the rampant heat.

"There it is," Kate said, her finger extended in the direction of a huge thermometer. The town came fully into sight as the endless, flat road suddenly dropped and cut through the land in a way that felt magical. Far into the distance, the highway shimmered once again, looking otherworldly. It was one of the most unforgettable visions I have ever witnessed.

Immediately, our fatigue and anxiousness disappeared and were replaced with glee. We were there. In the middle of the desert, in a small, nearly abandoned town called Baker. We had left the civilization and safety of Barstow to survey the unknown and the seldom seen. We had come in search of classic roadside Americana.

It stood tall—134 feet tall, to be exact—and was first introduced to the world in 1991. Now, that may seem like yesterday, but at the time of writing, that was close to thirty-one years ago. (And that is saying a lot in today's fast-moving world.) The sign weighs 76,812 pounds and is held together by 125 cubic yards of concrete. Impressive. Standing guard over the Mojave Desert night and day, the colossal creation was the brainchild of Willis Herron, a local businessman who paid $750,000 to have it constructed and placed next to his Bun Boy Restaurant. I'm sure he thought it would be a great investment, certain to call to holidayers and pull them into his motel and restaurant. But things would not go smoothly for Herron. After the thermometer's completion, but before it was ever lit, a windstorm knocked the behemoth over and almost put it out of business. Not one to be easily defeated, Herron simply had it rebuilt, made stronger and more wind resistant, and it has told the world the local temperature ever since. It once read up to 134 degrees, commemorating the hottest day ever on record in nearby Death Valley. Any warmer and we may well combust—I'm just saying.

Eventually, Herron sold his restaurant and the thermometer to a buyer who would go on to sell them again. In 2012, with a poor economy and an electric bill of a whopping $8,000 per month to keep the temperature taker on, the most recent owner simply shut it off. Soon the thermometer was in bad shape and ready to be brought down, but salvation was to come in the form of its "mother"—Barbara, Herron's wife. Determined to save her family's legacy, she found the money and vowed to repair the hulking structure and ensure that it would not be turned off again. And it has not!

"Can you believe that it's 106 degrees?" Kate said as we stared up, way up, at the wonderful example of human ingenuity and kitschy Americana.

"Look at the size of this thing," I responded. "I wonder if the temperature is accurate, though?"

"I think it is," she said, Googling the current warmth in Baker.

It was surreal to stand in a spot that we had long admired in pictures. Often, as awesome as real life can be, most experiences are better in the mind. A lot of attractions are a little disappointing in person. But not the giant thermometer.

A strong breeze picked up and blew dust into our eyes. Kate waved her hand in front of her face and coughed. "Phew!" she said. We stood in silence. Well, Kate and I did.

"That is really cool," Thembi commented, gazing around. "But now what? Is there anything else in Baker for us to see?"

"Sure, there is," I said.

"Like what?" he asked.

"Like . . . well, I don't know. But there must be something."

And so, after twenty glorious minutes with the world's largest thermometer, we got bored. Time to make a move. We jumped into the scalding vehicle and, after I burned my hands on the fiery wheel, continued slowly on down I-15, intent on discovering Baker.

"Holy cow! That is awesome. Look over there!" Thembi exclaimed. On our left stood numerous green aliens in shiny silver suits holding flying saucers over their heads with one hand and making peace signs with the other. It was not what we were expecting to see. The spacemen were standing guard over a large gray building that resembled a rectangular spacecraft. The building had enormous guns mounted on the roof, just in case, and looked to have made an emergency landing in the wilderness of California. This turned out to be the world-famous Alien Fresh Jerky.

"This is brilliant!" Kate said. "And a bit crazy."

Thembi was rushing around to take a look at the statues and the outside of the building while Kate was busy snapping selfies with her new friends. She had forgotten about Abraham Lincoln and his stuffy bench miles ago.

The jerky shop was opened in 2000 and was the grand idea of Luis Ramallo and his obviously supportive wife, Susana. The couple recognized the large market of road warriors who flew through Baker day in and day out on their way to Nevada, and they wanted to offer them healthier, fresher snacks. Inside, the shop is quirky and fun, packed with nuts, wild honey, dried olives, more aliens, and, of course, beef jerky in an abundance of flavors. They have Roadkill Original, Abducted Cow Pineapple Teriyaki, BBQ on the Moon, and, if I ate beef, what I imagine my personal favorite would be, Space Cowboy Pepper.

Soon it was two o'clock and the sun was impossibly bright. We were feeling a little tired. Funny how heat can wear one down. But there were some old signs I wanted to take a closer look at, so we slowly made our way back to the road, passing a few silver vehicles in the parking lot that had smiling aliens inside looking like they, too, were ready to roll. Cars flashed by, disappearing in the distance, and in the rearview mirror, I watched as a handful of Chinese tourists excitedly took pictures with the peace-loving space dudes. They must have been amazed with the weirdness of roadside America.

Faded beacons of hospitality loomed nearby among a cluster of leafy palm trees. Bun Boy Motel, with its grinning toddler holding an arrow pointing visitors toward the motel's entrance, stood decaying in the sunshine, long lost to history. Strangely, Bun Boy still appeared happy, oblivious perhaps that his once-frequented property was now forever shut down. Not far away, Arne's Royal Hawaiian Motel was equally forgotten and most certainly must have been an ambitious stab to attract patrons back in the day. Hawaii of the Mojave Desert. I truly love the way that America's two-lane highways have used—and still will use—almost any means to pull motorists off the road. Sadly, there in Baker, aspirations and efforts may have been larger than the payoff.

After a full day, we joined the traffic and headed back to Barstow to enjoy the serenity and placid atmosphere of the Route 66 Motel.

54

IT WAS ALREADY eighty-four degrees when we departed Barstow and drove past the turnoff toward Highway 93, revisiting Elmer Long's Bottle Tree Ranch and pushing toward modernity and the end of our westward journey. It was eight in the morning.

There was silence in the vehicle. After traveling close to three thousand miles toward something, after digesting so much of what America has to offer and meeting so many extraordinary and, at times, terribly strange people, after so many periods of laughing (and a few of arguing) together, several long moments of boredom and innumerable moments of awe, the trip was almost over. There were a mere 137 miles remaining of our Route 66 odyssey. We were exhilarated and melancholy.

It is always fascinating to me how a pervasive sadness fills the close of a journey, quickly replacing the palpable excitement of the commencement of a road trip. Starting out, there is tremendous expectation and hope. What will we see? Who will we encounter? There is anticipation about all that lies ahead. Toward the end, there is only the task of heading back, and what remains are merely memories. Recollections that begin to fade with time and become part of a beautiful but distant past.

The road was quiet, free of vehicles as we drove. Perhaps it was too early for traffic. A striking steel-truss bridge carried us across the Mojave River, and soon Emma Jean's Holland Burger Cafe came into sight.

"Do you want to stop and grab a coffee and maybe some breakfast?" Kate asked.

I did. I generally don't take breakfast until later in the morning, but that morning I was hungry. Or perhaps I was trying to prolong the trip.

A pickup truck had come out of nowhere and was riding my bumper. His impatience was going to cause an accident. But seeing my signal to turn right off the otherwise empty road, he slowed down. The faded lime-green-and-white restaurant was silent. It looked closed.

I watched as the Ford sped off into the distance, kicking up dust as he veered on and off the tarmac. The desert heat shimmered above the pavement.

"He's going to kill someone," I moaned. But Kate's attention was on the café.

"That is so odd," Kate commented. "Why would they be closed?"

"Not sure. Let me go and look at their hours on the door." But we should have known by then. Many small-town businesses maintain very odd hours, with some closing in the middle of the day, depending on how they feel at that moment. Route 66 had struck again.

The sun was hotter as I stepped down onto the faded concrete. The giant Emma Jean's Holland Burger Cafe sign is stunning in a classical manner, a true testament to a time that so much of Route 66 celebrates, but which Los Angeles, our destination, has largely forgotten. I tried the door, but it was indeed locked, and the lights were out. A notice indicated that they were closed on Sunday. *Wait*, I think. *Is this really Sunday?* After two months on the road, the days had morphed together.

Built in 1947, the café was initially the Holland Burger Cafe and Emma Jean Gentry was a waitress at the diner. In 1979, Richard Gentry purchased the café for his wife, and they renamed the venue Emma Jean's Holland Burger. The oldest standing structure in the Victorville area, the café still offers a safe and comfortable place to take a seat for hungry travelers and locals looking for some grub and gab. (Just not on Sundays, apparently.) Emma Jean passed away in 1996 and Richard shortly after in 2008, but the venue is still open and now run by their son Brian and his wife, Shawna. Adding to its claim to fame is its relationship to Hollywood. The café featured hilariously in *Kill Bill: Vol. 2* and romantically in Train's music video for the song "Bulletproof Picasso."

Alas, there would be no coffee and breakfast for us there that day.

The scenery was becoming more intense as we began to traverse Cajon Pass, a mountain pass through the San Bernardino and San

Gabriel Mountains that is believed to have been created by the movements of the San Andreas Fault.

The road began to pick up with a lot more cars; the slow meandering that made up the last few days coming down the Oatman Highway and across the Mojave was over. My heart began to beat faster. As the road opened up, we were descending quickly through hills with vivid, almost aggressive, natural beauty. I was not ready for what unfolded before me and I immediately felt boxed in by the intensity of the arid landscape and the rush of my fellow motorists, even though the actual highway is wide. The sky was so big and so blue and the hills so brown and shrubby, but barren and steep—and all around us—that there was an uncomfortable feeling of being able to drive right off the face of the earth. It felt as though we were on a whole different planet.

There was now a noticeable energy. This part of California's Route 66 was different. The Mother Road was gone, and people were intent on getting to where they were going; enjoying the road on a simple Sunday was not an option. Many motorists were returning from a weekend in Las Vegas, Nevada, and hurrying home before the start of the new week. Still, we tried to stay at a pace that allowed us to absorb our surroundings, without causing an accident.

"Get off on Cajon Boulevard," Kate suggested, studying a map. "That should lead us into San Bernardino." Doing so, we passed under CA 30 and followed directions to Foothill Boulevard. It was a very long road— over sixty miles—that led us into Rialto, a suburb of San Bernardino and home of the other Wigwam Motel on the route and its famous wooden Indian statue. It was a lovely setting located in an otherwise seedy area of town. Sad, as the community was once known for its picturesque groves of lemon and orange trees.

"Let's stop and get a picture here," Thembi requested. "That's cool how the Indian statue is sort of pointing. Do you think they've painted him? He looks much brighter than in the pictures."

It was still early, and it seemed as though all of the venue's guests had left. The Indian stood alone on the roadside in front of the rooms, pointing, as Thembi noted, toward the fifteen available tepees, beckoning travelers to stop for the night and sleep beneath some history. At one time, the motel's slogan was the classy "Do It in a Teepee." I wasn't sure if that was effective or not, but the vibe there was a bit different than at the Holbrook location, which carries a more vintage mood. But in the midst of a busy, crowded road, this small slice of Americana was soothing and welcome. This Wigwam Motel, built in 1947, is without a doubt the most famous landmark in the Rialto area and continues to draw visitors from near and far.

———

CONTINUING DOWN THE road into Fontana and only sixty miles away from Los Angeles, we had entered the land of ugly strip malls. The road was suddenly claustrophobic and somewhat overwhelming. There were too many people, too much generic scenery, a wide assortment of transients, and an infliction of urbanity in its rawest form. An unusual relic sat placidly on the roadside to our left, totally out of place. It was the Bono's Historic Orange, a roadside refreshment stand in the shape of a giant orange that once offered fresh orange juice to thirsty patrons. At one time, there were a great many of these orange stands on the streets. But today the venue is closed, and this representation of a more colorful past, itself built in 1936, stands to remind us of what once was. Of course, we pulled over to take some pictures.

As we stopped at one of a million traffic lights, a homeless man approached the vehicle and motioned that he was hungry, but when we offered him some food, he was not interested. "No, no! Money. I want money." He elongated the "ey" so it sounded like "moneeeee." We explained that we had no cash on hand and he grunted and waved his hand at us aggressively, dismissing us before moving off to the vehicle behind us. The light turned green and we motored on as the driver behind us desperately tried to put their window up.

Foothill Boulevard felt like it went on forever, as it moved us through Southern California toward the great blue ocean. In modern times, it is also known as CA 66 and is the Mother Road of yesteryear. Rancho Cucamonga came into sight. This town is obviously proud of its Route 66 heritage, as every other building celebrates its connection to the historical road. But like Rialto, its agricultural heritage seemed lost. The area was once famous for its fertile vineyards and aromatic orange groves. We saw none that day, but the area was still pretty in its own way, with mature trees and an air of suburbia.

"Look at that!" shouted Kate. "It's the Cucamonga Service Station."

Again, traffic was on my tail as I made a sharp right turn and crashed into the narrow driveway that led visitors to the rear of the museum. Any onlookers would have viewed me as I had the French motorists back in Wilmington, where we first began the journey. Originally a Richfield Oil service station, the bright-yellow building is pretty hard to miss and had been on our bucket list since beginning to plan the trip. With over a hundred years under its belt, the service station operated for the first half of the twentieth century, before closing its doors in the '70s. It sat, like so many venues and businesses along Route 66, decaying and in disrepair for many years, until a local nonprofit pulled people and funds together to refurbish the station and get it back to the look and vintage feel of 1915, when it first opened its doors. Now a museum and information center, the Cucamonga Service Station was a wonderful break from the road. And they even gave Thembi a lovely hand-drawn poster of the venue and its friendly town.

Back on Foothill Boulevard, we cruised on, a bit tired of the slow-moving—and plentiful—traffic, increasingly eager to get to the Pacific. The road got a bit confusing as we continued into the urban sprawl and congestion of Glendora and Azusa, Monrovia and Arcadia. Every time I thought that we were close to Santa Monica, we encountered another small town.

"Are we almost there?" Thembi asked, sweat forming on his forehead. "This road seems to never end."

"Are you excited to see the Pacific Ocean?" I asked. He had been in the cold water of the Atlantic and spent most of his life soaking in the balmy Indian Ocean but had not seen the Pacific.

"Yeah, I guess. But will it be very cold? Isn't California where a lot of great white shark attacks happen?"

That was a good question, and a fair assessment of the dangers that possibly lurk in the ocean. To local beachgoers, this assumption may seem a bit over the top and unlikely, but we had just finished watching the latest season of *Shark Week* and had been inundated with what can happen in the sea when things do go bad.

"It does happen from time to time," I cautioned, "but it's rare."

"You are more likely to get hit by lightning, right?" he responded.

Thembi has a large book collection, most of them being science and trivia based. He loves providing random facts.

"That's what they say! But personally, I'd rather get hit by the lightning."

"Me too," he said, laughing.

"I'm sure we will be just fine. There are thousands of people that swim in the ocean every year," Kate added. "And not many of them get eaten."

Soon we joined the Pasadena Freeway and entered into the madness of Los Angeles proper.

"Does any of this look familiar to you?" Kate asked, her eyes darting in every direction. LA really is an assault on the senses.

I was trying to reconnect with the city that I once called home, twenty-two years earlier. But everything looked so different that I felt little nostalgia for the place. It was just a big, anonymous, chaotic town to me now. Traffic is notorious in Southern California, and as we inched our way, bumper to bumper, through the million red lights that dot Santa Monica Boulevard, our anxiety increased, and we wanted to escape the confines of the vehicle. It had been our home for close to eight weeks now and our faithful ship down America's Main Street, but now we wanted out.

Finally, after another hour in congestion, we could sense that the sea was nearby. The mood changed as we traversed Beverly Hills and entered Santa Monica and turned onto Ocean Avenue. There was an energy and festivity in the air. Parking is limited around this area and we were forced to head to our hotel first, Fairmont Miramar Hotel & Bungalows, before making the final dash to the famous Santa Monica Pier. Beaches in Southern California are often lined with well-planned boardwalks that are intended for cyclists, skateboarders, rollerbladers, and pedestrians alike.

Santa Monica State Beach is beautiful, with soft, warm sand and ever-blue skies. But of course, being the mecca that it is, the beach was packed with people from all corners of the planet, soaking in the sun and reveling in the laid-back seaside mood. Kate and I kicked off our shoes and strolled hand in hand along the boardwalk, but Thembi was dashing around on the sand, breathing in the sweet, salty air and releasing hours of tension built up from sitting in LA gridlock.

Seagulls swooped down from above, crying out in the late-afternoon melee, while flags from perhaps every nation in the world fluttered in the breeze. Someone had created a lovely display to celebrate the area's international draw.

Stairs to the pier called to us in the distance as we pushed through a group of Chinese tourists taking selfies on the sand, dancing about as the heat burned their feet. A black man wearing only a cheetah-patterned loincloth, his body covered in a gallon of shiny lotion, urged passersby to stop and witness his ability to charm a giant black snake that he had in his hands, as he stood on one leg. "I doubt that's even a real snake," commented a tourist to his partner. "See how he's making it move himself? I'm sure it's a scam."

Artists sat cross-legged on the end of the pier, creating masterpieces and soliciting donations for their work, and homeless people slept peacefully underneath palm trees, totally oblivious of their surroundings. Police officers on foot patrol simply walked around their outstretched legs, ignoring their presence. It was shocking to see. We overheard some Europeans complaining that they were forced to step over a sleeping person's legs in order to enter the pier.

It was still daytime, but the mood on the pier was tremendously exciting. The world-famous Pier Burger was buzzing to our left, while the Ferris wheel rose above the single-level shops that line the pier. In the evening, the Ferris wheel would light up with an array of brilliant colors that would add to the rush of noise from the other rides on offer. It was going to be a sight.

The "End of the Trail" sign stood before us now as we waited to take our pictures and officially complete our 2,448-mile journey down Route 66. "Can I take your picture?" offered a young blond woman, pointing to the sign. "Then you can take ours." Like along the rest of the trip, there was camaraderie right until the very end. It was astounding to experience such unity and a sense of common purpose: to experience Route 66 and the essence of America.

We had traveled a great distance and been—for a short period—inserted into the lives of many. Most we would never speak to again. Most would forget about us the moment we parted ways. That's okay. It's the way of life. But still, all had impacted us in one way or another and, hopefully, we impacted them. We took the trip to chase some adventure and to get clearer direction in our lives. I'm not so sure that we finished with many answers, but our questions had somehow changed. And unknown to us at that time, on that celebratory afternoon, a new chapter had already started.

EPILOGUE

I have always found ending a journey to be quite disheartening. There is a finality, a sense of loss. I am an emotional traveler, and if you are like me, you plan extensively and devour information as you prepare to hit the open road. As the departure date draws near, my enthusiasm and eagerness increases, and my anticipation grows. So much time goes into planning and preparing that it all feels too fast when a journey comes to an end. While I look ahead, I am constantly finding myself looking back and struggling to enjoy a moment to its fullest. It is a weakness.

I have been on many travels in my life: I have slept under an enormous desert moon on top of the flowing dunes of northern Burkina Faso on the Niger border, cared for by the nomadic Tuareg tribe. I have voyaged across the dry, dusty landscape of mythical Timbuktu in Mali, where infrastructure, good health care, and education are but a dream, but the people are rich in their hospitality and age-old traditions. Kate and I have driven across the Great Lakes region of Africa, traversing Uganda; picturesque Rwanda, a land of a thousand hills, whose lushness conceals the ghosts of the country's bloodied genocidal past; and the beautiful Tanzanian highlands, visiting spice and coffee farms as we made our way to a nation with a mysterious name, Zambia. We have swum with dolphins in the Indian Ocean and been invited into the humble homes of Dogon, Maasai, and Rendille warriors. I have been on hundreds of safaris to game-rich areas, where I have been chased by enraged wildebeest, been treed by stampeding buffalo, and witnessed a lion and a leopard fighting to the death. Now I can say that we have ventured down America's Main Street and fallen in love with an endangered way of life, as well as a history that still entrances people from across the globe.

At the time of writing this epilogue, we have been down the Mother Road, from Illinois all the way to California, eight times—we have traversed every single mile possible many times—and are planning for a new adventure in the coming months. Every single time is different and unique. That is one of the things that makes an American road trip so exceptional—the diversity is endless.

Many times during this two-month journey down Route 66, I surprised myself by discovering how many more miles we still had yet to cover. I was never disappointed that so much of America lay before us, but rather felt exuberant that there was still so much more to see and experience, even after traveling for so long and so far. No two days were the same, and being out on the road, where no one knew our names or really cared about who we were, was freeing. Far away from the stress and cares of routine and daily life, away from the ordinary and planned, it was easy to let go, embrace existence as it came, and move on when it seemed right to do so. Time disappeared and instincts guided us. In this quietness, away from normal life, we were able to reorganize our thoughts and purge some of the contents that were weighing down our spirits. This happens when we slow down—which I find very hard to do—and get out of our own way. Getting out on the open road without a tight schedule to stick to was undeniably therapeutic. We simply watched and listened, observing the characters in the theater of life in action.

As we passed through quaint towns along the Mother Road, we began to find solace in their simplicity and tranquil atmosphere. Our souls discovered a healing balm in the genuineness of Middle America, as it is lived out along Route 66 and America's blue highways. We grew a new appreciation for and understanding of America—not just the gloss and shine and Hollywood glitter that is screened across the world but the real heart and soul of a diverse and divided nation. People and places I would have judged harshly only months earlier as being too rural or too content in the "smallness" of their lives took on a different hue. These were not folks living in the middle of nowhere or unsophisticated, small-town people clinging to a dying way of life. These were decent, hardworking, honest people from all sorts of backgrounds who were welcoming and relaxed with their lives and selves. That is saying something.

Kate and I embarked on this journey in order to create the distance and space we needed to get a proper understanding of our lives during a difficult period. We set out as a family to discover America and learn more about a way of life that many say is gone forever. Yet in some ways, after traveling almost three thousand miles, we were less certain of what tomorrow would bring than we were before the voyage. But soon after the trip down America's Main Street, we did begin to gain some clarity, and once again, our lives have been changed forever.

The following year, we found ourselves back on Route 66, this time playing tour guide with close friends from Africa. It was wonderful to watch the impact that the old road had on them as they discovered America themselves for the first time and wiped away many of the negative perceptions that they had about the United States and Americans before their arrival. More than anything else, it was the enormity of the country and the constant generosity of the people we met along the way that shocked and impressed them. They, too, went home changed, with a newfound appreciation for small-town America and a profoundly altered understanding of the land of the free. And they would fly back around the world the following year to tackle America's most famous highway once again with us.

A major outcome from our trip was the inspiration to launch a new print publication—*ROUTE Magazine*. Now we are amazingly blessed to work with Route 66 towns and cities and businesses every day, telling their stories and promoting their destinations. It is an honor to showcase their distinct locations and journeys. And best of all, it keeps us connected to the Mother Road each and every day.

We arrived in Canada exhausted, with little direction and quite apprehensive about the future. There were many questions and few answers. We decided to hit the road and seek out America in search of inspiration, but what we thought was a simple road trip turned out to be just the balm that our souls needed and the first step in charting out the next chapter of our story.

THERE HAVE BEEN many changes on the iconic highway since we did the initial road trip.

While almost lost forever, the Launching Pad has not fallen into merely becoming a historical footnote. A year after our first visit, the venue was purchased by an optimistic, energetic couple, Tully Garrett and Holly Barker, who serendipitously met at a grief support group after they both sadly lost their spouses to illness. The restaurant is now open and once again attracting curious travelers and hungry motorists from far and wide. Gemini himself is looking happier, with a new coat of paint and the removal of that blasted football. There is newfound energy in Wilmington as new history is, once again, made every day.

In November 2021, down in Carthage, Missouri, sisters Debye Harvey and Priscilla Bledsaw sold the Boots Court Motel to some local investors. We are not sure what the future holds for the vintage venue, but the sisters are hopeful that the new owners will maintain the motel and invest in continuing the work of love that they began in 2011.

New blood and enthusiasm have found their way into Tulsa, Oklahoma, with the birth of Buck Atom's Cosmic Curios, a fun, crazy visitors' center and gift shop that was opened on 66 by local entrepreneur Mary Beth Babcock. The center is also home to the newest Muffler Man on the route, Buck Atom. Like Gemini, he is a spaceman—but also a cowboy. He is a space cowboy. Buck Atom is a quirky, unusual giant who continues to attract thousands of visitors per year. He is very much an example of the continuous and constant growth and change along the road and of the reinvention of roadside America.

One more piece of wonderful news is that Claire, the young girl we spent time with at the Old Riverton Store in Riverton, Kansas, graduated high school with a 4.0 GPA! She is now in nursing school and her future is looking bright. Hers is a success story.

Sadly, there have been many losses as well.

Esteemed artist Lowell Davis of Red Oak II in Carthage, Missouri, died at the ripe old age of eighty-three. He passed in November 2020 but left a legacy and a small town that will continue to be preserved by his wife, Rose. Davis will be missed.

FourWay in Cuba, Missouri, shut its colorful doors for good in December 2020, becoming one more victim of small-town American economics.

The old man who had a good time poking fun at Thembi in the Old Riverton Store in Kansas, Forrest Nelson, passed away peacefully in January 2021. He was ninety-eight. His son Scott will continue to operate the popular destination and welcome local and Route 66 visitors.

Sadly, after our enjoyable visit, Angels on the Route in Baxter Springs, Kansas, closed its doors in early 2018. There was simply not enough business and Alan and Cheri could not afford to keep operating. It is a huge shame, as theirs was one of the truly memorable dining experiences on America's Main Street.

Kevin and Nancy Mueller decided to retire, and they moved to Tennessee in early 2020. They handed over the reins of the Blue Swallow Motel in Tucumcari, New Mexico, to a new couple—Robert and Dawn Federico of Crystal Lake, Illinois—who stumbled upon the unique opportunity in a similar manner as Kevin and Nancy. They are already making Lillian Redman proud.

The iconic twin arrows just outside of Winslow, Arizona, are now in jeopardy of being lost forever. In February 2021, the faded red arrowhead of one of the arrows was completely destroyed by vandals and weather, and in early 2022 the entire arrow fell to the dry ground. At the time of writing, there it still sits. This has been happening up and down Route 66 for years, but in recent days has gotten totally out of control. A little farther west down the highway, the incredibly picturesque KAMP building of Two Guns was brought down by vandals and bad weather. As of this writing, the structure is flattened on the ground.

The eccentric and rather reclusive Elmer Long from the Bottle Tree Ranch in California passed away on June 22, 2019, after a battle with lung cancer. He was seventy-two. For a time, there was uncertainty about the future of his strange roadside attraction, but since his death, family members have stepped up with a commitment to keep the colorful stop open.

So much more has happened since we first made this journey. There have been loads of gains and some losses, but my biggest takeaway is that time marches on and waits for no person. America is a land of adjustment and where one opportunity fails, another will quickly rise to fill its spot. I find that incredibly encouraging, both as a person and as a lover of history and the great American road trip.

Sometimes all it takes is seeing the world from a different angle to change your perspective and inspire an idea. We may not know for certain what tomorrow holds, but without a doubt, our time on Route 66 in the warm embrace of Middle America gave us the support and space we needed to find some of the answers we were looking for.

ACKNOWLEDGMENTS

Throughout my life, timing has been a constant factor. God's planning has always superseded my own, thank goodness! *Miles to Go* has come about later down the line than I had wanted, but exactly when it was meant to. This book may have been conceived from my first sojourn down Route 66, but its journey to fruition has been the result of several others who have helped to nurture and care for the story. In Africa, there is a proverb that says, "It takes a village to raise a child." I've discovered that it takes a "village" to rear a book too.

Route 66 has several talented writers and boosters who daily promote the old highway and remind us of its significance to America's growth and development, and work to ensure that Route 66 remains relevant for future generations to discover and enjoy. Perhaps the most passionate of these children of the Mother Road is the acclaimed author, speaker, and voice-over artist Michael Wallis. It was through his clear and dependable guidance that *Miles to Go* began to develop into the story that it is. Michael has been a dear friend and confidant for many years now, and his vision for the Mother Road is reflected in the book's pages. James Fitzgerald would be pleased, Michael.

It is always a challenge for an editor to take direction from someone else on our own stories, since we are used to working on and revising other people's work. I believe that editors make the worst receivers of literary critique! (They say that doctors make the worst patients.) It was not without a little trepidation, then, that I opened my editor's comments to the first draft of *Miles to Go*. I was fearful of his red pen and hoped he would not have too different of a vision for the story than I did. I need not have worried. Michael Millman and the University of New Mexico Press could not have been easier and more pleasant to work with. Michael's suggestions and wisdom were spot on and helped this writer tighten a story that became at times overly wide. His bird's-eye view of the book allowed me the freedom to tell the story in my own way, but with the reader in mind.

I would also like to thank one of the most talented photographers on Route 66 today, David Schwartz, for all of the amazing images he provided for the book. David is an Ohio native but lives and breathes American road travel and Route 66. I am forever indebted to him for his undeniable talent and passion. David, your shared vision for this book was evident from the start, and I am proud to call you my friend.

Thank you to Marshall Hawkins for the fantastic imagery that he shot on Route 66 and allowed me to use. A special thanks to Jim Hinckley, Cheryl Eichar Jett, Bill Thomas, Nick Gerlich, Ken Busby, and Ian McCloy for all of their words of encouragement and insights, and for always being stand-up, dependable, wonderful friends and counselors.

Most of all, I would like to thank my amazing wife, Kate, and my ever-curious son, Thembi. Both are very much the energy and drive behind *Miles to Go*. They are my constant companions and there is no one I would rather adventure down the road with. Kate's critical, insightful ideas and suggestions have made the book much stronger. As in traveling, she is my chief navigator in life.

ABOUT THE AUTHOR

Brennen Matthews is the editor of *ROUTE Magazine,* the nation's leading pop-culture magazine dedicated to Route 66 and classic Americana. He lives with his wife and son in Toronto, Ontario, but travels the Mother Road several times a year.